Islamic Perspectives on the New Millennium

The **Institute of Southeast Asian Studies (ISEAS)** was established as an autonomous organization in 1968. It is a regional research centre for scholars and other specialists concerned with modern Southeast Asia, particularly the many-faceted issues and challenges of stability and security, economic development, and political and social change.

The Institute's research programmes are the Regional Economic Studies (RES, including ASEAN and APEC), Regional Strategic and Political Studies (RSPS), and Regional Social and Cultural Studies (RSCS).

ISEAS Publications, an established academic press, has issued more than 1,000 books and journals. It is the largest scholarly publisher of research about Southeast Asia from within the region. ISEAS Publications works with many other academic and trade publishers and distributors to disseminate important research and analyses from and about Southeast Asia to the rest of the world.

AS Series on Islam

Islamic Perspectives on the New Millennium

edited by
Virginia Hooker
Amin Saikal

ISEAS

INSTITUTE OF SOUTHEAST ASIAN STUDIES
Singapore

First published in Singapore in 2004 by
ISEAS Publications
Institute of Southeast Asian Studies
30 Heng Mui Keng Terrace
Pasir Panjang
Singapore 119614

E-mail: publish@iseas.edu.sg
Website: <http://bookshop.iseas.edu.sg>

ISEAS Library Cataloguing-in-Publication Data

Islamic perspectives on the new millennium / edited by Virginia Hooker and Amin Saikal.
1. Islam—21st century.
2. Islam and state—Indonesia.
3. Islam and politics—Indonesia.
4. Islam—Economic aspects—Indonesia.
5. Women in Islam.
I. Hooker, Virginia Matheson, 1946–
II. Saikal, Amin, 1950–
BP63 I5I824 2004

ISBN 981-230-240-9 (soft cover)
ISBN 981-230-241-7 (hard cover)

Typeset by International Typesetters Pte Ltd
Printed in Singapore by Photoplates Pte Ltd

CONTENTS

Acknowledgements vii
Contributors ix

1. Islamic Perspectives on the New Millennium 1
   Virginia Hooker

The New World Order

2. Islam and the West: Challenges and Opportunities 19
   Amin Saikal

3. Indonesian Responses 32
   Samsu Rizal Panggabean

The New Age

4. Islam and Globalization: Arab World Perspectives 43
   Ahmad Shboul

5. Indonesian Muslims Enter a New Age 74
   Nurcholish Madjid

The Economy

6. Financial Activism among Indonesian Muslims 91
   Nur Ahmad Fadhil Lubis

7. Islamic Banking and Finance: In Search of a Pragmatic Model 113
   Abdullah Saeed

The Nation-State

8. Political Islam in Post-Soeharto Indonesia 133
   Azyumardi Azra

9. The Experience of the Islamic Republic of Iran 150
Gholamali Khoshroo

Muslim Women
10. Muslim Women and Human Rights in the Middle East and South Asia: Occupying Different Spaces 161
Samina Yasmeen

11. Islam, Gender, and Politics in Indonesia 183
Kathryn Robinson

Law and Knowledge
12. Perspectives on the *Shari'a* and the State: The Indonesian Debates 199
M. B. Hooker

13. The Role of Muslims in the New Millennium 221
Mohamed Aris Othman

Conclusion
14. Developing Islamic Arguments for Change through "Liberal Islam" 231
Virginia Hooker

Glossary 253

Index of Names 259

Index of Subjects 262

ACKNOWLEDGEMENTS

The assembling of a collection of essays requires patience from each contributor as well as from the publisher and, as editors, we have been most grateful for the collegial support they have generously given. Many of the contributors came together for preliminary discussions about the book, and the editors wish to thank the Ford Foundation, Jakarta; the Department of Foreign Affairs and Trade, Canberra; and the Australian Institute of International Affairs (especially its Executive Director Ross Cotterill) for sponsoring the travel of overseas visitors to the meeting.

The editors are grateful also to the Anglican Bishop of Canberra and Goulburn, the Rt Rev. George Browning; The Rev. Elaine Farmer; broadcaster and commentator Graeme Dobell; and Professor Peter Read for their thoughtful and perceptive responses to issues raised in the essays.

At the Australian National University, where the essays had their first editing, it is our pleasure to acknowledge the warm assistance of Vera Joveska, Andrea Haese, and Carol Laslett. Professor Anthony Milner and Professor James J. Fox, Dean of the Faculty of Asian Studies and Director of the Research School of Pacific and Asian Studies respectively, and Dr Khalifa M. Bakhit Alfalasi, former Ambassador to Australia of the United Arab Emirates, encouraged and supported the enterprise from start to finish. Professor Deanne Terrell, former Vice-Chancellor of the Australian National University provided a grant to assist with pre-publication preparation of the book, and by so doing underlined his commitment to improving general understanding about Islam. It remains to add our special thanks to Australian editor Belinda Henwood and to our publisher,

Mrs Triena Ong (Managing Editor, Institute of Southeast Asian Studies, Singapore) and Ms Rahilah Yusuf, Production Editor.

Virginia Hooker and Amin Saikal
Canberra
July 2004

CONTRIBUTORS

Azyumardi Azra is Professor of History and also Rector of the State Islamic University (UIN) Syarif Hidayatullah Jakarta. He is widely known for his many academic publications on Islam in Southeast Asia and for his media commentaries on contemporary Indonesian affairs.

M. B. Hooker is Professor of Law at the Australian National University and was formerly Professor of Comparative Law at the University of Kent, Canterbury. He is widely known for his writings on Islamic law in Southeast Asia. His *Indonesian Islam: Social Change through Contemporary Fatawa* has recently been published (Allen & Unwin, 2003).

Virginia Hooker is Professor of Indonesian and Malay at the Australian National University. Her published work includes studies of Islam and social change in Malaysia and in Indonesia.

Gholamali Khoshroo was formerly Deputy Foreign Minister for Research and Education in the Islamic Republic of Iran. He was a member of the delegation of the Islamic Republic of Iran to the United Nations before being appointed Ambassador to Australia for the Islamic Republic of Iran. His doctorate is in sociology and he has served as Dean of the Faculty of International Relations, affiliated with the Ministry of Foreign Affairs. Currently he serves as Deputy Foreign Minister for Legal and International Affairs in Tehran.

Nur Ahmad Fadhil Lubis is Professor of Islamic Law at the State Institute of Islamic Studies (IAIN), North Sumatra and is currently a Vice-Rector. He is well known for publications on Islamic law and finance.

Nurcholish Madjid is Professor of Islamic Studies and Rector of Paramadina Mulya University, Jakarta. An outstanding Indonesian scholar, speaker, public figure, and a prolific writer, he was also a candidate for the Indonesian presidential elections in 2004.

Mohamed Aris Othman is Dean of the Faculty of Islamic Revealed Knowledge and Human Sciences, International Islamic University, Kuala Lumpur. His published work includes studies of Malay identity, urbanization, and constitutional development in Malaysia.

Samsu Rizal Panggabean is Head of the Centre for Peace and Security Studies and member of the Department of International Relations, Gadjah Mada University, Yogyakarta. He is on the Editorial Board of prominent Islamic journals, and he researches peace initiatives in Indonesia and the Middle East as well as Southeast Asian pluralism and Islamic thought in the twentieth century.

Kathryn Robinson is Senior Fellow, Anthropology, Research School of Pacific and Asian Studies, Australian National University. She has published widely on gender relations in Southeast Asia and the anthropology of the Islamic peoples of Indonesia, especially in Sulawesi. She is the editor of *The Asia Pacific Journal of Anthropology* and consultant for numerous aid projects in Indonesia and editor (with Sharon Bessell) of *Women in Indonesia: Gender, Equity and Development* (Institute of Southeast Asian Studies, 2002).

Abdullah Saeed is Sultan of Oman Professor of Arab and Islamic Studies at the University of Melbourne. His recent publications include *Islamic Banking and Interest* (1999), *Muslim Communities in Australia* (co-edited, 2001), *Islam and Political Legitimacy* (co-edited, 2003), *Islam in Australia* (2003), and *Freedom of Religion, Apostasy and Islam* (co-authored, 2004).

Amin Saikal is Professor of Political Science and Director of the Centre for Arab and Islamic Studies (Middle East and Central Asia), Australian National University. He is a regular media commentator on crises in Afghanistan and the Middle East and has published many books on Islam and international relations. His most recent books are *Islam and the West: Conflict or Cooperation* (2003) and *Modern Afghanistan: A History of Survival and Struggle* (2004).

Ahmad Shboul is Associate Professor and Co-ordinator of Arab, Islamic and Middle Eastern Studies, School of Languages and Cultures, University of Sydney. His many writings include *A History of Arab Islamic Civilization* (Amman, 1992) and *Al-Mas'udi and His World: A Muslim Humanist and His Interest in Non-Muslims* (London, 1979).

Samina Yasmeen is Senior Lecturer in International Politics, Department of Political Science, University of Western Australia, Perth. She was formerly Senior Research Fellow for a UNESCO project at the Ministry of Education, Government of Pakistan, and Research Specialist in Defence for the Legislative Research Service of the Australian Parliament.

1

ISLAMIC PERSPECTIVES ON THE NEW MILLENNIUM

Virginia Hooker

The suicide bombings in the United States of America on 11 September 2001, executed by terrorists claiming they acted in the name of Islam, set in train events whose repercussions will influence world politics for the foreseeable future. Although the perpetrators were denounced by Muslim leaders around the world as criminals whose acts were not condoned by Islam, many non-Muslims nevertheless believed that somehow Islam was to blame for the September 11 tragedy. The Islamic terrorist group known as Al-Qaeda claimed responsibility for the bombings and was targeted by Western leaders for retribution, but care was taken to emphasize that the punitive action would be directed against Al-Qaeda and its allies, not against Islam and Muslims in general. However, when the United States and its allies bombed Taliban forces in Afghanistan (2001) and then proceeded against Saddam Hussein without the sanction of the United Nations Security Council (2003), increasing numbers of ordinary Muslims became suspicious about the motives of the administration of President George W. Bush. Heightened surveillance of Muslims in many Western countries, more stringent immigration controls, tight security in public venues and centres of mass travel, and alarmist reports in many media outlets produced a sense of fear among ordinary people, both Muslims and non-Muslims. The early years of the twenty-first century have therefore been characterized by widespread anxiety and fear of violence, state intrusion into personal lives (in the name of public safety) and perceived discrimination against individuals on the basis of their place of origin or religion.

The climate of fear which has grown and been fostered by the media, wherever it operates, is in sad contrast to the efforts of many intellectuals in the last decade of the twentieth century to find common ground between people of all faiths based on the universality of mankind. Possibly provoked by Samuel P. Huntington's controversial claim that "universal civilization" was the product of Western thought, there have been many responses from Muslim intellectuals who argued that it was Islamic civilization which became the first truly universal civilization. These intellectuals also promoted the concept of civilizational dialogue, recognizing that there are many religions and cultures and seeking a system of global ethics based on shared spiritual, moral, and ethical values.

This book, an analysis of Muslim attitudes to key areas of modern life, is a contribution to continuing the effort which Muslim intellectuals have already started, in making Muslim views on contemporary issues available to a wider audience. Although not all the authors are Muslims, each has written from a Muslim perspective and addressed their particular topic so as to give a sense of the internal Muslim points of view. The aim is to provide non-Muslims with a sense of the main debates within Islam on six important issues. As each chapter shows, there is no single "Muslim" position on issues such as Islamic banking, human rights, the public role of women, globalization, or the relationship between Islam and the state. The reader will discover the plurality of views Muslims hold on these topics, ranging from those based on literalist interpretations of the Qur'an to views which argue that contextual interpretations are the most appropriate for Muslims living in the twenty-first century. For many Muslims, the challenge of modernity rests on the question of how to be up-to-date with technological, medical, and financial advances and still remain true to the basic principles of Islam. Equally, many Muslims do not wish to see their religion being accused of holding back women or applying inhumane punishments under religious laws, and so they work within their own societies to persuade their fellow Muslims that the Qur'an supports full development of the potential of all human beings and that compassion and mercy are the principles underpinning Islamic law.

The critical question, as Associate Professor Ahmad Shboul emphasizes in his chapter on Islam and globalization, is the need to define our questions appropriately: which Islam, in which place, when, and for whom? This book has been planned to respond to the diversity of thinking across the Muslim world by bringing together views from the Middle East, South Asia, and

Indonesia, the state which now has the largest Muslim population in the world. This wide-ranging comparison of Muslim views on major issues is rarely attempted because most of the scholarship on the Islamic world focuses on particular nation-states and does not reflect fully the connections which Muslims have established throughout the *ummah* (all people who profess to follow Islam). These long-standing, trans-*ummah* connections were made by Muslim travellers and merchants from the thirteenth century onwards and were facilitated by the use of Arabic as a lingua franca and by the great intellectual capitals of Islamic scholarship, Mecca, Baghdad, Damascus, Constantinople (Istanbul), and Cairo where students from throughout the Muslim world congregated to study. Two-way interaction between South Asia, Southeast Asia, and the Middle East increased as systems of transportation improved and became almost instantaneous in the late twentieth century when information technology in the form of the Internet, satellite, and cable television became widely available. In the twenty-first century the borderless world of the *ummah* is divided only by barriers of its own making. The success and influence of the Arabic news network Al-Jazeera, which now rivals the American CNN network, is further proof of the global reach of Islam.

The religion of Islam, its followers believe, offers the spiritual and intellectual resources necessary for human life at all times. But how are these resources being used to meet the challenges of rapid political and social change, global business practices, and international concerns about human rights and democratization? These are questions which have been energetically debated among Muslims during the twentieth century but the discussions have rarely been reported in non-Muslim societies. This is despite the fact that the world's Muslim populations are influential, expanding, and concerned to establish inter-civilizational dialogues. As well, many young Muslims have increasingly become disillusioned with what they perceive as the materialistic and immoral behaviour of leading Western nations and, under the leadership of charismatic religious teachers, are taking steps to make their views heard both within their own societies and beyond. While the Western media is quick to report the more violent expressions of frustration and anger of the members of militant Muslim groups, they almost never present the debates and ideological positions which are circulating among the proliferating study groups and e-mail networks which are a prime means of communication between Muslims in the new millennium. Almost never reported by the Western media are the attempts by many young Muslims to define and articulate a moral vision for action in contemporary society.[1]

The chapters in this book are presented in pairs which offer Middle Eastern (and in one case South Asian) points of view which are matched by

Southeast Asian perspectives on each of the issues selected as being of importance for the twenty-first century. It is useful to understand that Islam, the most recent of the world's great religions, was received into societies with established customs and traditions. In its first historical context of Mecca and Medina, the societies were tribal Arab groups who had long associations with mixed communities, which included Jews and Christians. The earliest interpretations of the Qur'an were made in the particular context of the Middle East in the seventh and eighth centuries CE. As Muslims travelled the great trade routes to India, Southeast Asia, and China, they encountered complex and well-established local belief systems and societies which were very different from those of the Middle East. Those societies which over time accepted Islam did not necessarily abandon their own customs and traditions, and Islam outside its heartlands had to be translated, literally and symbolically, into local modes and languages. Although the chapters in this book do not describe the history of these translations, readers will appreciate the diversity which now exists on the practical level.[2]

The first two chapters address the topic of the New World Order[3] and describe how Muslims in the Middle East and in Indonesia have responded to the reconfiguration of world politics since the formal ending of the Cold War (1990). Professor Amin Saikal, political scientist and Director of the Centre for Arab and Islamic Studies at The Australian National University, looks at the tensions between Islam and the West and places them in historical perspective before moving into the present. He argues that during its first four centuries (seventh to tenth centuries CE), Islamic leaders had a good record of tolerance for non-Muslims. The wars with the Christian armies during the periods of the Crusades, however, and the massacres committed in the name of Christianity later followed by colonization of much of the Muslim world by Western nations, resulted in mutual distrust and suspicion. In the period following the Second World War, political and military domination of the United States underlined its influence in global affairs so that its attitudes to Islam were of crucial importance in international diplomacy. Amin Saikal identifies three issues which shaped U.S. perceptions of Islam and resulted in its attempts to marginalize Islam in world politics. This policy has created disillusion and resentment among many Islamic groups who have become openly critical of U.S. policies and hegemonic behaviour, and these groups provide fertile grounds for recruits for extremist organizations such as Al-Qaeda. The chapter concludes by emphasizing the responsibilities of the United States as the superpower of our times to promote peaceful interaction between Muslims and non-Muslims and to reassess its own attitudes to Islam.

Samsu Rizal Panggabean focuses on Indonesia to present a range of Muslim responses to the New World Order (NWO). A lecturer in International Relations at Indonesia's prestigious Gadjah Mada University and Director of its Centre for Security and Peace Studies, he argues that, in general, Indonesian Muslims' perceptions of the NWO are shaped by domestic factors. Because the condition of domestic politics and prevailing domestic economic situations influence how Indonesian Muslims react to issues related to the NWO, their views can change over time. In his chapter, Rizal provides examples of the range of views held by Indonesian Muslims. The attitude of Muslims in Aceh towards the United States, for example, is markedly different from some groups of Javanese Muslims. The difference is based on the political needs and aims of each group. Although Indonesian Muslims' attitudes to the NWO are influenced, in large measure, by domestic concerns, Rizal notes a tendency to use conspiracy theories (involving "unbelievers", Christians, Jews and/or "the West") to deflect blame for domestic crises to forces outside Indonesia.

Responses to the NWO are followed by two chapters that address the second of the book's six topics, "the New Age". Associate Professor Ahmad Shboul provides an extensive overview of current Islamic thinking about globalization in some of the leading nations of the Arab world and Professor Nurcholish Madjid discusses concepts of humanitarianism in the Qur'an before moving to the specific context of development in Indonesia. Both authors note that Muslims have inherited a civilization which has already functioned as a truly global civilization and that Muslims should draw from their past experiences and revive the Islamic spirit of universal humanitarianism.

Associate Professor Shboul, born in Jordan and a graduate of the University of London, is Co-ordinator of Arab, Islamic and Middle Eastern Studies at the University of Sydney, and has written widely on history, culture and political change in the Arab world. He carefully traces the variety of perceptions in the Arab world about the meaning and significance of "globalism" and its more negative derivative "globalization". While "globalism" as an Arabic term carries positive connotations of worldwide cultural and economic flows, "globalization" is understood by a majority of Arab intellectuals as "the latest manifestation of Western imperialism". Thus, many among the Arab Left identify "globalization" with the worst features of capitalism, neo-liberalism and neo-imperialism which they believe threaten to undermine Arab culture and, as also noted in Professor Saikal's chapter, they perceive it as a further attempt to marginalize the Arab world. Associate Professor Shboul describes the responses of some Arab thinkers who have suggested alternative systems to that of global capitalism and a few who can view globalization as a challenge and an opportunity for creative action.

Taking modernity as an issue of critical importance to the Arab world, Associate Professor Shboul uses it to describe the internal and external cultural and intellectual challenges it poses. The internal challenge, he explains, concerns the confrontation of views between Muslims of secularist orientation with those whose interpretations of Islam are fundamentalist in character, a confrontation which becomes very marked when dealing with "political Islam". The external challenge concerns the apparent supremacy of "the West" and the Arab world's dilemma about how to achieve its own version of modernity. Associate Professor Shboul suggests that an appreciation of the nature of the internal and external challenges provides a strong background for understanding Arab views on globalization.

In further elaborating the views of fundamentalist, extremist Muslim groups, Associate Professor Shboul describes the exclusivist nature of their world view which divides peoples into those who follow their restricted (and sometimes distorted) interpretations of Islam and those who do not, so that they cut themselves off from the *ummah* as a whole and are unreceptive to and critical of the contemporary world. Many Arab intellectuals have voiced concern about the motives of these groups and their divisive influence on the Muslim world, let alone their lack of intellectual vision. To balance this narrowness of outlook, Associate Professor Shboul provides examples of the lively intellectual debates which have been occurring throughout the Arab world since the mid-1970s, providing examples of the theories developed by activists such as Tunisia's Dr Rashid Ghannoushi and Morocco's Al-Jabiri.

For the resource-rich Gulf sates, in particular, globalization poses very practical problems. As one of his examples, Associate Professor Shboul cites the fact that some of those states depend on foreign powers for their security and defence needs, increasing the perception of ongoing Western dominance in the region, which has been exacerbated by the conduct of the Gulf War in 2003. Associate Professor Shboul concludes his chapter by reminding readers that the media focus on the views and behaviour of Muslim extremists should be balanced by an appreciation of the views of progressive and rationalist Arab thinkers who work more creatively for change.

Mankind's capacity for creative energy is also one of the themes of Professor Nurcholish Madjid's chapter. One of Indonesia's most famous intellectuals, Professor Madjid draws on his understanding of the classical texts of Islam to argue for a contextual interpretation of the Qur'an so that its essential principles can be applied to any time and any place. He has written extensively on Islam and modernization in Indonesia and in his chapter for this book his discussion of the application of Islamic values in contemporary life ranges widely to touch on globalization, the dynamic of economic and social development, mankind's capacity for innovation, and the need to balance freedom with responsibility.

Professor Madjid acknowledges the difficulties and complexities of life in the modern age but urges Muslims to live "actively", draw closer to God, and at the same time make a commitment to assist those who live in suffering. The quality of mutual care between individuals whatever their beliefs, and the protection of the religious freedom of all peoples are, he emphasizes, basic principles of Islam. Throughout the chapter he draws on the Qur'an to show how Islam teaches that people are essentially good because of their God-given natures and that all people should respect and recognize this innate goodness and maintain a positive view of each other. One of the values of globalization, he argues, is its potential to improve communication between people and increase the interchange of ideas. However, he cautions, it is essential for individuals to feel they have a strong spiritual underpinning and sense of identity which allows for the consolidation of pluralism and appreciation of diversity.

Both Associate Professor Shboul and Professor Madjid stress that the Qur'an encourages practical involvement in the problems and concerns of daily life. This aspect of Islam is explored from the perspective of banking and finance by the authors of the next two chapters. Professor Nur Ahmad Fadhil Lubis is Vice-Rector (Vice-President) of the State Islamic Institute of North Sumatra in Medan, Indonesia. His doctorate is from the United States and he has specialized in Islamic law. The topic of his recent research is the formation and operation of small credit groups which try to operate according to Islamic principles. In his chapter for this book, Professor Lubis begins with a brief account of the Islamization of Indonesia including the intensification of interest in "being a good Muslim" which developed in the 1980s and 1990s among the growing urban middle class. During that period, Professor Lubis explains, the focus of many of these Indonesian Muslims was on implementing Islamic values and the principles of Islamic law in ways which would improve social and economic conditions for their fellows. Like Professor Madjid, he notes that improving society for the benefit of those who were in need is considered a religious duty incumbent on all Muslims.

In the area of providing for the necessities of life, the Qur'an provides a number of guides, as discussed by Professor Lubis. Trade and business activities are honourable and beneficial if they are free of usury (lending money at a high rate of interest). The nature of the banking system of Indonesia was discussed before Independence and the Islamic principle of usury-free credit was endorsed.[4] However, "the concept of bank interest for productive loans or interest which was not excessively high" was allowed if the bank is licensed by the government.[5] Obviously, this compromise was not acceptable to many Muslim scholars, and from the late 1970s, Professor Lubis notes, Indonesian Muslims were actively exploring how Islamic principles could be applied more effectively to banking and finance.

During the 1990s, the renewed interest in applying Islamic principles to all aspects of social life (as mentioned above), resulted in the establishment of a range of banks and small credit organizations based on Islamic law. Legislation passed in the post-Soeharto era not only confirms the principles of Islamic law, but also extends them to "other *shari'a* based monetary transactions" such as *zakat*.

In his chapter, Professor Lubis claims that the topic of Islamic economics is one of the most difficult in contemporary Muslim debate. He writes, "[n]o subject in recent Islamic writings has been more open to honest misunderstanding on the one hand, and deliberate misrepresentations on the other". Hope for the future, in his view, lies with Muslims who are thoroughly trained in Islamic law and who have mastered the principles of contemporary economics. Professor Abdullah Saeed's chapter complements the points made by Professor Lubis by moving beyond Indonesia to trace the development of models for Islamic banking and finance in more general terms.

Professor Saeed is Sultan of Oman Professor of Arab and Islamic Studies at the University of Melbourne. He has an undergraduate degree from Saudi Arabia and a doctorate in Islamic studies from the University of Melbourne. Like Professor Lubis, he has published widely on Islamic finance with particular attention to various interpretations of the meaning of *riba* (usury). As Professor Saeed points out, the question of Islamic banking and financial practice raises some of the most practical issues about idealism versus pragmatism: how can Muslims remain true to Islamic principles and also participate fully in the commercial life of the twenty-first century. The chapter illustrates that there is no single answer to the question but rather a range of positions which Muslims have adopted to accommodate theory and practice.

Professor Saeed's chapter includes a brief history of Islamic banking principles from the 1950s until the present and explains the principles which now underpin financial dealings. Central to these is the concept of profit and loss sharing (PLS) which is based on the principle that a sharing of risk is balanced by a sharing of returns where effort, capital, and risk have been pooled to bring a return on an investment. To illustrate the accommodation some Muslim bankers have made to achieve a practical return while still adhering to Muslim principles, Professor Saeed describes four examples of actual practice. In doing so, these bankers and financiers demonstrate the creative abilities of mankind in their application of logic and reason, as described in Professor Madjid's chapter.

The fourth topic which the book addresses is ways in which Muslims are responding to the concept of the nation-state. The two chapters in this section describe experiences in Indonesia and in Iran. Professor Azyumardi Azra a historian, whose doctoral study was at Columbia University, New York, is President of Jakarta's highly regarded State Islamic University Syarif Hidayatullah (UIN). His chapter notes the increase in political activity by a number of Muslim groups in Indonesia following the relaxing of restrictions imposed by the government of former President Soeharto. He stresses that there is no one united political position held by all Muslim political groups and that only a small minority seriously debate the possibility of establishing an Islamic state in Indonesia. They are outnumbered by those who consider the concept impractical and unsuitable for the Republic of Indonesia.

The period of *reformasi* which followed Soeharto's stepping down as president (1998) saw a growth in the number of political parties which claimed links with Islam. Of the twenty Islamic parties which contested the 1999 general elections, Professor Azra notes that only ten claim Islam as their sole ideological basis. The poor performance of all parties claiming to be Islamic is strong evidence, Professor Azra says, that Indonesian Muslims separate their personal devotion to Islam from their political behaviour. And even though Muslim scholar Abdurrahman Wahid, leader of Indonesia's largest Muslim organization, became President of the Republic, he is not regarded as having promoted a specifically Muslim agenda. His successor, President Megawati Sukarnoputri has also not been seen as favouring increased Islamization of Indonesia; in fact, she has been criticized by some Muslim leaders for not doing enough to recognize the importance of Islam as the majority religion in Indonesia. Therefore, Professor Azra asks, "... what is the prospect of Islamic parties, or even political Islam? How viable is the idea of stronger and more formal connections between Islam and the Indonesian nation-state?"

Professor Azra warns that there has been an increase in violent activities initiated by splinter groups within the Muslim communities. He advocates four areas which require firm action by the central government if these activities by radical groups are to be controlled. Three of the areas he nominates are concerned with good governance and the enforcement of law and order. These are issues which are also discussed by Dr Gholamali

Khoshroo, Deputy Foreign Minister (Legal and International Affairs) in the Islamic Republic of Iran.

Dr Khoshroo begins his chapter with a survey of the history of the concept of the nation-state as it was developed in sixteenth and seventeenth century European thinking. He argues that the main characteristics of the nation-state are territorial sovereignty; national identity; and democratic legitimacy. The concept of nationalism, as personal loyalty to the nation above all else, he points out, runs counter to the Islamic ideal of the *ummah*, which transcends the concepts of all man-made affiliations and boundaries. One of the challenges for modern political entities is how to achieve a balance between the realities of the modern nation-state and the transcendency of the *ummah* as the group concept which takes precedence over all others.

Dr Khoshroo takes the example he knows best, that of the Islamic Republic of Iran, to show how its experiences since the Iranian revolution of 1978/79 have contributed to bringing together the concept of the nation and of the *ummah*.[6] Under President Khatami (1997–), there have been ongoing efforts to strengthen civil society and promote debate about how to formulate an Iranian identity, remain true to Islam, and express this through the political framework of a republic. The Constitution of the republic shows how the balance is being sought between God's law, human interpretations of that law and its implementation.

As already explained in Professor Madjid's chapter, God has given mankind the power to reason, and mankind therefore has the responsibility to shape society and politics in ways which will maintain the republic and the *ummah*. The Islamic Republic of Iran has instituted several procedures to ensure the rules of the Constitution are in line with Islamic law and also that the principles of Islamic law can be interpreted in a way which allows them to be followed in the contemporary world. Dr Khoshroo cites the Foreign Investment Bill and Iran's proposed membership of the WTO as issues which have tested the Parliament and the Councils, which have to rule on the balance between practicability and religious law.

The topic "Muslim women" is the subject of two chapters which approach the issues facing Muslim women in the early twenty-first century from the perspective of South Asia, the Middle East, and Indonesia. Dr Samina Yasmeen is a political scientist specializing in international politics at the University of Western Australia. She has also conducted large-scale research projects on Pakistani and Middle Eastern women and draws on some of that material for her chapter. Globalization, Dr Yasmeen argues, has been a productive factor in supporting the growth of social movements, particularly in the Middle East and in South Asia. These movements "are characterized by loose and often non-hierarchical networks of disparate individuals, groups or organizations" who aim to bring about, or sometimes to oppose social change through channels which lie outside the normal political structures. The question Dr Yasmeen asks is whether Muslim women are active in these social movements? She uses the issue of human rights to test whether women are involving themselves in groups working for social change and, if so, what positions they are taking.

In broad terms, Dr Yasmeen says data on the occupations of Muslim middle-class women in the Middle East and South Asia show they are moving out of their traditional roles as home-makers and nurturers, whose lives revolved around the private domain of their homes, to take up positions which bring them increasingly into the public domain. However, although these women may have similarities of background and share a common experience of seeking employment beyond the home, do they share the same attitudes to women's access to human rights?

Dr Yasmeen's findings support those of the earlier chapters: that is, there is no single "Muslim" position on critical issues, including that of rights for women. She provides details of the range of positions she encountered in her research. Using the example of a spectrum, she places those who view women's rights through secular lenses and use global terms to describe the issues at one end. These "secular feminists" often encounter resistance to their activities from other groups within their own societies and from their own government but in the process of their campaigns establish links with similar organizations in other parts of the world. At the opposite end of the spectrum are those whose views are shaped by what Dr Yasmeen terms "Islamic traditionalism". She refers to women with these views as "Islamic feminists" and describes their beliefs as being firmly grounded in Islamic principles, particularly the application of the rules which recognize the rights of women within Islam. Using the terminology of Islam (including adoption of *hijab* as an emblem of Muslim identity) most support women's participation in certain areas of public life although there are divisions concerning the role of women in politics.

Between the two ends of the spectrum lies a "middle space" which Dr Yasmeen describes as being occupied by women "who try to negotiate between their Islamic identity and the reality of living in a globalized era". Women in this "middle space" may not be so tied to the dictates of particular ideologies and therefore have greater flexibility to experiment with a variety of ways to achieve their aims of greater recognition of the rights of women. It is in this "middle space" that women mediate, on a personal and public level, between Islamic and secular identities, seeking ways of addressing critical issues such as family planning and women's health measures in terms which do not run counter to Islamic principles. Because the groups who work between extremes represent true moderation (rather than expressions of extremism), Dr Yasmeen sees them as extremely effective and important agents of change whose efforts deserve international recognition and support.

Dr Kathryn Robinson from The Australian National University, a noted anthropologist and analyst of women's issues in Indonesia, takes a longer view of Muslim women's participation in public life in Indonesia. The failure of Megawati Sukarnoputri to be appointed President immediately after being the popular winner of the 1999 Indonesian general elections, is her starting point for an analysis of the role of Islam in debates about women's participation in public life.

Dr Robinson takes examples of debates about women in the 1930s, the 1950s, and in the late 1990s to illustrate her points. As in the Middle East and South Asia, the Indonesian debates up to the late 1990s (the time of Megawati's candidature as President), focused on the ways in which Islam influenced women's positions in the family and the home. But concerning women's participation in public life, the Indonesian debates differ from those in the Middle East and South Asia by *not* influencing women's rights in that area.

The specific case of the possibility of a female president, however, as a result of Megawati's electoral success in 1999, stimulated debate about whether this aspect of women's participation in public life was acceptable under Islamic law. Dr Robinson chronicles the main themes of the debates that revolved around literalist or contextualist interpretations of Islamic texts. In the lead-up to the appointment of Abdurrahman Wahid as President, several influential Muslim groups argued that it was not permissible to have a woman as head of state. Less than two years later, when Abdurrahman Wahid had been impeached and stepped down, the majority of Muslim groups gave their support to Megawati. The issues concerning female leadership, it seems, were political rather than religious in nature.[7] Dr Robinson concludes her chapter by highlighting the fact that the "woman as president" issue in Indonesia actually strengthened support for the position of women by encouraging public discussion about gender equity and Islam. Many prominent Indonesian Muslims made statements which argued that Islam does not support the inferior status of women.

Dr Robinson refers to the influence of Islam on Indonesian family law in her chapter. Professor Azra also describes moves to implement Islamic law in several areas of Indonesia. The nature of Islamic law (*shari'a*) in Indonesia has aroused considerable interest both within Indonesia and more widely afield and is addressed in this book by Professor M. B. Hooker, an internationally acknowledged analyst of Islamic law in Southeast Asia. Indonesia is not an Islamic state and the Constitution defines Islam. However, Professor Hooker asks: how did the state come to dominate Islam and is this dominance permanent?

Presenting his responses in a historical context of the impact of colonial administration on the *shari'a* in the Netherlands East Indies, Professor Hooker describes some of the important debates which occurred before it was decided that the independent Republic of Indonesia would take the form of a secular state. Nevertheless, Islamic law was still enforceable for Indonesia's Muslim population, although its administration by colonial authorities had reduced its jurisdiction to a limited amount of family law. While in formal terms the *shari'a* has been dominated by the Indonesian state, Indonesian Muslim leaders throughout the twentieth century have been formulating *fatāwā* which reveal their attention to meeting the specific needs of Indonesians in their own time and place.[8] In this chapter, he selects just four of Indonesia's outstanding Muslims to argue that their views on the interpretation of Islam in an Indonesian context "suggests an original and Indonesian intellectualism". One of these figures is Nurcholish Madjid, author of an earlier chapter in this book, whom Professor Hooker suggests offers the beginnings of a new method for Islamic reasoning in Indonesia.

In concluding his chapter, Professor Hooker identifies two systems that he believes have resulted from efforts to translate the *shari'a* into a temporal context while maintaining the integrity of Prophetic Revelation. He refers to the first as "responsive scholasticism" which was characteristic of Indonesian Islamic scholarship during the colonial period when Muslims felt the need to defend Islam in the face of Dutch dominance over the administration of Islam. The second, he terms "creative scholasticism", which became evident in the second decade after Independence, and reveals a new confidence about ways of interpreting Islam in its Indonesian context. It is this second mode of scholasticism which Professor Hooker suggests carries its own inherent dangers but also indicates that the dominance of the state over Islamic law may be tested and contested.

In his chapter, Professor Aris Othman, an experienced Malaysian academic who is Dean of the Faculty of Islamic Revealed Knowledge and Human Sciences at the International Islamic University, Kuala Lumpur addresses the issue of reconstructing knowledge so that it reflects the principles of Islam. This is a project which gathered pace in the last quarter of the twentieth century and was initiated by Muslim social scientists to explore and define the relationship between revealed and acquired knowledge. There are similarities here with the Indonesian efforts, described by Professor M.B. Hooker, to interpret the *shari'a* in a way which was relevant to the contemporary needs of Indonesian Muslims (see also the book's concluding chapter). For the social scientists concerned with the decline in the status of Islamic knowledge systems (compared with their glory in the Medieval and Late Medieval periods), the challenge is to make all Islamic religious disciplines relevant to contemporary issues. For the new millennium, Professor Aris suggests, a specific contribution from Islamic thought to the common good would be a restoration of an integrated approach to life which Islam has maintained but the West has lost.

Professor Aris sees globalization as a means of facilitating better communications between Muslims and non-Muslims to increase mutual understanding. Finally, he sees the harmonious spirit of *jama'ah* (togetherness), a characteristic of Muslim social organization, as a positive contribution to improving harmony in other societies.

One of the themes which runs through each of the chapters in this book is the ongoing creativity of Muslim intellectuals and scholars. In Professor M. B. Hooker's words " 'the crisis of modernity' at the end of the twentieth century has in fact reinvigorated *ijtihad* to an unexpected degree". The book concludes with a chapter which presents a forward look into the twenty-first century by analysing the positions of a contemporary group of liberally-minded Muslims in Indonesia. Their debates draw on the thinking of Muslims in the Middle East, South Asia, Europe, and the United States to support their wide-ranging arguments for change to very literal interpretations of Islam. Although their ideas represent only one group among many who have strong opinions about how Muslims could embrace the opportunities of the twenty-first century, the vigour of their debates reflects the passion which currently surrounds most discussions of Islam in the early twenty-first century.

Notes

1. This atmosphere of lively polemics has received a warm welcome by groups of young Muslim intellectuals in Indonesia. One group, whose members have an e-mail network, write in the print media and appear on talk-back programmes, has published excerpts from a selection of its debates (which are discussed in the final chapter of this book). Entitled *Wajah Liberal Islam di Indonesia* (The Face of Liberal Islam in Indonesia), the publisher compares the contestation of interpretations of Islam which is currently taking place with the impact of printing on debates about Christianity in sixteenth century Europe, see "Sekapur Sirih" in *Wajah Liberal Islam di Indonesia*, edited by Luthfi Assyaukanie (Jakarta: Jaringan Islam Liberal and Teater Utan Kayu, 2002), p. vii.

2. For descriptions of the "coming of Islam" to Southeast Asia, see Peter Riddell, *Islam and the Malay-Indonesian World: Transmission and Responses* (London: Hurst & Company, 2001); P. M. Holt et al., *The Cambridge History of Islam*, Volume 2A, Part VI (Cambridge: Cambridge University Press, 1977), pp. 123–208; Azyumardi Azra, *The Origins of Islamic Reform in Southeast Asia: Networks of Middle Eastern and Malay-Indonesian 'Ulama in the Seventeenth and Eighteenth Centuries* (St Leonards: Allen & Unwin, 2004).
3. The "New World Order" was first used as an official term by George Bush Senior, former President of the United States, to describe international society, its shaping procedures and institutions, after Iraq annexed Kuwait in 1990. During the Gulf War (1991), the term was used to describe the collective opposition (led by the United States) to Iraq's behaviour which was conducted in the name of halting aggression, relieving civilian suffering and restoring law and order. See further B. V. Muralidhar, "The New World Order: The Concept in Historical Perspective", *Journal of Diplomacy and Foreign Relations* 2, no. 2 (December 2000): 61–66; Hilal Khashan, "The New World Order and the Tempo of Militant Islam", *British Journal of Middle Eastern Studies* 24, Issue 1 (May 1997): 5–24.
4. Further details are given in M. Dawam Rahardjo, "The Question of Islamic Banking in Indonesia", in *Islamic Banking in Southeast Asia*, edited by Mohamed Ariff (Singapore: Institute of Southeast Asian Studies, 1988, first reprint 1992), pp. 137–63.
5. Ibid., p. 140.
6. Analyses of the period in Iran leading up to the events described by Dr Khoshroo are given in the three essays which comprise Part Five, "Revolution in Iran", in Edmund Burke, III and Ira M. Lapidus, eds., *Islam, Politics and Social Movements* (Berkeley, Los Angeles, and London: University of California Press, 1988), pp. 263–314.
7. A broad overview of recent issues affecting all Indonesian women is given in the collection entitled *Women in Indonesia: Gender, Equity and Development*, edited by Kathryn Robinson and Sharon Bessell (Singapore: Institute of Southeast Asian Studies, 2002).
8. A detailed account of the range and topics of Indonesian *fatāwā* through the twentieth century is given in M. B. Hooker, *Indonesian Islam: Social Change through Contemporary Fatāwā* (St Leonards: Allen & Unwin, 2003).

References

Azra, Azyumardi. *The Origins of Islamic Reform in Southeast Asia: Networks of Middle Eastern and Malay-Indonesian 'Ulama in the Seventeenth and Eighteenth Centuries.* St Leonards: Allen & Unwin, 2004.

Assyaukanie, Luthfi. "Sekapur Sirih". In *Wajah Liberal Islam di Indonesia*, edited by Luthfi Assyaukanie. Jakarta: Jaringan Islam Liberal and Teater Utan Kayu, 2002.

Burke, Edmund, III, and Ira M. Lapidus eds. *Islam, Politics and Social Movements.* Berkeley, Los Angeles and London: University of California Press, 1988.

Holt, P. M., et al., *The Cambridge History of Islam.* Volume 2A, Part VI. Cambridge: Cambridge University Press, 1977.

Hooker, M. B. *Indonesian Islam: Social Change through Fatāwā* . St Leonards: Allen & Unwin, 2003.

Khashan, Hilal. "The New World Order and the Tempo of Militant Islam". *British Journal of Middle Eastern Studies* 24, Issue 1 (May 1997): 5–24.

Muralidhar, B. V. "The New World Order: The Concept in Historical Perspective". *Journal of Diplomacy and Foreign Relations* 2, no. 2 (December 2000): 61–66.

Rahardjo, M. Dawam. "The Question of Islamic Banking in Indonesia". In *Islamic Banking in Southeast Asia,* edited by Mohamed Ariff. Singapore: Institute of Southeast Asian Studies, 1988. Reprint 1992.

Riddell, Peter. *Islam and the Malay-Indonesian World: Transmission and Responses.* London: Hurst & Company, 2001.

Robinson, Kathryn and Sharon Bessell, eds. *Women in Indonesia: Gender, Equity and Development.* Singapore: Institute of Southeast Asian Studies, 2002.

The New World Order

2

ISLAM AND THE WEST
Challenges and Opportunities[1]

Amin Saikal

Whilst relations between the West and the world of Islam are today complex and multi-dimensional, with elements of both conflict and co-operation, in general they are very tense. This tension has its roots not so much in religious but in political and politically motivated perceptual differences, the intensity of which has fluctuated according to the political utility of the issues that have occasioned the two sides to expose their differences. Since the horrific attacks on the United States on 11 September 2001, the tension has sharply escalated. On the whole, two opposing views have come to dominate the Western and Islamic approaches to dealing with each other. One is a Western contention, which has resonated more strongly in Washington than in any other Western capital, that the forces of political Islam which have defied American control or influence constitute a brand of Islamic fundamentalism that threatens Western interests and must be combated. Another is a view, which is widespread among not only the political forces of Islam but also moderate Islamists and ordinary Muslims, that the U.S. "cold warrior" realists have deliberately fabricated the notion of an "Islamic threat" for one important purpose — to maintain a Western sense of superiority and hegemony over the Muslim world.

Yet amid all this, both sides — more out of necessity than anything else — have found it increasingly important to interlock in a globalized world in ways that can help them to minimize their political differences and improve relations. This, however, will only happen should the two sides be prepared to let principles of positive dialogue, based on the mutual accommodation of interests rather than those of opportunism and ideological supremacy, prevail in the conduct of their foreign relations.

This chapter has three main objectives. The first is to explore some of the features that the West and the Muslim world hold in common, which have helped them to pursue durable paths of peaceful coexistence. The second is to tease out the key factors that underlie the growth of tension in the relations between them in recent times. The third is to make a number of proposals for the easing of that tension.

That the relationship between the Muslim world and the largely Christian West has been far from smooth since the advent of Islam in the early seventh century is to state the obvious. This is despite the fact that Islam and Christianity, and for that matter Judaism, share a great deal of beliefs and values. They are the three main monotheistic faiths that not only embrace a common concept of God, but also give equal weight to the sanctity of life as a precious gift from God. They are all rich in fundamental social principles from which strong notions of universal ethics and justice can be drawn, and in relation to which a virtuous life can be lived on earth. These principles can be deployed to promote causes for reconciliation and reasons for coexistence based on a non-competitive and non-combative notion of justice and moral existence. One of the central elements of Christianity (and, for that matter, of Judaism) is "do justly, to love mercy, and to walk humbly with God". Christianity has evolved to stress justice based on the principle that one must not do to others what one does not want done to oneself. This is akin to the Islamic principles, as enshrined in the Qur'an, that strongly emphasize the notion of justice as the closest to that of piety, and the significance of compassion, forgiveness, mercy, and persuasion to a humane existence. Muslims are also guided by the command that they must respect all of God's apostles and revealed books before Muhammad and the Qur'an, and that they must be respectful to the followers of these religions and provide them with protection under their rule, while affirming that their own religion, prophet, and book are final. Thus, an overwhelming majority of Muslims have historically been respectful towards Christians and Jews.

Moreover, as with the other two revealed religions, Islam puts a high premium on the value of life, and in Islam only God as the creator and mover of the universe is empowered to give and take life. The Qur'an states that all Muslims will be rewarded or punished on the Day of Judgement according to their deeds. This, however, does not preclude the notion of "self-sacrifice" in the way of God or in the defence of Islam. Hence, the combative *jihad* (struggle, battle) is but one of the varieties of *jihad* in Islam. Whilst *jihad* generally carries "the basic connotation of an endeavour toward a praiseworthy aim", a combative *jihad* involves "a struggle against one's evil inclinations or an exertion for the sake of Islam and the *ummah*". Conceptually, a *jihad* is a defensive act and proportionate to the Islamic emphasis on the sanctity of life, and comes closest to what is described by the Western concept of "just war". In Islam only learned religious authorities who have reached the highest stage of *ijtihād,* with widespread recognition in the Muslim world, can declare a *jihad.* There is no such authority in the Muslim world today.

These common features and Islamic ordinances were important in fostering an initial period of highly tolerant coexistence among Muslims, Jews, and Christians during the first four centuries of Islam. They were manifested critically in the wake of the Islamic conquest of Jerusalem — which is, for Muslims, the third holiest site after Mecca and Medina — early in the mid-630s (CE). Under the "Omar Agreement", which was named after the second Caliph of Islam, Omar Ibn al-Khitab, Arab Muslim forces established Muslim political rule over Jerusalem, but accorded full recognition of the right to freedom of religion for Jews and Christians in the city. The employment of Jewish, Christian, and many other non-Muslim thinkers, scholars, and professionals alongside their Muslim counterparts in the court of the Abbassids (750–1250 CE) marked the height of this development. This is not to claim that these co-religionists lived in perfect harmony at all times, but it does indicate that a remarkable degree of peaceful coexistence, mutual respect, and tolerance prevailed among them. At the time, the Jewish biblical claim to Palestine as the "promised land" was not markedly pronounced, and the Arab Muslim rule of Palestine did not cause many Jews and Christians to feel ostracized. The Jewish claim to be the divinely chosen people, the Christian claim of precedence over Islam, and the Islamic exaltation of an authoritative nature as the seal of all revealed faiths did not override shared values and a largely harmonious coexistence. To a considerable extent, this remained the case for most of the Ottoman rule of the Arab world in general, and Palestine in particular (1350–1918 CE).

However, the situation changed with the Christian Crusades and the subsequent Western colonial and imperialist encroachment upon the Muslim world. The Crusades against Islam, the brutal capture of Jerusalem twice between 1099 and 1229 CE, and the final recapture of the city by Muslims by the mid-thirteenth century left lasting distrust and residual enmity between many of the orthodox followers of the two religions. European (especially British and French) colonialism, beginning in the wake of European expansionism from the sixteenth century CE, reinforced the painful residue of the Crusades. It caused widespread humiliation for Muslims, as many of their communities in the Middle East, South Asia, and Southeast Asia fell to European domination and cultural suppression.

The rise of the United States as a global power after the Second World War proved to be a double-edged phenomenon for Muslims. On the one hand, it helped them to free themselves of European colonial rule. On the other, it confronted them with difficult choices, especially in the context of American–Soviet Cold War rivalry. They were caught between a repugnance of godless Soviet socialism and American benevolent hegemonism. Whilst some Muslim countries found it necessary to walk a tightrope by leaning towards the Soviet Union and promoting non-alignment as a means to deflect their colonial past and counter America's imperialist reach, others rapidly drifted into the U.S. orbit. However, neither the first category, including such countries as Afghanistan, Egypt, and Somalia, nor the second category, including such states as Iran and Pakistan, found their experiences painless. In general, Muslim countries became highly distrustful, and in some cases resentful, of both powers, even though some of their ruling or opposition élites found comfort in alliances with one or the other.

European colonialism bifurcated the subjected Muslim societies into secularist élites that were dedicated to the goal of modernization along Western lines, and Islamic clusters that were devoted to reforming and reorganizing their societies according to Islamic teachings. In the late nineteenth and early twentieth centuries, the latter launched numerous ideological and combative challenges to Western domination. They ranged from Sayyed Jamal al-Din Al-Afghani's Pan-Islamic efforts to Hassan Al-Bana's endeavours with the Society of Muslim Brotherhood to unite Muslims at both national and regional levels against internal decay and outside intervention. They did not succeed in achieving their ultimate goals, but were important in germinating an awakening among Muslims that would gain deeper and wider salience after the Second World War.

In recent times, prior to the U.S.-led invasion of Iraq in March 2003, three developments have been instrumental in creating the necessary conditions for sharpening the enmities between the West and the Muslim world, and in motivating the West, more specifically the United States, to seek a geopolitical marginalization of Islam in world politics. The first was the Iranian revolution of 1978 that deposed one of America's key allies, Iran's absolute ruler Mohammed Reza Shah. The Iranian monarch had acted as the bridgehead for U.S. influence in Iran and the region since 1953, when the Central Intelligence Agency (CIA) reinstalled him on his throne. Although the revolution commenced as an anti-Shah phenomenon, it rapidly enabled the radical Iranian Shi'ite clerics, led by Ayatullah Khomeini, to seize the leadership and to establish a staunchly anti-American Islamic regime. Khomeini's Shi'ite Islamic regime was by no means widely emulated in the rest of the mainly Sunni-dominated Muslim countries. Nonetheless, in many ways it reflected the aspirations of all the Muslims in the region and beyond who felt humiliated and frustrated by their bitter experiences with the West. It inspired and emboldened many political forces of Islam from both sides of the Sunni-Shi'ite sectarian divide to challenge the influence of the West in the Middle East and elsewhere in the Muslim world. These forces were inspired as never before to seek either a peaceful or revolutionary political and social transformation of their societies along independent Islamic lines.

This, together with the seizure of fifty American diplomats for twenty months from November 1979 by Khomeini's Islamic militants, proved instrumental in moulding Washington's understanding of, and opposition to, radical or *jihadi* (exertive and combatant) political Islam. In the wake of its bitter experiences with Iranian and Iranian-inspired Islamism, Washington developed a particular mindset about radical political Islam that was shaped more by its own perceptions, experiences, and interests than by the reality of the phenomenon. It labelled as "fundamentalist" the political forces of Islam that either challenged or refused to recognize America's hegemonic interests and accord it the status of a global power. Washington considered these forces as an anomaly and a menace in the international system, and therefore liable to global suppression and isolation. Hence its deployment of "Islamic fundamentalism" as a pejorative term to disparage and discredit them as irrational, irresponsible, and extremist forces that were actually or potentially dedicated to the goal of international terrorism. This was a development that played into the hands of those who were keen, for one reason or another, to promote "Islamophobia", and those who had been, since the collapse of the Soviet Union, promoting the notion of a "clash of civilizations" in world politics.

The second development, which in its conception pre-dated the first, emanated from Western, and more importantly American, support of the Jewish state of Israel. Initially, the Western powers and the Soviet Union were driven more by moral and humanitarian considerations — given European persecution of the Jews in general and the Holocaust in particular — than by realpolitik to legitimize the creation of Israel out of the predominantly Arab-populated Palestine in 1948. However, the subsequent Western, especially American, behaviour in addressing the cost of creating an enduring Palestinian problem and Arab-Israeli conflict has had less moral and more realpolitik content. For the United States to embrace Israel within a few years of its creation as a strategic partner, with a commitment to guarantee its security and survival irrespective of its effect on the Palestinians in particular and the Arab-Muslim world in general, was a misdemeanour of gigantic proportions. It may have been beneficial to the pursuit of domestic and Cold War politics, but only at the cost of incalculable damage to relations with the Muslim world. Washington's massive financial and military assistance to enable Israel to maintain a strategic edge over its Arab neighbours, and its political protection of Israel at the United Nations and in other international forums, alienated the Arab masses and bred deep anti-American Islamic resentment in the region and beyond.

The turning point came with Israel's victory in the 1967 war, which enabled the Jewish state not only to occupy more land, but also to capture East Jerusalem. Israel's annexation of East Jerusalem to form, together with West Jerusalem, the "united capital" of Israel forever caused more anguish than ever before in the Muslim world's relations with the West. This, together with Washington's tepid reaction and the West's general sympathy for Israel, galvanized Muslim activists to grow more hostile towards Israel, and distrustful of the United States. Many viewed the whole development as a Jewish-Christian conspiracy that would ensure the continuation of the Palestinian problem and the Arab-Israeli conflict, and act as the main obstacle to finding a resolution. Although the Muslim Brotherhood had established cells in Palestine during the 1940s, it was now presented with a massive opportunity to expand its popular influence. By the late 1980s, the Muslim brothers found the necessary conditions to elevate the Palestinian radical Islamic group Hamas to the position of the major Islamist force in the Palestinian nationalist movement.

It has been suggested that Hamas was initially backed by Israel to counter the secularist Palestine Liberation Organization (PLO) under Yasser Arafat, which at the time was rejected as a "terrorist" organization. While this may have been so, Hamas was rapidly able to emerge as a strong anti-Israeli and anti-American movement. It drew not only on the PLO's failures and the increased suffering of Palestinians under Israeli occupation, but also the Islamic grievances of Palestinians and Muslims in general, to play a leading role in the *intifadeh* (uprising) that began late in 1987. In the end, whilst it felt threatened more by Hamas than by the PLO, Israel — with the backing of the United States — chose the PLO as a "partner" in the Oslo peace process, which the two sides initiated in September 1993. Yet, Hamas and its smaller sister organization Islamic Jihad, and many similar organizations in the region, were deeply troubled by the process and the United States' rejectionist attitude towards them. The advent of the second *intifadeh* against the continued occupation of Palestine in October 2000 magnified this sentiment.

From the perspective of the Palestinians, and that of most Islamists, the United States' strategic partnership with, and general Western sympathy for, Israel have enabled the Jewish state to defy any resolution of the Palestinian problem. It is their view that the U.S. maintenance of a monopoly on brokering the Middle East peace process has largely been designed to protect Israel. They argue that the United States cannot be a strategic ally of Israel and an impartial peace-broker at the same time. This view has never gained as much potency as it has in the current confrontation between the Israelis and the Palestinians, over which the United States and Israel have been condemned in almost equal terms throughout the region and beyond for Israel's use of excessive force against mostly unarmed Palestinian protestors. This, together with the way in which the U.S.-backed UN sanctions against Iraq have affected ordinary Iraqi people instead of Saddam Hussein's regime, has generated much anguish among Arabs, and has helped radical Islamic groups to serve as channels for the expression of this anguish against not only the United States, but also their own pro-American governments.

The third issue over which many Islamists and ordinary Muslims grew apprehensive was the U.S. counter-intervention strategy to address the Soviet occupation of Afghanistan in the 1980s, and its total neglect of post-communist Afghanistan. The Soviet invasion of Afghanistan in late December 1979 essentially confirmed all of the disdain that many Muslims had held for Marxist-Leninist Communism, and the perceived Soviet ambitions towards the region south of its borders. This was also an event that the United States, and other Western adversaries of the Soviet Union as well as the People's Republic of China, immediately used to achieve their long-standing goal of defeating Soviet Communism. However, in this instance Washington found it opportune to let realpolitik rather than ideological preferences determine its counter-interventionist strategy. Without any moral qualms, it welcomed the deployment of Islam as an ideology of resistance to Soviet occupation. It immediately embraced the Afghan Islamic resistance forces, the Mujahideen, which emerged as a mixture of radical and moderate groups, divided by personal, sectarian, tribal, ethnic, and linguistic differences. However, the United States confined its support to the main groups that were drawn from the majority Sunni Muslim population and based in Pakistan; it thus carefully avoided any action that could possibly help the Iranian-based Shi'ite Mujahideen groups or the Iranian regime.

Washington sprang into action to forge a regime of international assistance to the Pakistan-based Mujahideen, and helped Pakistan — the newly emerged frontline state in the fight against Soviet Communism — to act as the main conduit for anti-Soviet operations in Afghanistan. The CIA was given the prime responsibility for the conduct of America's proxy war. In a close alliance with Pakistan's military intelligence (ISI), the CIA trained and armed not only thousands of Afghans, but also hundreds of Muslims from Pakistan and the Arab world to join the Afghans in a *jihād* against the Soviets and their surrogates. It also developed contacts with, and forged an international network of, Islamic activists, some of whom were more radical and traditionalist than others, including some who were based in the United States.

However, when the Soviets withdrew and their surrogate regime in Kabul collapsed in the early 1990s, Washington turned its back on Afghanistan and left the country vulnerable to penetration by Pakistan's ISI. It turned a blind eye to Pakistan's creation in 1994 of an extremist Islamic militia — the Taliban — and its highly medievalist, discriminatory, and anti-human rights policies. It deferred to ISI's argument that such a militia was necessary to bring law and order to Afghanistan and protect it from Iran for the benefit of the United States in gaining access to the energy resources of the newly independent Central Asian states. This argument was also accepted by two of America's allies in the region, Saudi Arabia and the United Arab Emirates, which funded the Taliban.

Washington did not become substantially critical of the Taliban until mid-1998 when it accused Saudi Islamist dissident Osama Bin Laden of masterminding the bombing of American embassies in Nairobi and Dar-es-Salam. Bin Laden, who was once among those aided by the CIA to fight the Soviets in Afghanistan, but who subsequently turned against the United States for its support of what he called "the corrupt Saudi regime" and Israel's occupation of Palestine, especially East Jerusalem, had been protected by the Taliban in Afghanistan. It was the need to secure Bin Laden's extradition more than anything else that finally prompted the United States to become overtly critical of the Taliban. Even so, it continued to ignore repeated warnings by the Islamist leader of the Afghan anti-Taliban forces, Commander Ahmed Shah Massoud, who was assassinated two days before the 11 September attacks, that a dangerous and unprecedented alliance was developing in Afghanistan between extremist Arab and non-Arab groups, with the full patronage of Pakistan's ISI. While refusing to provide any assistance to Massoud, Washington refrained from criticizing Pakistan for creating and maintaining the Taliban and allowing its Arab allies to enter and exit

Afghanistan through Pakistan. In reality, Washington failed to develop a coherent policy of how to contain the Taliban and prevent Pakistan from making Afghans kill Afghans — all in the name of Islam, but for Pakistan's regional ambitions. It is plausible to argue that if it had not been for Bin Laden, the United States would have been quite content to see the Taliban operate as a force projecting an extremist image of the hostile political forces of Islam and dividing Muslims over what constituted an acceptable Islamism.

Although these three developments emerged from different bases and produced different outcomes, Washington's handling of them goes a long way towards explaining the tense state of relations that developed between the United States and political forces of Islam. It is clear that Iranian Islamic radicalism, the Afghan Islamic resistance, and Palestinian Islamic assertiveness interacted to induce an unprecedented degree of radicalization among Muslims, who have remained divided politically but have projected a semblance of unity in religious terms. Washington bears much responsibility for the way in which this radicalization has, at least from time to time, spawned and given rise to an anti-American and for that matter anti-Western upsurge in the Muslim world. The U.S. approach to these developments was from the start contradictory, naïve, and self-centred, devoid of any deep consideration for their long-term consequences. It showed little or no concern about the manner in which its policy actions could negatively affect the lives of ordinary Muslims and their perceptions of the West and relations with the West. Moreover, it failed to pay sufficient attention to the way in which its policy behaviour could play into the hands of those on both sides who, for political and ideological reasons, wanted the state of relations to remain confrontational.

No doubt the Clinton administration made visible efforts during its second term to come to grips with some of America's past mistakes in its dealings with the Muslim world, and introduced some perceptive changes in policy behaviour. While maintaining that adversarial forces of political Islam were threatening to Western interests, it endeavoured to be less belligerent in its disposition towards them than were its predecessors. It came to accept the fact that although these forces shared a common faith, they were nonetheless divided along sectarian, cultural, social, and political lines, which was reflected in their attitudes and operations in local circumstances. For example, whereas Hamas and its sister organization, Islamic Jihad (both Sunni) thrived very much on the Palestinian cause against Israel, Hezbullah (Shi'ite) was very much Lebanese in its opposition to Israel. Yet neither of them had any clear links with the Algerian Islamic Salvation Front, or with the Taliban and the Kashmiri Harakat al-Mujahideen.

Furthermore, the Clinton administration came to recognize the growing popularity of Islamic reformists in Iran, especially after Mohammed Khatami's landslide win in the 1997 election. It voiced support for President Khatami's push to generate an "Islamic civil society" and "Islamic democracy" in Iran, which contained many principles that underlined the operation of liberal democracy and the observance of human rights in the West. The Clinton administration was also attracted to Khatami's emphasis on the concept of a "dialogue of civilizations" and the use of humane co-operation to guide Iran's foreign relations. Although Khatami has faced serious domestic and international obstacles since that time, he has laid the necessary foundations for moderation in Iranian politics, and has made a marked contribution to relaxing the regional environment. If Khatami had succeeded in his politics, then his achievement could have had serious implications for regional and wider relations, and could result in an Iranian-American rapprochement.

In addition, the Clinton administration worked harder than its predecessors to remove a major anomaly in American foreign policy: one standard for Israel and another for the Arabs. Its efforts in finding a resolution to the Israeli-Palestinian conflict indicated that it wanted to diminish this anomaly as much as possible. However, its endeavours could not produce the desired result while the United States maintained its strategic alliance with Israel, East Jerusalem remained under the control of Israel, and the United States remained insensitive to the needs and aspirations of all Muslims beyond its own strategic power-plays. Clinton's Republican successor, George W. Bush, commenced his presidency with an aura of international defiance and global supremacy. Instead of building on Clinton's initiatives to address the root causes that gave rise to anti-Americanism in the Arab and Muslim world, his administration began to focus mainly on those issues that would underscore the position of the United States as the world's leading power.

It was against this backdrop that the condemnable attacks of 11 September materialized, and that Bin Laden and his Al-Qaeda network have been able to draw not only considerable support from radical Islamists but also an amount of quiet understanding and sympathy from many ordinary Muslims. This is not to suggest that that a majority of Muslims side with Bin Laden and his activists, and least of all the Taliban, whose theocratic rule was violently opposed even in Afghanistan. What it does convey is that there are plenty of anti-American grievances in the Muslim world that Bin Laden and his operatives can tap to galvanize public support. This is what they have precisely done to instigate a number of other subsequent attacks, such as those in Bali, Riyadh and Casablanca, in late 2002 and early 2003 at the cost of hundreds more civilian casualties. The Iraq War of March–April 2003, waged by the United States and two of its Anglo-Celtic allies (Britain and Australia) without the support of the UN Security Council and in defiance of international law to remove Saddam Hussein's regime from power has certainly aggravated the situation further. Without resulting either in the discovery of weapons of mass destruction or in linking Saddam Hussein's dictatorship to international terrorism, the war has deeply offended many Arabs/Muslims, giving people like Bin Laden and his supporters one more cause to harness wider public support for their anti-American stand.

To contain the situation from developing to a perpetual state of confrontation between the radical forces of political Islam and the United States and its allies, it is imperative for the United States and its supporters to focus on five urgent, interrelated political objectives.

The first must be to help rebuild Afghanistan and transform the country into a stable, secure, and viable state with a lasting participatory, pluralist political order as soon as possible. So far what has transpired is that the United States and its allies have won the battle in dismantling the Taliban regime and enabling the internationally-backed transitional government of President Hamid Karzai to take over, and in depriving Al-Qaeda of its Afghan sanctuaries. However, they have a long way to go to win the war in Afghanistan. The national situation is still so fragile in Afghanistan that any degree of international neglect could easily allow it to slip back to its pre-11 September conditions. The main criticism of the United States is that it has not invested enough in the area of reconstruction and security to ensure the long-term stability of Afghanistan.

The second objective must be to help Pakistan in achieving structural, political, social, economic, and security reforms and in restructuring the ISI in order to make it a responsible security organization with no powers to operate above the law either inside or outside Pakistan, and in returning to genuine democracy sooner rather than later. So far, all the Bush Administration has done is to prop up the position of Pakistan's military ruler, General Parvez Musharaf, and seek a political transformation of Pakistan in some kind of democracy under his leadership. As a consequence, it has done little to address the very factors which had made Pakistan in the first place a source of Islamic extremism and many of the problems that beset Afghanistan under the Taliban.

The third aim must be to secure a viable resolution of the Palestinian problem — a source of accumulated anti-American frustration and anger across the Arab and Muslim worlds. The Bush Administration has now endorsed a two-state solution to the problem, with a political roadmap to create a viable independent Palestinian state by 2005. But it is only lately that Washington has placed some urgency on the matter. Prior to that, President Bush allowed the right-wing Israeli Prime Minister Ariel Sharon to take advantage of the legitimacy of America's war on terror to intensify Israel's brutal suppression of the Palestinian resistance, involving Palestinian suicide bombing of civilian and military targets inside Israel. For a two-state solution to become a reality, it is now incumbent upon Washington to make Israel understand that its peace and security are ultimately intertwined with those of the Palestinians, and without a *viable* Palestinian state there can be no peace and security for Israel. If Washington fails to do this, there will be little chance of implementing the roadmap for peace: it may go down the same path to nowhere as did the Oslo peace process.

The fourth objective must be to empower the Iraqi people to determine their future and run their country, and thus to end occupation of Iraq, as quickly as possible. Most Iraqis, like their counterparts in the Arab and Muslim worlds, had little time for Saddam Hussein's dictatorship, but they are also equally indignant of any attempt by the United States and its allies to transform Iraq into a client state. Given the level of public opposition inside Iraq and in the region to a prolonged occupation of Iraq, the best option for the United States is now to pass on the process of transition of Iraq to the United Nations as the only international body with the necessary degree of legitimacy to do the job. A failure to do so could land the United States and its allies with more distrust and opposition in the Muslim world than has been the case so far.

The fifth goal must be to work together with both secular and religious democratic forces to help foster the necessary conditions for wider democratization in the Arab world. More than ever before the Arab regimes need to widen public participation in both policy-making and policy-implementation processes with pluralist, responsible, and transparent governmental frameworks. A failure in this respect will ensure the continuation of the popular political and social frustrations that make many people, especially the young, susceptible to Islamic radicalization. It is a fact that political disillusionment in the Arab world is widespread, and often it is this disillusionment that find channels of expression through other causes, most importantly anti-Israeli and anti-American causes. As long as this remains the case, many more like Bin Laden will have ground on which to defend their position and focus regional discontent on the United States and its allies.

In short, the removal of Bin Laden, the Al-Qaeda, the Taliban regime and Saddam Hussein's dictatorship will not in itself ensure the changes necessary to reduce the rising tide of anti-U.S. and in some cases anti-Western sentiments in the Muslim world. It will not eliminate the danger from groups that are, or will be, gripped by apocalyptic missions. However, if the United States and its allies cast their net wider and develop a sound political strategy to address the principle causes from which people like Bin Laden find motivation and sources for recruitment, then the world will be closer to eliminating such acts as those of 11 September and of what followed. There will also be fewer reasons to typecast a figure like Bin Laden as a "hero" in the eyes of those who identify their causes with his actions.

To change the situation and promote a peaceful coexistence between Muslims and the West, there is an urgent need for meaningful attitude shifts on both sides. Even so, the United States, as the world's most powerful actor, bears the major responsibility to avoid its past mistakes in the new millennium, and reach out to moderate Islamists, who outnumber radical Islamists by a large margin in the Muslim world, to build bridges of understanding and trust as a basis for a new, equitable world order.

Notes

1. Part of this chapter is based on Amin Saikal, "Islam and the West: Conflict or Cooperation?", in *Religion and Culture in Asia Pacific: Violence or Headline?*, edited by Joseph Camilleri (Melbourne: Vista Publications, 2001), pp. 74–83.

3

INDONESIAN RESPONSES

Samsu Rizal Panggabean

This chapter describes Indonesian Muslim responses to, and perspectives of, "the new world order", and shows how they are shaped by a set of historical, economic, and political conditions, including the recent *reformasi* (reform) movement. The perspectives and responses are not necessarily consistent over time or substantially monolithic. All Muslims do not share them. In addition, Muslim perspectives of the new world order are closely related to perceptions of roles and positions within the domestic, national order.

At the outset, it should be stated that the "Islamic factor" has historically been of secondary importance to the foreign policy of Indonesia. This was especially true during the Soeharto era. Many groups and leaders within the Muslim community in Indonesia, however, have been very much concerned about problems and issues in the Islamic world, such as the Israeli-Palestinian conflict, the Gulf War, the conflict in Bosnia, and the problems of various Muslim minorities. They have argued that as the world's largest Muslim nation, Indonesia should have a more activist foreign policy towards the Islamic world. For instance, Amien Rais, former chairman of Muhammadiyah and now the Speaker of People's Consultative Assembly, has argued that Indonesia should identify itself more with the Islamic world than with the Far Eastern nations.[1] In 1987, the Indonesian Committee for the Islamic World's Solidarity (KISDI) was established to foster ties between Indonesian Muslims and the larger Islamic world.

When Abdurrahman Wahid, the former chairman of Nahdlatul Ulama, ascended to the Indonesian presidency, there was an expectation among

Muslims that his rule would be a turning point in the history of Islamic political representation in Indonesia, including in the diplomacy and foreign policy sectors. His choice of Alwi Shihab, a scholar in Islamic studies, as the Minister of Foreign Affairs further strengthened this expectation. However, to the disappointment of many Muslims, President Wahid did not address the above concerns. On the contrary, in the first weeks of his rule, he created a widespread controversy among Indonesian Muslims, including Nahdlatul Ulama, when he publicly endorsed the possibility of opening trade and diplomatic relations with Israel. In the first month of his presidency, rallies were held in many cities to protest against this proposal. The protesters accused Wahid of being "the mouthpiece of Zionism, begging Jewish money".[2]

Politicians such as Faisal Basri maintained that trade relations with Israel were plausible. Basri, who was a former Secretary General of Amien Rais's People's Mandate Party, also criticized the *ulama* for fanning religious sentiment to achieve political gains. Others argued that several Muslim countries, such as Egypt, Jordan, and Turkey, maintained diplomatic relations with Israel, and the controversy that surrounded the issue indicated the reluctance of Indonesian Muslims to face the possibility of a peace deal in the Israel-Palestine conflict. However, in the end President Wahid backed down. In November 1999, Foreign Minister Alwi Shihab announced that the establishment of relations with Israel was not a government policy.

This controversy indicated how Muslim groups approached the issues and logic of the new international order, and how they identified specific Islamic dimensions of the situation. These dimensions included the incompatibility between Islam and the West, and the absolute and unconditional clash between the two civilizations. Many Muslim groups and leaders quoted Samuel Huntington's gloomy vision of civilizational conflict with approval. After defeating Communism, the Christian West was seen as turning on Islam in a tumultuous, zero-sum characterization of the world order.[3] Wars involving Muslim communities in the Middle East, the former Yugoslavia, and other parts of the world were perceived within the larger image of incompatible relations between the West and the Muslim world. In this scenario, the dominant Western actor was the United States, and the U.S.-controlled United Nations sought international dominance at the expense of Muslim interests.

Another dimension of this Muslim perspective was related to the domestic instability in Indonesia. From 1997, Indonesia faced economic crises, popular protests, and dissatisfaction with the state's performance, all of which added fuel to the *reformasi* (reform) processes. Whilst popular protest had long been an intermittent feature of Indonesian politics, the frequency and magnitude of protest during the last years of the Soeharto era challenged the government as never before, and led to the fall of Soeharto on 21 May 1998. Further communal violence then erupted in many parts of the archipelago, and demands from restive provinces such as Aceh and Irian Jaya for greater autonomy or even outright independence increased. These crises were viewed as the creations of powerful actors and institutions on the world stage.

Hence, the domestic and the global dimensions of the situation were closely intertwined. The problem of secessionist movements in Irian Jaya, otherwise known as West Papua, is a case in point. In response to the Congress of the People of Papua in 2000, some Muslims critically reviewed the integration of the province into Indonesia. They argued that the United Nation's support for the West Papuan integration referendum on 2 August 1969 was part of the U.S. struggle against global Communism. Yet when the global political climate changed with the fall of Communist regimes in the former Soviet Union and Eastern Europe, the U.S. policy changed accordingly. This indicated that the United States was not at all interested in the unity and territorial integrity of Indonesia. It was only concerned with its own interests, the most important of which was to secure the operations of Freeport, an American mining company with considerable interests in Irian Jaya.[4]

Similarly, some Muslim groups claimed that the so-called Rambo Country and other Western nations had supported the integration of East Timor into Indonesia, but then forced President Habibie to organize the independence referendum of September 1999. In their view, international non-government organizations and powerful media interests such as *Time* and *Newsweek* "cornered" the Indonesian Government by fabricating images of human rights violations that were perpetrated by Indonesian security forces and pro-Indonesian militias in East Timor. Moreover, so the logic of this argument went, the result of the referendum was obviously false because the process was administered by UNAMET and pro-independence East Timorese. Nurmahmudi Ismail, the former chief of the Justice Party and the Forestry Minister, raised another dimension of unfair treatment by the United Nations. He claimed that the death of three UNHCR workers in Atambua prompted the United Nation's condemnation of Indonesia's failure to deal with the militias in the refugee camps that were close to the East Timor border. He also lamented the U.S. threat to implement sanctions on Indonesia. In contrast, he claimed, the United Nations and the United States had done nothing to retaliate on behalf of the Palestinian victims of Israeli occupation.[5]

The position of Australia on East Timor was also accommodated in this scenario. Australia was seen as "the United States' deputy in the Asia Pacific".[6]

Similar to the United States, Australia was considered as an arrogant country when dealing with the pro-autonomy (that is, pro-Indonesian) militias of East Timor. According to this logic, Australia conspired with the United States to either weaken Indonesia or divide it into smaller, more pliant countries. Hence, the United States would have been faced with a weak group of small nations instead of an Islamic power with a population of 180 million.[7]

Similar thinking was offered in the periodical *Risalah*, the media outlet for the conservative movement Persatuan Islam or Persis. Muslims were told to be watchful of Australia's motives, with its non-Muslim "white arrogance" and "spirit of colonialism". To quote from one of its articles from October 1999:

> Once again, we should be vigilant of international conspiracies to divide this nation and state. Verse 120 of the *Sura al-Baqarah* mentions that "never will the Jews or the Christians be satisfied with thee unless thou follow their form of religion". In addition, Verse 109 of the *Sura* says, "quite a number of the People of Book wish they could turn you back to infidelity after you have believed". In Verse 32 of the *Sura al-Tawbah*, the Almighty God made it clear that the infidels wanted to extinguish His religion with their mouths.[8]

Indonesia's experience was viewed as part of the larger plight of the mainly Islamic Third World. Foreign parties were thought to be instigating the upheavals in Indonesia, as well as in other countries. For instance, the Taliban militia in Afghanistan was supposedly formed by the Central Intelligence Agency, and in East Timor the United States was said to have supported the Falintil. This indicated that infidel *(kafir)* foreigners were united in opposing Muslims all over the world. To substantiate this point, Verse 73 of *Sura al-Anfal* was quoted, to the effect that, "the Unbelievers are protectors, one of another". The motive behind this interference was to gain economic benefits from Muslim countries, which were generally rich in natural resources but without the technological capacity to exploit them. Moreover, the turmoil in Aceh, Moluccas, Irian Jaya, and East Timor were seen as excuses for UN intervention into Indonesia's sovereign affairs.[9]

One must bear in mind how this perspective blended the West, Unbelievers, Christians, and Jews. Indonesian Muslims were criticized for not realizing the acute danger of encroaching Western domination. Even worse, some Muslims were making friends with those who should have been their enemies. This was counter to the Islamic injunctions against relations with Christians and Jews. In Verse 54 of the *Sura al-Ma'idah*, God proclaims, "O ye who believe! Take not the Jews and the Christians for your friends and protectors.... And he amongst you that turns to them (for friendship) is of them." Muslims were reminded of the basic tenets of their faith and the need to insist that their rulers oppose Western domination in the economic, political, social, and cultural spheres.[10]

A combination of a failure to follow Islam and the control or exploitation of Muslim countries by various Western actors provided the basic explanation for economic problems in Indonesia. The Indonesian economy was in crisis because it was not Islamic. Instead, it was based on the interest system, or *riba.* An Islamic economy would have offered an interest-free banking system, such as those provided in small part by Bank Muamalah Indonesia (BMI), Baitul Mal wat Tamwil (BMT), or Bank Perkreditan Rakyat Syariah (BPRS). These banks were established in many cities of Indonesia, but they did not perform well due to the "lack of support from Muslims themselves".[11] In contrast, the International Monetary Fund (IMF) and the World Bank fostered Indonesia's dependence on the West through debt and financial aid, which again compromised the country's sovereignty.[12]

However, in the province of Aceh, this conception did not apply. Another face of injustice was more apparent after the emergence of the Acehnese secessionist movement in 1976 — Indonesia itself. Acehnese Muslims suffered, as they continue to suffer, from the worst examples of state violence in Indonesia, and pointed to the hypocrisy of their Javanese co-religionists and the Indonesian Government who were strident in their criticism of Israeli brutality in Palestine. With some irony it was stated that the Indonesian security apparatus in Aceh had "killed thousands of Acehnese people whom they called brothers".[13]

As far as Acehnese Muslims were concerned, the conflict between Islam and the West was neither absolute nor protracted. Compromise or even co-operation with the West was possible when a Muslim community needed the help of outsiders in their struggle for freedom and autonomy. For example, a pro-independence Acehnese rally in front of the UN office in Jakarta demanded international intervention to stop the violence in Aceh, and to seek a peaceful end to the violent conflict. The question that was raised was whether Islam would countenance a *jihad* that would have to be fought with the help of the United Nations, the United States, and other Western countries. A related question was whether the Muslim rebels in Aceh should avoid co-operation with the West and call on *jihad* groups in other, especially Arab, Muslim countries.

In response to these questions, it was argued that a *jihad* with American help was not forbidden by Islam, especially if it would help to save the lives of Acehnese Muslims. Moreover, help from Arab countries was deemed to be of no use, as they had already failed to defend Palestinian rights. This led to the interesting, perhaps even bizarre, argument that "Javanese Islam" was a deviant and impure form of Islam, as it was mixed with traditional and Hindu beliefs. Javanese Muslims were infidels in Islamic garb, and it was considered better to befriend helpful infidels such as the powerful Americans.[14]

However, the United States has a very different perspective of its interests in Indonesia. Regretting what he calls the miscommunication and disinformation between Indonesia and the United States, and a tendency in Indonesia to make the United States a scapegoat for domestic problems, the U.S. ambassador emphasize the similarity of interests between the two countries:

> The single most important fact is that the United States firmly supports the same goals as Indonesians themselves do for this vast and diverse country — democratization, sustainable economic growth, and territorial integrity. A democratic and prosperous Indonesia that extends from Sabang to Merauke is not only in Indonesia's national interest. It is squarely in the U.S. national interest as well.... Those who claim that foreign governments seek to destabilize or encourage the disintegration of Indonesia in order to promote some undefined goal of their own clearly have not thought the matter through rationally. A moment's reflection reveals that instability in Indonesia would serve no national interest of the United States or other friends of Indonesia.[15]

One might wonder whether this statement will succeed in banishing the prejudice and false images that have accumulated. The Muslim perspective of the new world order is marked by a propensity to believe in conspiracy theories. As a way of making sense of the world, belief in "an invisible, insidious, uncanny force, plotting various kinds of evil" can be found in many societies, from the United States to Iran.[16] In the Indonesian context, this mode of thought finds a scapegoat for all manner of Indonesian disturbances.[17] It explains many of the unfavourable circumstances that have occurred during the *reformasi*, especially because the process of reform has not improved the welfare of the population.

Conspiracy theories represent "a narrow, distorted, and oversimplified view of the social and political world, and lead to unrealistic assessments of the state of things and unrealistic expectations for the future".[18] Hence, the view of the West that emerges from the above discussion is essentially a restricted caricature of an outright civilizational aggressor that is to blame for many Muslim failures. However, there is a far more reasonable approach to this situation. Students of international relations are now discussing the role that a hegemonic actor with revisionist statecraft would play in the new world order. One of the questions that is asked is whether the United States plays such a role.

The answer to this question lies very much in notions such as "exporting democracy" and "political liberalization", the expansion of the North Atlantic Treaty Organization (NATO), and the promotion of economic liberalization and structural adjustment programmes for developing countries, which indicate that the United States does behave as a revisionist superpower. It should be emphasized that these notions are based on the assumption that the most pressing global concerns lie not in the United States or the West but in the rest of the world, which is the exact reverse of the Indonesian perceptions that were mentioned above. Furthermore, the current behaviour of the United States derives from its status as a world hegemon.

Fifty years after it emerged as a hegemonic power, the United States is still the dominant world power at the centre of a relatively stable and expanding democratic capitalist order. This is surprising. Most observers have expected dramatic shifts in world politics after the Cold War — such as the disappearance of American hegemony, the return of great power balancing, the rise of competing regional blocs, and the decay of multilateralism. Yet despite expectations of great transformations and new world orders, the half-century-old American order is still the dominant reality in world politics today.[19]

In conclusion, the perspectives of the new world order that are held by Indonesian Muslims have been shaped within an environment of increasing political and economic hardship. This hardship originated in the breakdown of the New Order rule that lasted three decades. During the last decade of that rule, state institutions were riddled with corruption, collusion, and nepotism that weakened democratic practice, perpetuated economic inequality, and eroded social capital. The riots and secessionist movements in several regions bolstered the destitution. Muslim perspectives of the new world order were built in this environment, and continue to mirror the hardships therein. A new and more positive perspective may emerge should that environment change and Indonesian Muslims begin to live in a functionally democratic state, a perspective in which mutual concern and shared reflection between cultures and civilizations presides.

Notes

1. Rizal Sukma, "Islam and Foreign Policy in Indonesia: Internal Weaknesses and the Dilemma of Dual Identity", Working Paper (Jakarta: The Asia Foundation, September 1999).

2. The Muslim opinions quoted in this chapter draw on four media outlets which represent rather conservative positions in Indonesian Islam. *Risalah*, the outlet for Persis; *Media Dakwah*; *Pandji Masyarakat*; and *Sabili*. "Hubungan Indonesia-Israel harus dibatalkan", *Media Dakwah*, December 1999, pp. 8–9; "Kebiadaban Israel harusnya menjadi pelajaran bagi Abdurrahman Wahid", *Media Dakwah*, November 2000, p. 7; *Panji Masyarakat* no. 51, 12 April 2000, p. 75.
3. *Risalah*, April 2000, p. 44; *Suara Muhammadiyah* no. 15, 2000, p. 37; *Media Dakwah*, September 1999, pp. 12–13; For Abdurrahman Wahid's view on the possibility of the convergence and not clash of civilizations, see *Far Eastern Economic Review*, 1 May 1997, pp. 38–39.
4. "Negara Kristen Indonesia Timur?", *Media Dakwah*, July 2000, pp. 16–17.
5. *Kompas*, 26 October 2000.
6. "Australia kini deputi AS di Asia Pasifik", *Media Dakwah*, October 1999, p. 40.
7. "Australia lebih biadab dari komunis", *Media Dakwah*, October 1999.
8. "Umat Islam wajib mewaspadai gerak-gerik neo-kolonialisme", *Risalah*, October 1999, p. 13.
9. *Panji Masyarakat*, 16 February 2000, pp. 8–9; *Sabili*, 18 October 2000, pp. 8–9.
10. Ibid.
11. *Risalah*, September 1999, pp. 61–62; *Risalah*, March 2000, p. 56.
12. *Risalah*, March 2000, pp. 15, 26; Dr. Fuad Bawazier, who was a Minister of Finance during the Soeharto era, likened the IMF to a *dukun cabul*, or an indecent medical man who treats but at the same time harasses his patient. See *Risalah*, July 2000, pp. 20–21.
13. Lantak-owner@egroups.com.
14. Ibid. During the first months of the communal violence in the Moluccas, Amien Rais — the Chairman of the National Mandate Party — stirred controversy in the media when, during the visit of the United States Secretary of State Madeline Albright, he "requested the intervention of the United States" to help the Indonesian Government to stop the killing in the Moluccas.
15. Remarks by Ambassador Robert S. Gelbard in a seminar that was organized by the GOLKAR Party, Jakarta, 14 November 2000; *Berita Buana*, 15 November 2000.
16. Ted Goertzel, "Belief in Conspiracy Theories", *Political Psychology* 15, no. 4 (1994): 731–42; Marvin Zonis and Craig M. Joseph, "Conspiracy Thinking in the Middle East", *Political Psychology* 15, no. 3 (1994): 443–59.
17. *Sabili*, no. 9, 18 October 2000, p. 8–9; *Risalah*, no. 1, March 2000, p. 24; *Media Dakwah*, October 1999, p. 40; *Panji Masyarakat*, no. 43, 16 February 2000, p. 8–9; *Panji Masyarakat*, no. 26, 18 October 2000, p. 11; *Suara Muhammadiyah*, no. 15, 1999, p. 37.
18. Zonis and Joseph, "Conspiracy Thinking", p. 450.
19. G. John Ikenberry, "Liberal Hegemony and the future of American Postwar Order", in *International Order and the Future of World Politics*, edited by

T. V. Paul and John A. Hall (Cambridge: Cambridge University Press, 1999), p. 123.

References

Berita Buana, 15 November 2000.

Far Eastern Economic Review, 1 May 1997, pp. 38–39.

Goertzel, Ted. "Belief in Conspiracy Theories". *Political Psychology* 15, no. 4 (1994): 731–42.

Ikenberry, G. John. "Liberal Hegemony and the future of American Postwar Order". In *International Order and the Future of World Politics,* edited by T. V. Paul and John A. Hall. Cambridge: Cambridge University Press, 1999.

Kompas, 26 October 2000.

Lantak-owner@egroups.com.

Media Dakwah, September 1999, October 1999, December 1999, November 2000.

"Negara Kristen Indonesia Timur?". *Media Dakwah,* July 2000, pp. 16–17.

Panji Masyarakat, 16 February 2000, 12 April 2000, 18 October 2000.

Risalah, September 1999, October 1999, March 2000, April 2000, July 2000.

Rizal Sukma, "Islam and Foreign Policy in Indonesia: Internal Weaknesses and the Dilemma of Dual Identity". Working Paper. Jakarta: The Asia Foundation, September 1999.

Sabili, 18 October 2000.

Suara Muhammadiyah, no. 15 (1999), no. 15 (2000).

Zonis, Marvin and Craig M. Joseph. "Conspiracy Thinking in the Middle East". *Political Psychology* 15, no. 3 (1994): 443–59.

The New Age

4

ISLAM AND GLOBALIZATION
Arab World Perspectives

Ahmad Shboul

It has become rather difficult to distinguish the dividing line at which American influence ends and globalization begins, whether globalization be simply a form of global Americanisation, or a genuinely independent phenomenon, although it tends to be viewed as American hegemony. ('Abd al-'Aziz al-Duri, 1999).[1]

As an Islamic movement ... we call [among other things] for a global democratic front against tyranny and against the suppression of peoples' freedoms, in order to have a world in which liberty is sovereign, and in which free and equitable circulation (*jawalan*) of benefits and ideas is facilitated. (Rashid Ghannoushi, 1993).[2]

ISLAM AND THE DIVERSITY OF VOICES IN THE ARAB WORLD

There is no doubt that globalization, with all of the ambiguities and disconnections that it involves, has become the new grand narrative of our times, particularly in the social sciences and in the media. In attempting to appraise "Islamic perspectives" within the regional context of the Middle East, I view the "Islamic factor" as one of several factors at work in the Arab world.

My approach belongs to cultural-intellectual history and sociology, rather than religious studies, economics, or realpolitik concerns. I am aware of the unfortunate tendency of many Islamists and certain Western observers to speak of Islam as if it were a changeless, closed system, inherently "unique" and remotely different from Christianity, and to view Islamic societies as antithetical to the modern values that are associated with the West. Such presentations are epistemologically unsound and tend to hinder comprehension of our common human reality. Apart from anything else, we need to remind ourselves that there are several "Islams" in our world.[3] Islam represents not only a "civilization" and a "culture of reference" in general, but also various regional, socio-economic, and ideological "cultures". Both Islamic teachings and history can be, and have been, interpreted in diverse ways. Contemporary Islamic movements, even within the same country, do not all share the same attitudes to such crucial issues as "religion and politics", the role of reason, the Islamic heritage, modernity, and the "other".[4] We need to remember that a century or so ago, Jamal al-Din al-Afghani, Muhammad 'Abduh, and Rashid Rida, for example, though considered as one school of thought, actually differed in their approaches to the *means* and *orientations* of Islamic reform.[5]

The diversity of historical experience, sociological complexity, and political realities that affect Islamic regions, countries, and groups can be reflected in how the "Islamic factor" has been played out, represented, and used in different contemporary contexts. Hence, the need to make clear which "Islam" we are talking about, when, where, and in what context. For example, within the Arab world, is it devotional "Islam", the "Islam" of political regimes seeking legitimacy with the help of domesticated "clerics", the "Islam" of the "modernized" élite or the "Islam" of the "fundamentalist" groups — the "Islamists" for short? In the latter case, Islamists may ally themselves with a political regime (Sudan), may be in violent opposition (Algeria), or may interact within a pluralist context (Egypt, Jordan). They can act as resistance movements (e.g. Hizbullah, Hamas) or they can appear (or go underground) as terrorist splinter groups of the Jihad, Jama'at, or Bin Laden's Al-Qaeda variety, the latter increasingly hijacking the image of Islam in recent years. It makes more methodological sense to acknowledge the reality of this diversity within the global Islamic scene, than to resort to medieval paradigms such as the "relationship between the Household of Islam and the sphere of war" if we wish to "understand the recent political and cultural history of Islamic societies".[6] I suggest that the "Islamic factor" is inadequate by itself to explain all manifestations and problems in Muslim countries, which should be understood and explained in concrete historical and sociological terms. We need to keep in mind that neither globalization nor "Islam" is a monolith, and that "Islam" and the "West" are not two inevitable and perpetual opposites. We also need to guard against intellectual fuzziness in dealing with such terms as *ummah, shari'a, fatwa*, and the ubiquitous and emotive *jihad*, as used by Islamists and by the world media. "*Jihad*" has even been sensationally used as shorthand by some popular writers on globalization, "quite independently from its Islamic theological origins".[7]

DIVERSE APPROACHES TO GLOBALIZATION

Globalization has been discussed from different perspectives, in both Western and Arabic discourses.[8] Even a cursory survey of the relevant literature would reveal that a number of important questions recur across the board. For example, is globalization a neutral phenomenon? Is it simply a "network society", or an open contest for "cosmopolitan" cultural interaction? Is it a panacea for the world economy, or a capitalist-driven worldview? Or is it a co-ordinated economic, strategic, and cultural programme to subjugate the whole world to American interests and those of transnational corporations? Globalization, understood as policies and programmes that are controlled by a hegemonic capitalist American centrality, is usually differentiated from "globalism" as a worldwide reality of economic, communication, and cultural flows. Both globalism and globalization are often rendered as *'awlamah* in Arabic. Occasionally, globalism is expressed as *'alamiyyah*, or *kawniyyah*, with hints of "cosmopolitanism" and "universalism". Universalism with the implication of "reciprocity" is often contrasted with "material globalization", which also suggests imposition or "intervention".[9] Even universalism (*'alamiyyah*) can be perceived negatively if it is only "defined by Western centrism".[10]

In its modern version, globalism can claim possible antecedents, though with different and varying centralities. From an Islamic world history perspective, we can refer to such phenomena as the early Arab Islamic empire across the three old continents, global trade across the Indian Ocean and the Mediterranean worlds,[11] Sufi orders and their far-reaching networks, and Muslim globetrotters such as the fourteenth century Ibn Battuta. Today, the Muslim pilgrimage (*hajj*), with its geographical, cultural, ethnic and linguistic diversity and reach, continues to present an annual event with global dimensions. Thus, Islamic civilization itself can be described as "truly a global-local phenomenon".[12] At the conceptual level, a "universalism", as shared or claimed by Islam and Christianity for example, can reflect a conscious solidarity of globalist "imagined communities". Whilst the complex issue of "universalism" is never far from the agenda of global modernity, it is difficult to separate claims of "universalism" from overt or latent ideology, whether religious, cultural, political, or economic. Like "cosmopolitanism" but unlike "globalization", true universalism is more of an outlook, a cultural recourse, a mode of meaning.[13] Neither economic globalization nor a strategic "world order" can in themselves guarantee, or necessarily sustain, true universalism or cosmopolitanism.

Before either "globalism" or "globalization" entered the English language, the adjective "global" in the sense of "worldwide", like its French equivalent "*mondial*", had been essentially associated with "conflict", before the advent of the term "global warming". Marshall McLuhan's often-quoted "global village" (1961) signalled the significant "communications" dimension of a new age. Certain analysts view global conflict both as the main reality of our world and as the major driving force behind scientific and technological development. It is worthwhile keeping this in mind as some "experts" continue to unduly single out "Islam" in the context of actual or potential conflict on the global scene today. Apart from the official strategic, political, and security concerns of the global order, Western discourse on globalization appears to place greater emphasis on economic and communications aspects than on cultural issues. On the whole, Arab discourse on globalization tends to focus more on cultural and societal issues. The divergence in emphasis may reflect different perceptions in the context of different stages of development and underdevelopment, rather than inherent religious or ideational orientations. In what follows, I attempt to indicate the diversity of voices within current Arab discourse, including the place of the Islamic factor therein, and to highlight the salient issues that are associated with globalization as reflected in this discourse.

GLOBALIZATION IN ARAB "PROGRESSIVE" AND "ISLAMIST" DISCOURSES: PRAGMATISM AND IDEOLOGICAL DIVERSITY

In focusing on the Arab world, we should not confine our analysis to a narrowly defined "Islamic" perspective as perceived by fundamentalists. One cannot exclude or downplay the modernist views of non-fundamentalist Muslims, under the pretext that they are perceived as "Westernized". In general, Arab intellectuals (both Muslim and Christian) share much common ground in the current Arab political and cultural discourse. In this context, the fundamentalist proponents of "political Islam", who are often labelled as *Islamawiyyun* (Islamists), as distinct from ordinary Muslims, need to be viewed in the light of their relative significance, rather than their often-exaggerated media profile.

Arabic commentators, for example in the daily and weekly press and the electronic media, regularly discuss aspects of globalization, and questions are sometimes raised as to whether globalization should be viewed as a choice or an inevitable fate for the Arab world; whether it is a hobby horse or a dangerous wild beast. At one level, there is a pragmatic attitude towards globalism among future-oriented Arab development experts. For example, alternative "global models" are sometimes analysed as possible "tools with which to probe the future of the Arab world".[14] Apart from this aspect, certain professional Arab economists seem realistically enthusiastic about perceived positive aspects of economic globalization. Such pragmatic business-oriented experts simply argue that it is better to join the global order (often conjured up as a fast train) than to be left out and behind by it. Similar enthusiasm can also be discerned among Arab experts in computers, communications, tourism, and employment, as well as international education "consultants", professional linguists, and translators. Here, globalization is accepted as a fact; the question becomes simply confined to how to make use of it.[15] Nevertheless, several Arab economists and intellectuals have warned against the dangers of globalization as it operates now. In this, their views often echo, or coincide with, Western critics of the so-called neo-liberalism of the unbridled market economy. Some Arab intellectuals thus paint a gloomy picture of their societies in the shadow of globalization, which is seen as a replay of earlier dramas of exploitative capitalism, except that the wheels of economic globalization can now move much faster, and do more damage, in view of the sophisticated technology and one-sided protectionism.[16]

GLOBALIZATION AND THE PERENNIAL PROBLEMATIC OF "WESTERNIZATION"/"MODERNIZATION"

In attempting to indicate the range of attitudes of Arab intellectuals to globalization, and the distinction between "Muslim" and "Islamist" voices, we can consider them against the ongoing debate about the "impact of the West" and "modernization". A majority of Arab intellectuals and analysts, across the ideological spectrum, seem to agree that globalization is "the latest manifestation of Western imperialism". At one end of the spectrum, we find a historical view that reflects a certain anti-capitalist Third World outlook, expressed by both progressive Islamic and Marxist writers. At the other end, we encounter the inflexible fundamentalist Islamist worldview. In between, we find more or less liberal tendencies, including pan-Arab nationalist and moderate Islamic. All three perspectives include different hues of Islamic representation; all three share elements of a perception of continued Western domination of the Arab world.

In relation to modernity, the Arab world faces two types of intellectual and cultural challenge. One of these is internal, and is represented by the secularist versus fundamentalist confrontation, with the perennial question of how to deal with "political Islam" and its obscurantism. The other is external, and is represented by the historical encounter with the West and how to define the Arab world's interaction with it.[17] Arab social scientists are generally conscious of the significant distinction between "modernization" (Arabic: *tahdith*) as a process of only superficial change, for example in material infrastructure and consumer culture, and "modernity" (*hadathah*) as a dynamic cultural project that is associated with deep structural and productive change which affects individual and society orientations both intellectually and in terms of organization and civilization. Jürgen Habermas's celebrated concept of the "unfinished project of modernity" would inevitably assume a radically different signification, and more urgency, in the Arab world.[18] In the attempts by progressive Arab intellectuals, both Muslim and Christian, to analyse the problems that are facing the Arab world, an important running theme is modernity without Western strategic or cultural hegemony. The problem has been complicated by the wish to embrace parts of the complex package of Western modernity while rejecting other parts.[19] It is against such a background that the more recent Arab discourse about globalization can mainly be appreciated.

The Arab Left in general, including a self-defined Islamic Left, identify globalization with a triumphant greedy capitalism that masquerades as neo-liberalism, and with a neo-imperialism that threatens Arab cultural identity. Thus, the influential Egyptian Marxist cultural critic Mahmud Amin al-'Alim condemns globalization, in rather sweeping terms, as "the end of ends"; and warns that submission to "this globalization and capitalist hegemony" is the most serious threat to "our Arab culture and our humanity".[20] The Egyptian economist and intellectual Samir Amin approaches the problem from the perspective of "Third World dependency" versus "global capitalist hegemony", and "traditional patriarchal cultures" versus "global capitalist culture". He sees the "Western" attribute of globalism as an "external feature or form (*mazhar* or *shakl*) in the simplest sense of the word". Thus, the problem facing the Arab or Islamic world should not be seen in the context of confrontation with the "West" and its culture as such. Rather, it is part of the process of polarization between modern Western centres of global capitalist culture, on the one hand, and the traditional patriarchal Third World peripheries on the other. In this capitalist global scheme, the peripheries, including Arab and Islamic countries, are expected to be open to the free movement of foreign capital and goods, whilst the markets of the developed countries remain closed to Third World labour (and refugees). Indeed, Samir Amin, who has long advocated the concept of "de-linking" and a "polycentric" world instead of a centralized world that is controlled by the capitalist market, has recently described the Arab region as a likely "fourth world", in terms of its position in the hierarchy of development and its place in the periphery away from the controlling centre, while remaining directly under its hegemony.[21]

GLOBALIZATION AND THE "ISLAMIC FACTOR" IN THE ARAB WORLD

Certain scholars have pointed to a strong connection between globalization and religious fundamentalism, particularly the Islamic brand.[22] Various forms of discourse, including fundamentalism, are seen as symptoms of processes of globalization reabsorbed and reproduced in the political fabric of local life. In so far as responses to globalization have been expressed in "Islamic" terms at all, a distinction needs to be made between the open Islamic discourse that engages the progressive secularists, and the closed fundamentalist discourse that clings to its own exclusivist worldview. This extremist Islamism seems at odds with both the modern realities of the wider world and the creative streams of classical and contemporary Islamic theological thought.

It does not require much effort to gauge or analyse the extremist view *vis-à-vis* globalization, as it is essentially similar to the classical position of hardened extremists of any faith or ideology towards the rest of the world. In this perspective, the world is not seen in terms of nation-states, religious communities, or civilizations, not in regional, spatial, or socio-economic terms, and not even as simply divided between Muslim and non-Muslim societies. The extremists see the world as divided in abstract confrontational, more or less apocalyptic terms, between their own version of "Islam" on the one side, and the totality of the rest of humanity, including all other Muslims, on the other. They see a stark division between "belief" and "unbelief", wherein "unbelief" is supposed to exist everywhere outside the narrow circle of their own fundamentalist group, which could number a few hundred or even no more than a few dozen devotees. What defines the realm of "belief" here is membership of the small group under a self-proclaimed shadowy amir, or commander, armed with a willingness to fight for a vision derived from his own narrow and weird interpretation of a few Qur'anic verses and Hadith texts. These are usually supplemented by odd bits quoted from a couple of fourteenth-century works on *jihad* and a few fundamentalist statements from Mawdudi, and perhaps from Sayyid Qutb.[23] As a rule, these quotations are taken totally out of context.

Sayyid Qutb (executed in Cairo on 29 August 1966) has been rightly claimed as the undisputed leading ideologue of the Muslim Brothers; some observers have even dubbed him, perhaps with a little exaggeration, as the father of contemporary Islamic extremism. His extremist admirers often misread him and concentrate only on certain passages, not from his earlier aesthetic studies on the Qur'an or his important *Social Justice in Islam*, but rather from the emotively expressed *Ma'alim fi al-Tariq* (Signposts on the Way). The two key concepts here are the sovereignty (*hakimiyyah*) of God and the division between a pristine utopian Islam and the *jahiliyyah* (arrogant ignorance) of the real world. The latter would include modern and indeed most pre-modern-Muslim societies.[24] Zealots with little comprehension of Islamic principles often adopt statements by Qutb or other fundamentalist writers as emblematical mottoes. In such a context, "Islam" becomes unnaturally reduced to a force that appears afraid of, and hostile to, the modern world.

The Islamist political phenomenon is often emotively described by its representatives as the "Islamic awakening" (*al-Sahwah al-Islamiyyah*). Enthusiasts perceive it with inflated hope, often in utopian and even eschatological terms. Certain Arab intellectuals, including many progressive Muslims, view it with apprehension. Others, including some moderate committed Muslim thinkers, whilst giving it the benefit of the doubt, raise serious questions concerning its "remaining unknowns". There is widespread suspicion among concerned Muslims about the many self-proclaimed shadowy splinter groups that masquerade as representatives of an "Islamic awakening". The late Professor Shukri Faysal (Damascus, Syria) has suggested that this so-called awakening is not necessarily a genuine, internally motivated renaissance, but rather an externally induced one. The appeal of the drummed up "awakening" with its paradoxical self-perpetuating "narcotic" effect, especially among the young, must not hide the fact that it is "a confused and ultimately intellectually barren movement; a self-perpetuating myth that has proclaimed itself as a life-jacket in the surrounding waves of change". Other equally concerned Muslim intellectuals have pointed out the lack of a cultural project among most fundamentalist movements.[25] Even certain leaders of the mainstream Islamist movements have expressed concern about the danger of discord and violence, which extremists are capable of causing. Thus, Shaykh Yusuf al-Qaradawi, a prominent leader of the Egyptian Muslim Brothers with followers throughout the Arab world, distinguishes between what he calls "legitimate difference of opinion and objectionable discord" within the Islamic "awakening" groups.[26]

We need to remember that among those who speak in the name of the Islamic awakening, there is wide diversity and contradiction. At one end of the Islamist spectrum we find a number of extremist groups who are generally unwilling to articulate any programme or provide answers to complex problems beyond the vague slogan of "*al-Islam huwa al-hall*" ("Islam is the answer"). These people seem to get most of the international media exposure. At the other end of the spectrum are those who share much of the ground with progressive secularist Arab liberals (both Muslim and Christian), in terms of acceptance of plurality and open constructive debate. In the middle are active representatives of the Muslim Brothers in Egypt, Sudan, and Jordan, for example, who in their different ways attempt rationalist dialogue with representatives of the secularist Arab tendencies. However, most, but not all, of the Brothers prefer to conduct the discussion in their own terms. Even their most articulate scholars and activists, such as the Egyptians Ghazali and Qaradawi and the Sudanese Turabi, are often ready to dismiss what they do not like by describing it as "imported", "Western", or "un-Islamic".

Apart from Islamist political activism, whether extremist or moderate, there is an important epistemological dimension of the broader Islamic discourse, which has been articulated by certain committed individual Muslim scholars, including social scientists and philosophers, since the mid-1970s. Examples of this can be seen in the Arabic monthly, *al-Muslim al-Mu'asir* (the Contemporary Muslim, Kuwait, 1975–), and the ambitious project of the Egyptian Islamic Leftist philosopher Hasan Hanafi on "Heritage and Modernity", as well as his public dialogue with the Moroccan pan-Arab thinker Muhammad 'Abid al-Jabiri. The more controversial project of the so-called Islamization of Knowledge, which is associated with the late Ismail al Farouqi and his disciples, mostly in the United States and Malaysia, should be mentioned here, although its influence is less significant in the Arab countries.[27] Despite the exceptional talent that is devoted to this project, it may run the risk of being a mere intellectual exercise leading to a cul-de-sac, or at best to reinventing the wheel.

By way of contrast, we can see in the founder of the Tunisian Islamic Renaissance Party, Dr Rashid Ghannoushi, an outstanding example of a more open pragmatic approach among Islamic activists. Through participation in symposia and publications, particularly his critical study of "Public Liberties in the Islamic State", he has systematically addressed practical questions relevant to contemporary Muslim societies, placing them in a proper sociological and indeed global context. He advocates a purpose-oriented comprehension (*al-fahm al-maqasidi*) of Islam, as opposed to the text-bound or demagogic tendencies of extremists. His insights into the different responses of diverse Islamic political movements are quite illuminating. He argues that contemporary Islamist discourse needs to be seen in its dialectical relationship with its environment. If the latter is open and relaxed, then Islamists tend to be moderate, accepting of co-existence, and of the adherence to the rules of the democratic game. However, if Islamists are deprived of their rights and are treated violently, then they may fall back on the concept of *jihad* as a means of defending themselves and their faith, although in his view the majority of Islamists would take refuge in patience and forbearance. Like other rationalist Muslim intellectuals, Ghannoushi is uncertain of the intentions of the various "awakening" groups, and he is quite clear and outspoken in urging Islamist activists to abandon ambiguity and obscurantism. As he bluntly puts it, the Islamists, including the Muslim Brothers, should make it clear to everyone that they are on the side of freedom. This should include "freedom of thought, of conscience, of expression, of publication, of progress, of scientific advancement, and of the growth of arts and aesthetics, and that these groups would support the freedom of initiative, provide social security and welfare (*damanat ijtima'iyyah*), and guarantee the freedom of ethnic and religious minorities, intellectual freedom, and the freedom and dignity of women".[28]

Ghannoushi's critical stance and his insistence on a purpose-oriented understanding of Islamic teachings are also reflected in the writings of a number of prominent independent and committed Muslim intellectuals. These intellectuals argue that religious texts should be understood in the light of modern social concerns (such as justice, freedom, and humanity), and not the reverse. Moreover, the soundness or weakness of Hadith texts should be judged not by the old pre-modern criteria of transmission, but by the relevance of their actual content to the needs of modern Islamic reform.[29] Enlightened Muslim intellectuals, who can hardly be described simply as "Westernized", have highlighted the importance for the future of Islam of intellectual and cultural communication (*tawasul*), as the Palestinian-Jordanian philosopher Fehmi Jadaane has strongly advocated in a positive Habermasian sense. They have also emphasized the need for Muslims, including those in Islamist movements, to learn from the West, not only in the fields of science and technology, but also in the humanities, and in the realms of organization, institutions, and culture generally.[30] Unlike the extreme fundamentalists, these independent Muslim intellectuals and activists do not divide the world between "believers" and "non-believers"; rather, they see it in political and socio-economic terms. Ghannoushi in particular identifies the enlightened Left in Western countries, as well as international human rights movements, as the natural allies of reformist Islamic movements, especially those who are denied a voice in the political process, such as his own Tunisian Renaissance Party. Other concerned modernist Muslim intellectuals, including some public figures close to the official élite, even in conservative societies such as Bahrain and Saudi Arabia, have also criticized extremists and openly and strongly advocated the promotion of rational thinking congruent with Islamic principles. They have also stressed the need to build the education system on modern rationalist foundations, and have supported the liberation of women.[31]

That progressive Muslim intellectuals share aspects of the critical view of globalization with secular critics can be seen in the views of the Tunisian Islamist Abu Ya'rub al-Marzuqi, who considers globalization, as "a European or Western malady, which has not attained the level of a metaphysical problem and should not be confused with universalism". To him, globalization constitutes an attempt at the spiritual liquidation of others, whereby imitators find a misleading model in the one that they emulate.[32] This is reminiscent of the views that are articulated by the Moroccan secular thinker, Muhammad 'Abid al-Jabiri, who contrasts globalization (associated with cultural hegemony and the diminution of particularity) with universalism (associated with openness towards others and defined as an attempt to sublimate particularity into universal ideals). Al-Jabiri's distinction, however, is essentially based on epistemological rather than judgemental grounds.[33]

A number of concerned Muslim intellectuals have warned against the long-term dangers of certain brands of religious fundamentalist movements. Such movements are seen as posing "a grave challenge to world politics, security, and stability", as having engaged in "the mythologization and ideologization of Islam", and as having the potential to bring their own Muslim countries "to the abyss through their infiltration of the legal system and the state".[34] The high profile of the Islamic fundamentalists has caused many Muslim intellectuals to warn against the potential of extremist tendencies not only to strengthen narrow isolationist concepts of identity, but also to accentuate the marginalization of the Arab world in the global context. Hisham Sharabi has expressed the dilemma quite succinctly, from the perspective of progressive Arab intellectuals who advocate constructive interaction with genuine creative Islamic thought. He contrasts the discourses of extreme Islamists and progressive Arab secularists. The former present a monological discourse of an absolutist, traditional position, advocating total hegemony and an ethic of ultimate ends; whilst the latter offer a dialectical discourse of a self-limiting, rationalist position advocating free pluralism and an ethic of responsibility.[35]

The apprehension of Islamist extremism and demands for political, social, and cultural liberalization, are not confined to Arab Muslim intellectuals living in Western countries. Important progressive voices, of both men and women, can be heard in most Arab countries from Morocco to the Gulf, including conservative countries. As might be expected, the approach and style of discourse of these Muslim critics of Islamist extremism vary in emphasis according to their respective contexts. Such critical views, which are also shared by many Christian Arab intellectuals, have regularly been aired in lectures, conferences, and published in journals and books over the past two or three decades. The two influential monthly journals, *al-Naqid* (London and Beirut, 1989–5) and *al-Mustaqbal al-'Arabi* (Beirut, 1978–), as well as the quarterly *Mawaqif* (London, 1976–93) and *Abwab* (London and Beirut, 1994–), and the collected essays and monographs that are regularly published by the MDWA, Riad El-Rayyes, al-Saqi Books, and Dar Sina, among others, provide important wide-ranging examples.

GLOBALIZATION, THE NATION-STATE, AND POLITICAL LIBERALIZATION

Despite the considerable analysis of the effect of economic globalization and global governance on the nation-state and national sovereignty, much ambiguity persists. Such ambiguity is also reflected in Arab discourse, although Arab social scientists have produced substantial analytical work on the problem of "Arab society and the state".[36] There is clearly a pervasive apprehension among Arab intellectuals about the political, strategic, economic, and cultural processes of globalization and the so-called new world order. A number of Arab writers have warned against allowing external interference in the role of the state in Arab countries. In the affluent Arab Gulf states, two additional fears exist in connection with globalization. One of these reflects conservative attitudes and has to do with the problem of guest workers and the likelihood of external intervention in labour and employment practices and regulations.[37] The other fear is more serious. It stems from the dependence of the "security needs" of certain Arab states, or regimes, upon foreign military presence, which is widely perceived as tangible proof of a persistent Western "neo-imperialism".

Both the much proclaimed new world order and globalization, as two sides of the same coin, are seen to have spawned a configuration of unpopular programmes and policies. These include constant pressure for more privatization even in the vital public services of education and health, more government spending on defence and internal security, cultural penetration by foreign media and communication corporations, favouring foreign languages, especially English, at the expense of Arabic, and the encouragement of foreign investment and transnational companies, as well as excessive consumerism, in the name of neo-liberalism. There is a strong perception among Arab intellectuals that these invasive policies have been imposed under the umbrella of globalization and the neo-liberalism of the market, without any guarantees (in some cases hardly a serious sign) of political and social liberalization. The realization of how much, or rather how little, American and other proponents of neo-liberalism care about the progress of democracy and human rights in non-Western societies in this global scheme of things has led to serious questions.[38] Whether openly or furtively, there are now many voices in the Arab world calling for the expansion of the public sphere of political debate, and the promotion of genuine democratic processes, bureaucratic and fiscal transparency, freedom of expression, human rights, including rights of women and minorities. While some Arab intellectuals optimistically anticipate some progress in these areas, others remain sceptical, especially in relation to certain religiously conservative oil-rich states and totalitarian republics.

The challenge of globalization affects not only the ambivalently perceived "nation-state", but also, and perhaps more seriously, the entire Arab regional system. Globalization threatens or challenges Arab capacity to maintain any freedom to affect positive change in the economic, political, social, and cultural spheres in the region. While this signifies a serious *threat* in the eyes of some bemoaning Arab intellectuals, including Islamists, certain Arab analysts and political leaders prefer to view it more positively as a *challenge* that must be faced creatively. Specifically, this relates to whether the Arab League should evolve towards, or perhaps be superseded by, a more appropriate Arab (or Middle Eastern?) regional system in line with such regional "global models" as the European Union (EU) and other economic and strategic regional systems in the Asia-Pacific or the Americas. This has implications for the type of interaction of an integrated (or disintegrated?) Arab world with the outside world, including the two non-Arab Muslim neighbours, Iran and Turkey, and particularly the close regional ally of the United States, Israel. If such a challenge is not positively met, then a likely alternative will be for the Arab states and their societies to accept as inevitable what the new world order, globalization and the other, more astute, regional players are willing to offer them, or rather impose on them in a new Middle East.

Among various "what if" scenarios that are discussed by Arab analysts, and by some visionaries in the ruling élites (also by international Arab world specialists), there is a recurrent emphasis on the need to work more pragmatically towards Arab regional integration. However, equally important is the urgent need to promote existing, or in most cases hardly existent, "civil society" institutions, democracy, and broader political participation. These powerful emblems of modernity should become essential features of Arab political culture and practice, no matter what becomes of the role of the "nation-state" in the economic, political, and cultural spheres under the ostensible global order.[39] However, while some concerned progressive Muslim intellectuals join in the debate over such practical problems, most Islamists continue to dogmatically repeat undefined emotive slogans, including their utopia of the "Islamic State".

GLOBALIZATION AS A THREAT TO CULTURAL IDENTITY

It is essentially in the cultural sphere that most of the apprehension about globalization is to be found in current Arab discourse. To a certain extent, several Western thinkers have expressed such apprehension from their own "developed world" perspective.[40] In the Arab world, this has to do with the perennial debate about the Arab "cultural identity" (*al-huwiyyah al-thaqafiyyah*) in the face of the "Western impact" and "modernization". There is fear that certain aspects of globalization, particularly the increasing dependency of Arab countries in the economic, communications, and cultural spheres, will lead to more social fragmentation, and more negative effects on family ties, moral values, and cultural character. Even when the discussion concerns the cultural identity of a well-defined nation-state, such as Egypt, globalization is perceived as contributing to the weakening of national allegiance, the destabilization of traditional work and career orientations, and affecting individual identity. Thus, university graduates are seen to give priority to individual rather than national or societal interests, and the young and talented prefer to work in an oil country, or with a transnational company, or to emigrate. This tends to be seen as a modern interpretation of an old maxim (sometimes attributed to Imam 'Ali) to the effect that "wealth in exile is a homeland (*watan*), poverty at home is alienation".[41]

Among the more emotive expressions in current Arab discourse about cultural identity is that of "cultural invasion or assault" (*al-ghazw al-thaqafi*). In the context of globalization, we can take the following articulation as representative of a general outlook among progressive intellectuals:

> today we are living a reality (disturbing and painful) of a single cultural project that controls the whole world, stamping it with its own personality, within a global strategy whose project of "totalitarian technology" devours spatial and historical distances as well as national characteristics in order to establish "the New World Order" in a grand global (*kawniyyiah*) drama in which different actors play their assigned parts under its sole direction.[42]

As globalization is seen as a strategy of hegemony, absorption, and the negation of non-Western cultures, it is natural to associate it with a stark form of cultural assault, indicated by a more emotive expression: "cultural infiltration or penetration" (*al-ikhtiraq al-thaqafi*). This may appear to echo the well-known political science assessment of the region as "the most penetrated international relations subsystem in today's world".[43] It may also indicate a more specific apprehension of perceived Israeli cultural and economic infiltration under the umbrella of the "New Middle East", and within the broader context of globalization or the new world order.

However, the problem has been articulated in broader socio-cultural and global terms. Thus Muhammad 'Abid al-Jabiri, whilst agreeing that "the culture of globalisation has affected every corner of the planet, and has continued the process of penetration and weakening of cultural identity", sees "cultural penetration" as a much more specific and complex problem facing developing societies, including the Arab world.[44] Similarly, 'Abd al-Ilah Balqziz, another Moroccan intellectual, sees globalization as "representing no less than the domination of other cultures through controlling science, education and communication technology" and as a "historical culmination of a long experience of domination that had begun with the colonial invasions some centuries ago … ultimately decimating or disfiguring several cultures of the 'South', particularly in Asia, Africa and Latin America".[45]

To some extent, the perennial problem of cultural insecurity in the face of "cultural invasion" is not unconnected with the phenomenon of "guided" — that is controlled — cultural orientations by Arab political regimes. While new ministries of "Culture" and/or "National Guidance" became arms of "progressive" regimes in the mid-1950s, cultural defensiveness has always been second nature to "conservative" leadership. Some independent liberal Arab intellectuals have warned against the official strategy of "fending off (*sadd*) cultural invasion". The late Egyptian journalist Ahmad Baha' al-Din, writing as the editor-in-chief of the wide-circulation pan-Arab monthly, *al-'Arabi*, has argued that the question should not be "how to repel cultural *invasion*", as a 1977 pan-Arab meeting of ministers of culture had assumed, but rather "how to face and address cultural *challenge*".[46] His call that the people should "read everything, listen to everything, and discuss everything", has by and large been ignored. Instead, the cultural defence syndrome has more or less persisted, together with censorship by governments, by religious functionaries who are controlled or co-opted by the state, and by self-appointed guardians of "morality". Unfortunately, this can still operate in the most bizarre ways, not only against outside influences but also, and indeed mostly, against indigenous and culturally committed liberal innovative talents.[47]

In traditional regimes, earlier expressions of this defensiveness can be seen, for example, in a statement that was attributed to the founder of modern Saudi Arabia during the late 1930s: "We want Europe's products and inventions, not its ideas"; and in a similar pronouncement by the ruler of Yemen in the 1950s, that he did not want from the West anything that might infect his country, "neither whisky nor parliaments".[48] It can still be encountered in recent, officially sponsored, advertisements in leading Western newspapers, proclaiming the success of a leading Arab oil state in achieving the miracle of "Sixty Years of Progress Without Change!" with an official quotation in the same newspaper, that "our society is unique, democracy is not suitable for us".[49] Whilst not so expensive in financial terms, such pronouncements could prove quite costly in other ways. Political leaders will have to face the paradox of accepting the imposition of economic and strategic consequences of globalization and the new world order, while rejecting democracy, freedom of expression, and human rights for their own people.

Thus, the current fear of certain aspects of globalization by political leaders and others can be said to reflect a deep-seated resistance to the opening up of society, fear of political, social, cultural, and intellectual liberalization and democracy, and fear of change. As the Moroccan sociologist Fatima Mernissi has aptly put it, it is "fear of the modern world".[50] This seems to include fear of the erosion of the father figure's position, and of the weakening of patriarchal political culture in general, as has been convincingly argued by Hisham Sharabi. Here the Islamists are not the only backward-looking opponents of real modernity. Such fear has long been discernible in the ranks of both conservative and ostensibly revolutionary political élites, as well as those who claim to speak in the name of traditions, morals, religious faith, and cultural particularity, often in atavistic and static terms. This is one of the unfortunate ways to react to the challenge of modernity. As a prominent visionary Arab statesman has recently observed, "cultural particularities are emerging as defensive identities".[51]

GLOBALIZATION AS A VEHICLE OF BRASH CONSUMERISM

There is another level of response. This indicates the negative evaluation of the perceived cultural offerings of globalization itself. Edward Said has observed, albeit in a somewhat different context, that "culture" has to be seen as having to do with both "excluding" and "exporting".[52] Moreover, several Western analysts have observed that globalization helps to promote a culture of consumerism and decadence.[53] The point has been cogently made by a number of concerned Arab intellectuals. Thus, the eminent Iraqi historian 'Abd al-'Aziz al-Duri (Professor at the University of Jordan since 1970), points out that the hegemonic implications of globalization are associated with "the dissemination of American cultural exports, often reflecting no more than the lower levels of American cultural activities, a typical American lifestyle in clothes, fast food and other consumer goods". It is America's common culture, not its élite culture, that is being exported. Similarly, other writers have associated globalization with exporting the commodities of "a cheap decadent culture that would spread a superficial consciousness among its consumers, and promote the mania of stardom and the daily consumerism and style of American street life".[54] Such a culture, it is often inferred, can hardly be expected to promise a civilized or enlightened vision for the future of humanity.

An indicative category of popular views, usually ignored by researchers but admired by intelligent readers, is that of the press cartoon. Examples from the work of the Palestinian-Jordanian artist "Mahjoob", which are published in Amman newspapers, can be cited as relevant in our present context. In one non-captioned cartoon, Uncle Sam, standing tall and identified by the stars and stripes, is shaking all the continents of the world through a large round sieve, causing many national flags and lesser human identities to disappear below (see Figure 4.1). A second cartoon entitled "Government Advertisement and Warning", admonishes people to "Drink More" [Cola], "Watch More" [foreign films on the special movie channel], "Chat More" [on mobile phones], but "Keep Away from the Allahu Akbar Group" (see Figure 4.2). Thirdly, under the heading "Technology in the Age of Abject Poverty", an ATM machine acts as an automatic beggar, appropriately

FIGURE 4.1

Source: Cartoon by Mahjoob (Copyright), published in *Ad-Dustour* (Amman, Jordan), 22 February 1999.

FIGURE 4.2

Government Announcement and Warning:
Chat more!... View More!... Drink More!...
And Keep Away from the People of Allahu Akbar!

Source: Cartoon by Mahjoob (Copyright), published in *Ad-Dustour* (Amman, Jordan), 21 June 2001.

bandaged: "Kindly insert whatever you can pay into the slot as indicated, press 'Enter' and wait to hear the thank you prayer" — "May God Protect Your Children" (see Figure 4.3). Finally, the fifty-six-year-old Arab League appears as a lost baby between the gigantic feet of the G7, the EU, and the WTO (see Figure 4.4).[55] A more optimistic cartoon by "Sadeddine" from Egypt, the Arab country that is richest in political humour, depicts a fellah instructing a relative by mobile: "buy the buffalo on Visa Card and meet me at the Internet Café".[56]

FIGURE 4.3
"Technology in the time of abject poverty"

Welcome to the Automatic Beggar
----------XXXXXXXXXX----------

Insert the amount you feel generous enough to give in
the specified place, then press ENTER
*** Wait to hear the "thank you" prayer ***

"May God preserve your children"

Source: Cartoon by Mahjoob (Copyright), published in *Ad-Dustour* (Amman, Jordan), 30 May 2001.

FIGURE 4.4

Source: Cartoon by Mahjoob (Copyright), published in *Ad-Dustour* (Amman, Jordan), 2000.

In a real sense, current Arab intellectual and popular discourse, whether Islamic or nationalist, conservative or progressive, indicates a dialectical relationship between a sense of fear of external dangers and influences — strategic, economic, and cultural — and a sense of awareness of acute internal problems. This is significantly reflected in the discussions at frequently held conferences and symposia, including those that are concerned with dialogue between nationalist and Islamic tendencies.[57] There is no doubt that, at least in certain spheres, notably the attention of the world media, Islamist extremists have succeeded in taking advantage of globalism and of highjacking the image of Islam in the world. They are also able to exploit the highly significant space of mosques and other local arenas in many Arab societies.

In their pursuit of illusive legitimacy, certain traditional as well as ostensibly progressive political élites (in Saudi Arabia, Egypt, Algeria, and the Sudan, for example) have often cynically manipulated Islamic sentiments and attempted to outdo the fundamentalists, by ambiguously appealing to the role of the Islamic *shari'a* and by using theocratic political vocabulary.[58] These, together with the inability of moderate Muslim and secularist progressive voices to present practical reform programmes, have greatly contributed to the apparent popularity of the Islamists in the eyes of the largely impoverished and disenfranchised Arab public opinion. In a way, the ostensible global order could in these circumstances exacerbate the Arab world's old problems, while adding its own new discontents. If not addressed in positive and creative ways, whereby human energy is directed to addressing political and socio-economic problems as well as cultural and spiritual concerns of Arab societies, then the real dangers of isolationism, extremism, disorder, and disintegration will persist.

Finally, the current high profile of the religious extremists in the public eye should not make us ignore the more rationalist progressive voices of modern Islam. The extremism of Islamists may continue to demand media attention, often disproportionately, for some time to come. However, their narrow atavistic "interpretation" of Islamic teachings will not illuminate or provide real answers for the complex problems of their societies, let alone the rest of the world. Early modern European thinkers may have *imagined* a utopia in Promethean terms; contemporary Islamists seem to want to *impose* their own utopia, based on a claimed divine political order, as they simplistically and crudely perceive it with little scope for human reason. Some violent-minded Islamist groups might even continue to "think narrowly and act globally", if I may put a familiar motto in this way. Concerned Muslim intellectuals and political élites need to face the challenge of the modern world in the light of the Qur'anic dictum: "God will not change the situation of a people until they change what is in themselves".[59] Thus, the Qur'an itself teaches that change is human driven. If we accept that ours is a truly global age, then we need to engage in analysing creative ways in which we can all be drawn together into new forms of interdependence and mutual acceptance to enable us to understand change, manage risks, and face uncertainties with confidence. In this way, Arabs and Muslims, like other members of our common humanity, can participate, not in Huntington's negative "clash of civilizations", but as the late Arab thinker and educator Constantine Zurayk taught, in a positive "venture for a common human civilization".[60]

Notes

1. 'Abd al-'Aziz al-Duri, "al-Huwiyyah al-'Arabiyyah wal-Tahaddiyat" [Arab Cultural Identity and [its] Challenges"], *al-Mustaqbal al-'Arabi* 248 (October 1999): 6.

2. Rashid Ghannoushi, *al-Hurriyyat al-'Ammah fi al-Dawlah al-Islamiyyah* [Public Liberties in the Islamic State], (Beirut: MDWA, 1993), pp. 315–16.
3. The point has been quite poignantly made by Aziz Al-Azmeh in *Islams and Modernities* (London: Verso, 1993); see also Mohammed Arkoun, *Rethinking Islam: Common Questions, Uncommon Answers*, translated and edited by Robert D. Lee (Boulder: Westview Press, 1994), p. 1 and *passim*; Ann Elizabeth Mayer, *Islam and Human Rights: Tradition and Politics* (Boulder: Westview Press, 1995), p. xi; Samir Amin, "Is there a Political Economy of Islamic Fundamentalism?", in his *Delinking: Towards a Polycentric World*, translated from French by M. Wolfers (London: Zed Books, 1990), p. 175.
4. See further Ahmad Shboul, "Islamic Radicalism in the Arab World", in *The Middle East: Prospects for Settlement and Stability?*, edited by A. Saikal and J. Jukes (Canberra: Australian National University, 1995), pp. 29–68; Rashid Ghannoushi, *al-Hurriyyat al-'Ammah*; also Ghannoushi, "*Tahlil lil-'Anasir al-Mukawwinah lil-Zahirah al-Islamiyyah bi-Tunis* [Analysis of the Constituent Factors in the Islamist Phenomenon in Tunisia], in *al-Harakat al-Islamiyyah al-Mu'asirah fi al-Watan al-'Arabi* [Contemporary Islamic Movements in the Arab World], edited by Ismail Sabri Abdalla (Beirut: MDWA, 1987), pp. 300–308; Abubaker A. Bagader, "Contemporary Islamic Movements in the Arab World", in *Islam, Globalization and Postmodernity*, edited by Akbar S. Ahmed and Donnan Hastings (London: Routledge, 1994), pp. 114–26.
5. Ahmad Shboul, "Islamic Radicalism in the Arab World", pp. 53–54; see also H.A.R. Gibb, *Modern Trends in Islam* (Chicago: University Press, 1947; reprint Beirut: Librairie du Liban, 1975), pp. 29–38; Albert Hourani, *Arabic Thought in the Liberal Age* (London: Oxford University Press, 1962, 1983), chapters 5, 6, and 9.
6. See, for example, Bryan S. Turner, "Politics and Culture in Islamic Globalism", in his *Orientalism, Postmodernism and Globalism* (London: Routledge, 1994), pp. 77–94.
7. See Benjamin R. Barber, *Jihad Vs. McWorld: How Globalism and Tribalism are Reshaping the World* (New York: Ballantine Books, 1995, 1996).
8. For example, see relevant works under A. Ahmed, S. Amin, M. Bamyeh, B. Barber, N. Chomsky, El Hassan Bin Talal, E. Gellner, A. Giddens, D. Held, M. 'A. Jabiri, F Jameson, B. Najjar, F. Rajaee, R. Rorty, G. Salamé, J. Tomlinson, B. Turner, listed in the References.
9. See HRH Prince El Hassan Bin Talal of Jordan, "Universalization/Globalization: Address", at the Forum 2000 Conference: "Education, Culture and Spiritual Values in the Age of Globalisation", Prague, 15–18 October 2000; El Hassan Bin Talal, "Address", at the conference on Counterfeiting and Piracy: (Enforcement of Intellectual Property Rights) Stockholm, 23 April 2001; John Tomlinson, *Globalisation and Culture* (Oxford: Polity, 1999), p. 183.
10. Hasan Hanafi, *Muqaddimah fi 'Ilm al-Istighrab* [Introduction to Occidentalism] (Beirut: al-Mu'assasah al-Jami'iyyah, 1992), pp. 18–43.

11. Janet L. Abu-Lughod, *Before European Hegemony: the World System AD 1250–1350,* (New York: Oxford University Press, 1989); K. N. Chaudhuri, *Asia Before Europe: Economy and Civilisation of the Indian Ocean from the Rise of Islam to 1750* (Cambridge: Cambridge University Press), 1990.
12. For example, Farhang Rajaee, *Globalization on Trial: the Human Condition and the Information Civilization* (Ottawa: International Development Research Centre, 2000), p. 55.
13. Tomlinson, *Globalisation and Culture*, pp. 183–84.
14. See, for example, Ismail Sabri Abdalla et al., *Images of the Arab Future*, translated from Arabic by Maissa Taldat (London: Frances Pinter and The United Nations University, 1983), pp. 14–64.
15. See, for example, Usamah al-Khuli et al., *al-Tarjamah fi al-Watan al-'Arabi* [Translation in the Arab World] (Beirut: MDWA, 2000).
16. See, for example, the Egyptian economist Ramzi Zaki, "Tanaqudat Hakimah li-Mustaqbal al-'Awlamah" [Contradictions Governing the Future of Globalization], *al-Ijtihad* 39 (Winter 1998): 57; idem, "Introduction" to the Arabic translation of H. P. Martins, *The Globalisation Trap* (Kuwait: 'Alam al-Ma'rifah Series no. 339, October 1998), p. 8; cited by Baqir al-Najjar "al-'Arab wal-'Awlamah: al-Makhawif wal-Tahaddiyat" [The Arabs and Globalization: Fears and Challenges], *Abwab* 26 (Autumn 2000): p. 13.
17. See, for example, Hisham Sharabi, "al-Muthaqqafun al-'Arab wal-Gharb fi Nihayat al-Qarn al-'Ishrin" [Arab Intellectuals and the West at the End of the Twentieth Century], *al-Mustaqbal al-'Arabi* 175 (September 1993): 29–35.
18. Jürgen Habermas, "Modernity: An Unfinished Project", in *Habermas and the Unfinished Project of Modernity*, edited by M. P. d'Entrëves and S. Benhabib (Cambridge: Polity, 1996).
19. For example, Georges Corm, *L'Europe et l'Orient de la balcanisation à la libanisation: histoire d'une modernitè inaccomplie* (Paris: la Dècouverte, 1989). Arabic translation *Awrubba wal-Mashriq al-'Arabi: min al-Balqanah ila al-Labnanah: Tarikh Hadathah Ghayr Munjazah* (Beirut: Dar al-Tali'ah, 1990); also his studies on religious diversity and political systems, on the Arab economy in the face of challenges, and on the "Missing Development"; Hasan Hanafi, *Muqaddimah fi 'Ilm al-Istighrab* [Introduction to Occidentalism]; Hisham Sharabi, *Neopatriarchy: A Theory of Distorted Change in Arab Society* (New York and Oxford: Oxford University Press, 1988), Arabic translation Beirut, 1989; see also Michael C. Hudson, "Introduction: Arab Integration: An Overview", in *Middle East Dilemma: The Politics and Economics of Arab Integration*, edited by C. Hudson (London: I.B. Tauris, 1999).
20. Mahmud Amin al-'Alim, "al-'Awlamah wal-Huwiyyah al-Thaqafiyyah" [Globalisation and Cultural Identity], *Jusur*, vol. 1 (February 1999), p. 5; cited by Baqir al-Najjar, *Abwab* 26 (Autumn 2000): 12.
21. Samir Amin, "Ba'da Harb al-Khalij: al-Haymanah al-Amrikiyyah, ila Ayn?" [After the Gulf War: American Hegemony, Where to?], *al-Mustaqbal al-'Arabi* 170

(April 1993): 4–22; see H. Sharabi's comments in *al-Mustaqbal al-'Arabi* 175 (September 1993): 30–31; see also Samir Amin, in *Hiwar al-Dawlah wal-Din* [Dialogue on State and Religion], by Samir Amin and Burhan Ghalyun (Beirut: al-Markaz al-Thaqafi al-'Arabi, 1996); Samir Amin, *Delinking: Towards a Polycentric World.*

22. Ernest Gellner, *Postmodernism, Reason and Religion* (London: Routledge, 1992); Akbar S. Ahmed and Donnan Hastings, eds. *Islam, Globalization, and Postmodernity.*
23. Radwan al-Sayyid, "al-Islamawiyyun wal-'Awlamah" [The Islamists and Globalization], paper presented to the symposium on Issues of Cultural Identity and Globalisation, Cairo, April 1998, cited by Baqir al-Najjar, "al-'Arab wal-'Awlamah" [The Arabs and Globalisation], *Abwab* 26 (Autumn 2000): 12.
24. Sayyid Qutb, *al-'Adalah al-Ijtima'iyyah fi al-Islam* (Cairo: 1949); Sayyid Qutb, *Ma'alim fi al-Tariq* [Signposts on the Way] (Beirut: Dar al-Shuruq, 1983); for a critical assessment, see Samir Amin, "Is There a Political Economy of Islamic Fundamentalism?", in his *Delinking: Towards a Polycentric World*, pp. 174–88.
25. See, for example, Ismail Sabri Abdalla, ed., *al-Harakat al-Islamiyyah* [Contemporary Islamic Movements], especially editor's Prologue, pp. 7–8; Shukri Faysal, "al-Sahwah al-Islamiyyah Bayn al-Waqi' wal-Tumuh" [The Islamic Awakening Between Reality and Ambition], ibid., p. 312; M. Filali, "Taqrir Tajmi'i: al-Sahwah al-Diniyyah al-Islamiyyah: Khasa'isuha — Atwaruha — Mustaqbaluha" [Summing up the Islamic Religious Awakening: Its Characteristics, Stages and Future], ibid., pp. 335–408.
26. Yusuf al-Qaradawi, *al-Sahwah al-Islamiyyah Bayn al-Ikhtilaf al-Mashru' wal-Tafarruq al-Madhmum* [The Islamic Awakening Between Legitimate Difference and Objectionable Discord] (Beirut: al-Risalah, 1990).
27. See 'Ali Sayf al-Nasr, "al-Sahwah al-Islamiyyah al-Mu'asirah wal-'Ulum al-Insaniyyah" [The Contemporary Islamic Awakening and the Humanities], *al-Mustaqbal al-'Arabi* 170 (April 1993): 116–32; Hasan Hanafi, *al-Turath wal-Tajdid* [Heritage and Modernity] (Beirut: Dar al-Tanwir, 1981); and *Muqaddimah fi 'Ilm al-Istighrab* [An Introduction to Occidentalism].
28. Rashid Ghannoushi, *al-Hurriyyat al-'Ammah*, pp. 287 and 315–16.
29. Ghannoushi, in I. S. Abdalla, ed., *al-Harakat*, p. 302; see also Muhammad Shahrur, "*al-Uswah al-Hasanah: al-Ta'ah li-Muhammad al-Insan am li-Muhammad al-Rasul*"(The Good Example: Is Obedience Due to Muhammad the Human Being, or Muhammad the Apostle?], in *al-'Unf al-Usuli: Nuwwab al-Ard wal-Sama'* [Fundamentalist Violence: Representatives of Heaven and Earth], by various authors, *Kitab al-Naqid* Series (London: Riad El-Rayyes Books, 1995), pp. 57–72.
30. Fehmi Jadaane, *al-Tariq ila al-Mustaqbal: Afkar wa Qiwa lil-Azminah al-'Arabiyyah al-Manzurah* [The Way to the Future: Ideas and Forces for the Anticipated Arab Times] (Beirut: al-Mu'assasah al-'Arabiyyah, 1996): especially chapter 4: "al-Islam fi al-'Asifah" [Islam in the Storm], pp. 207–342; and

chapter 5: "al-Tawasul" [Communication], pp. 343–430; Ghannoushi, *al-Hurriyyat al-'Ammah*, pp. 315–16.

31. For example, the Bahraini physician and former Minister of Health and of Education, Dr 'Ali Fakhru, "Ru'yah Thaqafiyyah fi Duwal Majlis al-Ta'awun" [A Cultural Perspective on the States of the [Gulf] Cooperation Council], *al-Mustaqbal al-'Arabi* 234 (August 1998): 31–39; and the leading Saudi economist and finance expert, 'Abd al-'Aziz Muhammad al-Dakhil, "'Arab al-Khalij wa Qadaya Qutriyyah wa Qawmiyyah [The Gulf Arabs and Some Regional and Pan-Arab Issues], *al-Mustaqbal al-'Arabi* 234 (August 1998): 40–57.
32. Abu Ya'rub al-Marzuqi, "al-'Awlamah wal-Kawniyyah" [Globalization and Universalism], *al-Tajdid*, 3rd Year (August 1998), p. 16; and idem, *Afaq al-Nahdah al-'Arabiyyah* [Horizons of Arab Renaissance] (Beirut: Dar al-Tali'ah, 1999), p. 120; cited by Baqir al-Najjar, in *Abwab* 26 (Autumn 2000): 12.
33. M. 'A. al-Jabiri, "al-'Awlamah wal-Huwiyyah al-Thaqafiyyah" [Globalization and Cultural Identity], *al-Mustaqbal al-'Arabi* 228 (February 1998): 17; see Muhammad Fahim Yusuf, "Huquq al-Insan fi Daw' al-Tajaliyyat al-Siyasiyyah lil-'Awlamah" [Human Rights in the Light of the Political Manifestations of Globalisation], in B. Ghalyun et al., *Huquq al-Insan al-'Arabi* [The Arab's Human Rights] (Beirut: MDWA, 1999), pp. 224.
34. B. Tibi, *The Challenge of Fundamentalism* (Berkeley, CA: California University Press, 1998), p. ix; Mohammed Arkoun, *Rethinking Islam*, p. 2; Nasr Hamid Abu-Zaid, in *Der Speigel*, issue 27 (1995); cited by B. Tibi, p. xi.
35. Hisham Sharabi, *Neopatriarchy*, pp. 11–12; see also Sharabi, "*al-Muthaqqafun al-'Arab*" [Arab Intellectuals], *al-Mustaqbal al-'Arabi* 175 (September 1993): 30–31.
36. For example, Saad Eddine Ibrahim, ed., *al-Mujtama' wal-Dawlah fi al-Watan al-'Arabi* [Society and the State in the Arab World] (Beirut: MDWA, Arab Future Studies Series, 1988); see also three regional studies by 'Abd al-Baqi al-Hirmassi, Khaldun al-Naqib, and Ghassan Salamé in the same series, listed in the References; also Halim Barakat, *The Arab World: Society, Culture and State* (Berkeley, CA: University of California Press, 1993).
37. Husayn Ahmad Amin, "Azmat al-Fard fi Misr" [The Crisis of the Individual in Egypt], *Abwab*, 27 (Winter 2001): 9–28; 'Ali Fakhru, in *al-Mustaqbal al-'Arabi* 234 (August 1998): 31–39; 'Abd al-'Aziz al-Dakhil, in *al-Mustaqbal al-'Arabi* 234 (August 1998): 40–57.
38. See, for example, Noam Chomsky, *Profit Over People: Neoliberalism and Global Order* (New York: Seven Stories Press, 1999).
39. See, for example, HRH Prince El Hassan Bin Talal of Jordan, "A Pragmatic Vision of the Arab Future", Egyptian Cultural Forum Seminar, Cairo, 28 January 2001; Saad Eddine Ibrahim, ed., *al-Mujtama' wal-Dawlah*, pp. 30–33 and p. 165ff.; Baqir al-Najjar, in *Abwab* 26 (Autumn 2000): 15; Ghassan Salamé, ed., *Democracy Without Democrats?* (London and New York: I. B. Tauris, 1994); for a fresh consideration of the ambiguities of globalization, see Mohammed

Bamyeh, *The Ends of Globalization* (Minneapolis: University of Minnesota Press, 2000).

40. See, for example, Richard Rorty, "Globalisation, the Politics of Identity and Social Hope", in his *Philosophy and Social Hope* (London: Penguin Books, 1999), pp. 229–39; Anthony Giddens, *Runaway World: How Globalisation is Reshaping Our Lives* (London: Profile Books, 1999); Fredric Jameson and Masao Miyoshi, eds., *The Cultures of Globalisation* (Durham, USA: Duke University Press, 1998); John Tomlinson, *Globalisation and Culture.*
41. Husayn Ahmad Amin, "Azmat al-Fard fi Misr" [The Crisis of the Individual in Egypt], *Abwab* 27 (Winter 2001): especially pp. 26–28; for a comparative anthropological perspective, see Gordon Mathews, *Global Culture/Individual Identity* (London: Routledge, 2000).
42. Muta' Safadi, "Mitafizya al-Shabah wal-Huwiyyah" [The Metaphysics of Resemblance and Identity], *al-Fikr al-'Arabi al-Mu'asir* 17 (December 1981–January 1982): 8; cited by Kamal 'Abd al-Latif, "Fi al-Tajdid al-Thaqafi: Mulahazat Awwaliyyah Hawla Mafhum al-Ghazw al-Thaqafi" [On Cultural Renewal: Preliminary Remarks on the Notion of Cultural Invasion], *al-Mustaqbal al-'Arabi* 109 (March 1988): 3–12; see also Khalaf Muhammad al-Jarad, "*al-'Alaqah al-Ishkaliyyah Bayn al-Muthaqafah wal-Ghazw al-Thaqafi fi al-Khitab al-'Arabi al-Mu'asir*" [The Problematic Relationship Between Acculturation and Cultural Invasion in the Contemporary Arab Discourse], *al-Mustaqbal al-'Arabi* 176 (October 1993): 66–78, and further references cited there.
43. L. Carl Brown, *International Relations and the Middle East: Old Rules, Dangerous Games* (London: I. B. Tauris, 1984), p. 4.
44. M. 'A. al-Jabiri, *al-Mas'alah al-Thaqafiyyah* [The Cultural Question] (Beirut: MDWA, 1994), part 4, pp. 171–248.
45. 'A. Balqziz, "al-'Awlamah wal-Huwiyyah al-Thaqafiyyah: 'Awlamat al-Thaqafah aw Thaqafat al-'Awlamah" [Globalization and Cultural Identity: Globalization of Culture or the Culture of Globalization], in *al-'Arab wal-'Awlamah*, by S. Yasin et al. (Beirut, MDWA, 1998), p. 319; cited by Baqir al-Najjar, *Abwab*, pp. 15–16.
46. Ahmad Baha' al-Din, "Muhawalat 'Sadd' al-Ghazw al-Hadari" [Attempts to "Repel" Cultural Invasion], *al-'Arabi* 219 (February 1977): 6–15.
47. See, for example, Ahmad Shboul, "Marcel Khalifé wa Mahmud Darwish wa Yusuf al-Husn" [Marcel Khalifé, Mahmud Darwish and Joseph of Excellence], *al-Quds al-'Arabi* (London), 26 September 1996.
48. See Ahmad Baha' al-Din, in *al-'Arabi*.
49. For the advertisement, "60 Years of Progress Without Change", as well as the quotation, see *The Times* (London), 23 September 1992; see also Allan M. Findlay, *The Arab World* (London: Routledge, 1994), p. 192ff.
50. Fatima Mernissi, *Islam and Democracy, Fear of the Modern World* (New York: Addison-Wesley, 1992).

51. HRH Prince El Hassan Bin Tilal of Jordan, "A Pragmatic Vision of the Arab Future", Address at the Cairo Forum on the Arab Future, 28 January 2001.
52. Raymond Williams and Edward Said, "Media, Margins and Modernity", in *The Politics of Modernity*, edited by R. Williams (London: Verso, 1989, 1996), p. 196.
53. Fredric Jameson and Masao Miyoshi, eds, *The Cultures of Globalisation*; John Tomlinson, *Globalisation and Culture*; David Held and Anthony McGrew, eds, *The Global Transformation Reader* (Cambridge: Polity, 2000), part iii.
54. 'A. 'A. al-Duri, "al-Huwiyyah al-Thaqafiyyah", p. 7; also Idris Hani, "Kayfa Yaqra' al-Muthaqqafun al-'Arab al-'Awlamah" [How Arab Intellectuals Read Globalisation], *al-Kalimah*, 19 (Spring 1998), p. 26; cited by Baqir al-Najjar, *Abwab*, 26 (Autumn 2000), p. 15.
55. <www.Mahjoob.com/archive>.
56. I owe this reference to my student Roslyn Philips.
57. For example, "Nahwa Mu'tamar Qawmi-Islami" [Towards a Nationalist-Islamist Conference], *al-Mustaqbal al-'Arabi* 161 (July 1992): 96–119.
58. For an Algerian perspective on this, see Azerradj Omar, *Manazil Min Khazaf* [Houses Made of Ceramics] (London: Riad El-Rayyes Books, 1991).
59. Qur'an 13:11.
60. Samuel P. Huntington, *The Clash of Civilizations and the Remaking of World Order* (London: Schuster, 1997); Constantine Zurayk, *Fi Ma'rakat al-Hadarah* [In the Battle of Civilization] (Beirut: Dar al-'Ilm lil-Malayin, 1964).

References

'Abd al-Latif, Kamal. "Fi al-Tajdid al-Thaqafi: Mulahazat Awwaliyyah Hawla Mafhum al-Ghazw al-Thaqafi" [On Cultural Renewal: Preliminary Remarks on the Notion of Cultural Invasion]. *al-Mustaqbal al-'Arabi* 109 (March 1988).

Abdalla, Ismail Sabri, ed. *al-Harakat al-Islamiyyah al-Mu'asirah fi al-Watan al-'Arabi* [Contemporary Islamic Movements in the Arab World]. Beirut: MDWA, 1987.

Abdalla, Ismail Sabri et al. *Images of the Arab Future*. Translated from Arabic by Maissa Taldat. London: Frances Pinter and The United Nations University, 1983.

Abu-Lughod, Janet L. *Before European Hegemony: The World System AD 1250–1350*. New York: Oxford University Press, 1989.

Ahmed, Akbar S. and D. Hastings, eds. *Islam, Globalization and Postmodernity*. London and New York: Routledge, 1994.

Al-Azmeh, Aziz. *Islams and Modernities*. London: Verso, 1993.

Amin, Husayn Ahmad. "Azmat al-Fard fi Misr" [The Crisis of the Individual in Egypt]. *Abwab*, 27 (Winter 2001).

Amin, S. and B. Ghalyun. *Hiwar al-Dawlah wal-Din* [Dialogue on State and Religion]. Beirut and Casablanca: al-Markaz al-Thaqafi al-'Arabi, 1996.

Amin, Samir. "Ba'da Harb al-Khalij: al-Haymanah al-Amrikiyyah, ila Ayn?" [After the Gulf War: American Hegemony, Where to?]. *al-Mustaqbal al-'Arabi* 170 (April 1993).

————. *Delinking: Towards a Polycentric World*. Translated from French by M. Wolfers. London: Zed Books, 1990.

Arkoun, Mohammed. *Rethinking Islam: Common Questions, Uncommon Answers*. Translated and edited by Robert D. Lee. Boulder: Westview Press, 1994.

Bagader, Abubaker A. "Contemporary Islamic Movements in the Arab World". In *Islam, Globalization and Postmodernity*, edited by Akbar S. Ahmed and Donnan Hastings. London and New York: Routledge, 1994.

Baha' al-Din, Ahmad. "Muhawalat 'Sadd' al-Ghazw al-Hadari" [Attempts to 'Repel' Cultural Invasion]. *al-'Arabi*, 219 (February 1977).

Bamyeh, Mohammed A. *The Ends of Globalisation*. Minneapolis: University of Minnesota Press, 2000.

Barakat, Halim. *The Arab World: Society, Culture and State*. Berkeley, CA: University of California Press, 1993.

Barber, Benjamin R. *Jihad Vs. McWorld: How Globalism and Tribalism are Reshaping the World*. New York: Ballantine Books, 1996.

Brown, L. Carl. *International Relations and the Middle East: Old Rules, Dangerous Games*. London: I. B. Tauris, 1984.

Chaudhuri, K. N. *Asia Before Europe: Economy and Civilisation of the Indian Ocean from the Rise of Islam to 1750*. Cambridge: Cambridge University Press, 1990.

Chomsky, Noam. *Profit Over People: Neoliberalism and Global Order*. New York: Seven Stories Press, 1999.

Corm, Georges. *L'Europe et l'Orient de la balcanisation à la libanisation: histoire d'une modernitè inaccomplie*. Paris: la Dècouverte, 1989. Arabic edition, *Awrubba wal-Mashriq al-'Arabi: min al-Balqanah ila al-Labnanah: Tarikh Hadathah Ghayr Munjazah*. Beirut: Dar al-Tali'ah, 1990.

Dakhil (al-), 'Abd al-'Aziz Muhammad. "'Arab al-Khalij wa Qadaya Qutriyyah wa Qawmiyyah" [The Gulf Arabs and Some Regional and Pan-Arab Issues]. *al-Mustaqbal al-'Arabi* 234 (August 1998).

Duri (al-), 'Abd al-'Aziz. "al-Huwiyyah al-'Arabiyyah wal-Tahaddiyat" [Arab Cultural Identity and [its] Challenges]. *al-Mustaqbal al-'Arabi* 248 (October 1999).

El Hassan Bin Talal of Jordan. "Universalization/Globalization". Address at the Forum 2000 Conference: Education, Culture and Spiritual Values in the Age of Globalisation, Prague, 15–18 October 2000.

————. "A Pragmatic Vision of the Arab Future". Address at the Egyptian Cultural Forum Seminar, Cairo, 28 January 2001.

————. Address at the Conference on Counterfeiting and Piracy: (Enforcement of Intellectual Property Rights), Stockholm, 23 April 2001.

Fakhru, 'Ali. "Ru'yah Thaqafiyyah fi Duwal Majlis al-Ta'awun" [A Cultural Perspective on the States of the [Gulf] Cooperation Council]. *al-Mustaqbal al-'Arabi* 234 (August 1998).

Faysal, Shukri. "al-Sahwah al-Islamiyyah Bayn al-Waqi' wal-Tumuh" [The Islamic Awakening Between Reality and Ambition]. In *al-Harakat al-Islamiyyah al-Mu'asirah fi al-Watan al-'Arabi* [Contemporary Islamic Movements in the Arab World], edited by Ismail Sabri Abdalla. Beirut: MDWA, 1987.

Filali (al-), Mustafa. "Taqrir Tajmi'i: al-Sahwah al-Diniyyah al-Islamiyyah: Khasa'isuha — Atwaruha — Mustaqbaluha" [Summing up the Islamic Religious Awakening: Its Characteristics, Stages and Future]. In *al-Harakat al-Islamiyyah al-Mu'asirah fi al-Watan al-'Arabi* [Contemporary Islamic Movements in the Arab World], edited by Ismail Sabri Abdalla. Beirut: MDWA, 1987.

Findlay, Allan M. *The Arab World.* London: Routledge, 1994.

Gellner, Ernest. *Postmodernism, Reason and Religion.* London: Routledge, 1992.

Ghalyun, Burhan et al. *Huquq al-Insan al-'Arabi* [The Arab's Human Rights]. Beirut: MDWA, 1999.

Ghannoushi, Rashid. "Tahlil lil-'Anasir al-Mukawwinah lil-Zahirah al-Islamiyyah bi-Tunis" [Analysis of the Constituent Factors in the Islamist Phenomenon in Tunisia]. In *al-Harakat al-Islamiyyah al-Mu'asirah fi al-Watan al-'Arabi* [Contemporary Islamic Movements in the Arab World], edited by Ismail Sabri Abdalla. Beirut: MDWA, 1987.

————. *al-Hurriyyat al-'Ammah fi al-Dawlah al-Islamiyyah* [Public Liberties in the Islamic State]. Beirut: MDWA, 1993.

Gibb, H.A.R. *Modern Trends in Islam.* Chicago: University Press, 1947; reprint Beirut: Librairie du Liban, 1975.

Giddens, Anthony. *Runaway World: How Globalisation is Reshaping Our Lives.* London: Profile Books, 1999.

Habermas, Jürgen. "Modernity: An Unfinished Project". In *Habermas and the Unfinished Project of Modernity*, edited by M. P. d'Entrëves and S. Benhabib. Cambridge: Polity, 1996.

Hanafi, Hasan. *al-Turath wal-Tajdid* [Heritage and Modernity]. Beirut: Dar al-Tanwir, 1981.

————. *Muqaddimah fi 'Ilm al-Istighrab* [Introduction to Occidentalism]. Beirut: al-Mu'assasah al-Jami'iyyah, 1992.

Held, David and Anthony McGrew, eds. *The Global Transformation Reader.* Cambridge: Polity, 2000.

Hirmassi (al-), 'Abd al-Baqi. *al-Mujtama' wal-Dawlah fi al-Maghrib al-'Arabi* [Society and the State in the Arab Maghrib]. Beirut: MDWA, 1987.

Hourani, Albert. *Arabic Thought in the Liberal Age.* London: Oxford University Press, 1962, 1983.

Hudson, Michael C. ed. *Middle East Dilemma: The Politics and Economics of Arab Integration.* London: Tauris, 1999.

Huntington, Samuel P. *The Clash of Civilizations and the Remaking of World Order.* London: Simon Schuster, 1997.

Ibrahim, Saad Eddine, ed. *al-Mujtama' wal-Dawlah fi al-Watan al-'Arabi* [Society and the State in the Arab World]. Beirut: MDWA, 1988.

Jabiri (al-), Muhammad 'Abid. *al-Mas'alah al-Thaqafiyyah* [The Cultural Question]. Beirut: MDWA, 1994.

———. "al-'Awlamah wal-Huwiyyah al-Thaqafiyyah: 'Ashr Turuhat" [Globalisation and Cultural Identity: Ten Hypotheses]. *al-Mustaqbal al-'Arabi* (February 1998).

Jadaane, Fehmi. *al-Tariq ila al-Mustaqbal: Afkar wa Qiwa lil-Azminah al-'Arabiyyah al-Manzurah* [The Way to the Future: Ideas and Forces for the Anticipated Arab Times]. Beirut: al-Mu'assasah al-'Arabiyyah, 1996.

Jameson, Fredric and Masao Miyoshi, eds. *The Cultures of Globalisation*. Duke University Press, 1998.

Jarad (al-), Khalaf Muhammad. "al-'Alaqah al-Ishkaliyyah Bayn al-Muthaqafah wal-Ghazw al-Thaqafi fi al-Khitab al-'Arabi al-Mu'asir" [The Problematic Relationship Between Acculturation and Cultural Invasion in the Contemporary Arab Discourse]. *al-Mustaqbal al-'Arabi* 176 (October 1993).

Khuli (al-), Usamah et al. *al-Tarjamah fi al-Watan al-'Arabi* [Translation in the Arab World]. Beirut: MDWA, 2000.

Mathews, Gordon. *Global Culture/Individual Identity*. London: Routledge, 2000.

Mayer, Ann Elizabeth. *Islam and Human Rights: Tradition and Politics*. Boulder: Westview Press, 1995.

Mernissi, Fatima. *Islam and Democracy, Fear of the Modern World*. New York: Addison-Wesley, 1992.

Najjar (al-), Baqir. "al-'Arab wal-'Awlamah: al-Makhawif wal-Tahaddiyat" [The Arabs and Globalisation: Fears and Challenges]". *Abwab* 26 (Autumn 2000).

Naqib (al-), Khaldun. *al-Mujtama' wal-Dawlah fi al-Khalij wal-Jazirah al-'Arabiyyah* [Society and the State in the Gulf and the Arabian Peninsula]. Beirut: MDWA, 1987.

Nasr (al-), 'Ali Sayf. "al-Sahwah al-Islamiyyah al-Mu'asirah wal-'Ulum al-Insaniyyah" [The Contemporary Islamic Awakening and the Humanities]. *al-Mustaqbal al-'Arabi* 170 (April 1993).

Omar, Azerradj. *Manazil Min Khazaf: Dirash fi al-Wa'i al-Jazairi al-Mu'asir* [Houses Made of Ceramics: A Study in Contemporary Algerian Consciousness]. London: Riad El-Rayyes Books, 1991.

Qaradawi (al-), Yusuf. *al-Sahwah al-Islamiyyah Bayn al-Ikhtilaf al-Mashru' wal-Tafarruq al-Madhmum* [The Islamic Awakening Between Legitimate Difference and Objectionable Discord]. Beirut: al-Risalah, 1990.

Qutb, Sayyid. *al-'Adalah al-Ijtima'iyyah fi al-Islam* [Social Justice in Islam]. Cairo: 1949.

———. *Ma'alim fi al-Tariq* [Signposts on the Way]. Beirut: Dar al-Shuruq, 1983.

Rajaee, Fahrang. *Globalisation on Trial: The Human Condition and the Information Civilization*. Ottawa: International Development Research Centre, 2000.

Rorty, Richard. *Philosophy and Social Hope*. London: Penguin Books, 1999.

Safadi, Muta'. "Mitafizya al-Shabah wal-Huwiyyah" [The Metaphysics of Resemblance and Identity]. *al-Fikr al-'Arabi al-Mu'asir* 17 (December 1981–January 1982).

Salamé, Ghassan. *al-Mujtama' wal-Dawlah fi al-Mashriq al-'Arabi* (Society and the State in the Arab East). Beirut: MDWA, 1987.

————. *Appels d'empire: Ingèrences et resistances à l'age de mondialism*. Paris: Fayard, 1996.

————. ed. *Democracy Without Democrats: The Renewal of Politics in The Muslim World*. London: Tauris, 1987.

Shahrur, Muhammad. "al-Uswah al-Hasanah: al-Ta'ah li-Muhammad al-Insan am li-Muhammad al-Rasul" [The Good Example: Is Obedience Due to Muhammad the Human Being, or Muhammad the Apostle?]. In *al-'Unf al-Usuli: Nuwwab al-Ard wal-Sama'* [Fundamentalist Violence: Representatives of Heaven and Earth], by various authors. Kitab al-Naqid Series, London: Riad El-Rayyes Books, 1995.

Sharabi, Hisham. "al-Muthaqqafun al-'Arab wal-Gharb fi Nihayat al-Qarn al-'Ishrin" [Arab Intellectuals and the West at the End of the Twentieth Century]. *al-Mustaqbal al-'Arabi* 175 (September 1993).

————. *Neopatriarchy: A Theory of Distorted Change in Arab Society*. New York: Oxford University Press, 1988.

Shboul, Ahmad. "Islamic Radicalism in the Arab World". In *The Middle East: Prospects for Settlement and Stability?*, edited by A. Saikal and J. Jukes. Canberra: Australian National University, 1995.

————. "Marcel Khalifé wa Mahmud Darwish wa Yusuf al-Husn" [Marcel Khalifé, Mahmud Darwish and Joseph of Excellence]. *al-Quds al-'Arabi* (London) 26 September 1996.

Tibi, Bassam. *The Challenge of Fundamentalism: Political Islam and the New World Order*. Berkeley, CA: University of California Press, 1998.

Tomlinson, John. *Globalisation and Culture*. Oxford: Polity, 1999.

Turner, Bryan, S. *Orientalism, Postmodernism and Globalism*. London: Routledge, 1994.

Williams, Raymond, and Edward Said. "Media, Margins and Modernity". In *The Politics of Modernity*, edited by R. Williams. London: Verso, 1989, 1996.

Yusuf, Muhammad Fahim. "Huquq al-Insan fi Daw' al-Tajaliyyat al-Siyasiyyah lil-'Awlamah" [Human Rights in the Light of the Political Manifestations of Globalisation]. In *Huquq al-Insan al-'Arabi* [The Arab's Human Rights], edited by Burhan Ghalyun et al. Beirut: MDWA, 1999.

Zurayk, Constantine. *Fi Ma'rakat al-Hadarah* [In the Battle of Civilization]. Beirut: Dar al-'Ilm lil-Malayin, 1964.

5

INDONESIAN MUSLIMS ENTER A NEW AGE

Nurcholish Madjid

The Holy Book teaches that all the faithful are brothers. It is also commanded that *ishlāḥ* (reconciliation) should always be sought among believers in disagreement as an aspect of devotion to Allah. These teachings about brotherhood are followed by an injunction about the first and foremost principle for the preservation of the brotherhood of Muslims (*Ukhuwwah Islāmiyyah*), namely, that among the faithful no one group should put down others. This primary principle is followed by several other injunctions explaining things which can destroy brotherhood, like insulting one another, referring to other believers by unpleasant names, being prejudiced, looking for faults in others, and bad-mouthing people (committing *ghībah*, that is, discussing the flaws of someone not present). This series of divine commandments about brotherhood is followed by an affirmation of the principle that all mankind are brothers, and that the division of mankind into different races and ethnic groups was meant to provide markers of self-identification (identity), which must be borne in a broader humanitarian environment with an attitude of absolute mutual respect. It is also stressed that a person's dignity and worth cannot be measured by external factors such as nationality or language, for dignity and worth consist in a truer philosophy of life, subsisting in man's deepest self, namely piety — and only Allah knows and can measure piety (Q. 49:10–13). Thus God alone has the right to measure and determine someone's worth, whereas a man must appraise other men in the spirit of equality.

If we consider aspects of Islam which could be the focus for reinterpretation, the noble spirit of humanitarianism (*ḥabl min al-nās*) should receive greater attention. It constitutes the second aspect of Islamic teachings after the spirit of godliness (*ḥabl min-Allāh*). This is, in fact, widely known among Muslims. So what is needed are substantiations, indicating the foundations in sacred sources (the Holy Book and Sunna) and reinvestigating a range of historical evidence, because no matter how exalted a teaching, what really influences society is its concrete realization in history, that is, in man's social and cultural life in the context of a particular place and time. So the approach to teachings as far as possible is not dogmatic, but analytical, even in the approach to understanding sacred sources.

An understanding of cultural aspects has the effect of widening one's horizons and freeing oneself from dogmatism and normativism. We are in great need of historical awareness, without becoming "historified" in the sense of making absolute what existed in the past, but rather seeing it as an actual example of the realization and implementation of a moral value within the demands of period and place. In this history of civilization the "link with Allah" is actually translated into a "link with fellow man". Muslim civilizations assume that a turning point in their creation was a commitment to Islamic values, the essence of which is devotion to Allah. However, these civilizations themselves also assume man's creative energy and his endeavour in the course of communal life. So their nature is truly humanitarian.

Civilization is a function of men's status as caliphs; as God's agents on earth. This status was given to man because of his ability to know and understand his living environment ("to know the names of the forms around him"), and was not given to angels even though they are very religious ("always chanting in praise of God to worship and sanctify Him") (see Q. 2:31–33). However, it transpired that, although he had knowledge, the first man, Adam, was not exempt from the possibility of going astray. He could not control his desires, and was still tempted by Satan to disobey God's prohibitions. Adam and his wife Ḥawā' (Eve) fell from a life of contentment in heaven to endure a life on earth filled with obstacles and difficulties.

However, Allah still demonstrated his love for Adam by giving him an assortment of teachings (*Kalimāt*). These teachings became a guide for Adam and his descendants, so that they were able to live without fear (Q. 2:35–39). These *Kalimāt* were the very earliest form of God's lessons in life to mankind, and thus also constituted the beginnings of "religion". From the narrative surrounding Adam (and his wife Ḥawā') we can conclude that these various lessons (*Kalimāt*) from God were to equip mankind so that the knowledge which had caused them to be appointed rulers on earth didn't, in fact, lead them astray. Or in contemporary terms, humanity's scientific orientation must be guided by spiritual values; values which issue from feelings of the deepest and truest meaning, founded on the consciousness of creatures originating from God who will surely return to Him (*Innā li-'l-Lāhi wa innā ilayhi rāji'ūn)* (Q. 2:156).

According to the above definition, religion remains humanitarian by nature, for it guides mankind towards happiness. It is not, however, detached humanitarianism but rather humanitarianism which springs from divinity (*ḥabl min al-nās* emanating from (*ḥabl min Allāh*). This humanitarianism is achieved not by limiting man's existence to transient values (*al-dunyā*) in this earthly life, but by reaching beyond the sky to achieve the most exalted of values (*al-matsal al-a'lā*) eternal in the afterlife (Q. 16:60). That is, the approval of God who appointed him ruler on earth.

The humanitarian side of religion can also be approached from the perspective that religion is referred to as a "revealed disposition" (*fithrah munazzalah* — Ibn Taymiyyah) to strengthen man's natural disposition (*fithrah majbūlah*). Because of this, man's calling to the true religion is linked to the nature of Allah, on account of which mankind was created (Q. 30:30). Taken from another point of view, this means that religion is an extension of man's own nature, being the concrete realization of his natural tendencies. Thus, just as it is impossible for humanitarian values to conflict with religious values, so too is it inconceivable that religious values should come into opposition with humanitarian values. Religion was not created as an obstacle to humanitarianism (Q. 22:78). Thus something concordant with humanitarianism (being useful to mankind) will undoubtedly be preserved on earth, whilst things not concordant (not being useful to mankind) will surely disappear (Q. 13:17). Religion originates from God, but for the sake of humanity. Humans must act well in order to earn the approval of God, and in fact, by trying to earn God's approval or blessing humans do what is best for themselves (Q. 41:46). Thus whilst God does not need mankind, man, for the sake of his own humanity, needs God's blessing (Q. 47:38). An appreciation of divinity gives rise to an appreciation of humanitarianism (Q. 31:12). Neither of these two aspects can make the other false or untrue. Godliness without humanitarianism is condemned by God himself (Q. 107:1–7), and humanitarianism without godliness is like a mirage (Q. 24:39).

If we return to the metaphorical narrative about Adam, mankind was essentially given total freedom to live life, but in such a way as not to transgress religious norms. Adam and Ḥawā' were given freedom to eat the fruit in the "garden" where they lived "freely and as they desired", but they were forbidden to approach a certain tree (Q. 2:35). They were given this freedom after they had been made Allah's caliphs on earth. This narrative clearly indicates that fundamentally life must be lived in total freedom, limited only by that which is clearly prohibited, hence the principle of Islamic jurisprudence (*'Ilm Ushūl al-Fiqh*), "In essence all things are permitted, unless there be a directive to the contrary" (*Al-ashl fi al-asy'yā' al-ibāḥ ah illā idzā mā dalla al-dalīl 'alā khilāfihī*). This principle becomes clearer when contrasted with another: "In essence [formal] acts of devotion are forbidden, unless there be a directive to the contrary" (*Al-ashl fi al-'ibādah al-taḥrīm illā idzā idzā mā dalla al-dalil'alā khilāfihī*).

The first principle emphasizes the existence of a basic freedom to live the life bestowed by Allah upon mankind (*Banī Ādam* — "Descendants of Adam") with certain prohibitions which must be observed. The second principle stresses that mankind is forbidden to "create" religion, including means of worship, which is the absolute right of Allah and His Prophets charged with transmitting religion to society. So, just as forbidding something which is permitted is heresy (first principle), creating one's own method of worship is also heresy (second principle).

Forbidden things, compared with those which are allowed, are relatively few. (Adam and Ḥawā', whilst being given freedom to eat the garden's fruit unreservedly, were only forbidden to approach one particular tree.) And it is hoped we will know the limits by our conscience. For the conscience is the seat of our natural appreciation of good and evil, consistent with God's revelation to each individual (Q. 91:8). Our inner voice is primordial capital, which we obtain from God before we are born into the world to enlighten our path by its natural ability to differentiate good, which it "knows" (*al-ma'rūf*) from bad, which it "rejects" (*al-munkar*).

This lesson constitutes an optimistic and positive source of vision for mankind. If it is true that man is essentially good because of his God-given nature, and if it is true that this God-given nature is the basis of his natural disposition to seek and side with what is right and good (*ḥanīf*), our view of our fellow man cannot be otherwise, and in principle must be entirely optimistic and positive. Therefore our attitude towards our fellow man must be based on positive expectations (*ḥusn al-dhann*), not negative expectations (*sū' al-dhann*). Negative expectations are only consistent with a pessimistic and negative understanding of mankind, arising from teachings that man is essentially evil.

RELIGION AND HUMANITARIANISM

The emphasis on the humanitarian side of religion has become increasingly relevant, even pressing, in coming to terms with the era of globalization, an age which has seen the increasing synthesis of human civilizations through developments in communications, technology, and transport. Human civilizations may never be totally unified. Each place has its own demands, which produce cultural patterns specific to the local community. But clearly there is no way to avoid the effect of improvements in communication and mobility, namely a necessity for interaction and mutual exchange between various groups of people. As a result, a firm spiritual basis is necessary to maintain identity in a positive way, whilst simultaneously consolidating notions of plurality and mutual appreciation.

In connection with this, Muslims may feel fortunate because they have inherited a civilization which has genuinely functioned as a global civilization. Muslim cosmopolitanism has in the past been a historical reality, which opened the way to the creation of a humanitarian legacy unconstrained by narrow and parochial conceptions of nationalism. So, if we now have to foster a universal humanitarian spirit among Muslims, it means most of the task is a repetition of history, for it means reviving views and experiences which were once held by Muslims themselves. Recognizing this problem as a repetition of history will undoubtedly have the effect of reducing the psychological burden of social change associated with the switch from existing views to a more global vision.

If globalism is an unavoidable necessity, why must it be approached through religion? If the problem is universal humanitarianism, why not approach it more efficiently by immediately introducing it simply as a general humanitarian problem? Or is "religion without revelation" consistent with the understanding of Western humanists who reject organized religion, such as Julian Huxley, for example? After all, notions of humanitarianism or humanism which developed in the West and have now become a "blessing" for all mankind were always conceived of and cultivated by thinkers who rejected, were indifferent to, or had their own ideas about religion.

Remembering man's global situation with regard to the problem of religiosity in the modern age, dominated by the West and with all the views currently developing, a similarly sceptical attitude is quite normal. Perhaps the answers to questions such as these have now become a little easier because of the possibilities of interpretation and lessons which have emerged from the bankruptcy of the Eastern European bloc. From one perspective, the Marxist-Leninist system of Eastern Europe was the greatest attempt to wipe out religions and to free mankind of the role religion played. This attempt, though Marx and his supporters claimed it was "scientific", ultimately met with failure. Firstly, the Marxists were unable to completely eradicate religion there, even though all funds and energies had been mobilized. Secondly, it is ironic that Marxism itself became a more basic and unrefined, if not primitive, quasi religion. While those convinced by communist doctrine may indeed have successfully freed themselves from a belief in objects of worship because, in their view, worship leads to the enslavement and loss of man's independence, they nevertheless fell headlong into the practice of worshipping objects which shackled, enslaved, and robbed them of their freedom to a greater extent, namely tyrannical and authoritarian leaders. Their leaders were regarded as personifications of "holy" teachings, such that it was natural for their doctrines to be named after a leader, as evidenced by the terms "Marxism", "Leninism", "Stalinism", "Maoism", etc. They fell into the practice of polytheism, or worse. Even though Marxism may be viewed as a "religion equivalent" or quasi religion, because it consciously and systematically rejects every possibility of believing in an Almighty, it grew to become a false religion, more base and unrefined than conventional religions, enslaving people and shackling their independence to a greater extent. Marxism, especially in its dogmatic and closed-off form within communism, was a tragic influence for people in their efforts to discover the meaning of their lives and a scientific solution for life's problems.

FAITH, KNOWLEDGE, AND GOOD WORKS

Any system of teachings, including religion, is of no benefit, and will not bring the improvements to life that it promises, unless it is put into practice. From this perspective, among other things, we have to understand the admonition in the Holy Book that it is a great sin against God if we say something (including saying that we embrace a particular system of teachings) but don't carry it out (Q. 61:3). Thus Islam, which promises happiness in this world and the next, will fulfil its promise only when it is wholly put into practice. Of course a person's ability to put teachings into practice depends on his or her respective circumstances. History shows that there has been no period in the social application of Islam which has been entirely free of deficiencies, not even the period known as the "Golden Age". This fact is also acknowledged by the Holy Book, as indicated in Allah's word instructing us to be devout unto Him "as best one can" (Q. 64:16), and that Allah never places a burden on someone unless it is appropriate to their ability (Q. 2:286).

Consequently the consideration regarding a man's deeds is: which are greater, his virtues or his vices (Q. 101:6–7).

Yet in the precise interpretation of "as best one can" and "appropriate to their ability" we find an exhortation that people, in carrying out God's teachings, should not take a minimalist attitude, but rather make an effort wholeheartedly to the best of their ability. This is the true nature of *ijtihād*, a form of moral responsibility towards a person's obligation to practise the teachings in which he or she believes. As a moral responsibility, *ijtihād* brings its own merits, so one still obtains spiritual rewards even if it later transpires that it produced something wrong or inappropriate. Should the product of *ijtihād* be fitting and appropriate, its rewards are twofold: first, because of the engagement in the moral responsibility of *ijtihād*; and second, because of the appropriate application of the teaching. Thus the Prophet (blessings and peace be upon Him) stressed that those who conduct *ijtihād* properly will earn two rewards, and those who conduct it inappropriately earn one reward.

The exercise of *ijtihād* to implement a teaching will inevitably involve a necessity to know precisely the social and cultural environment where the teaching is to be put into practice. Of course, first it is necessary to have an appropriate knowledge of the teaching itself, for an inappropriate knowledge will result in an inappropriate implementation, such that it may become a source of major errors. However an appropriate knowledge of a doctrine is no guarantee of appropriate implementation. At the level of implementation accurate knowledge of the associated social and cultural environment is needed, with an understanding also of the specific demands and restrictions these cause. Without such knowledge and understanding, all efforts to implement a teaching will plunge headlong into normativism, thinking according to what should be, and not about what is possible. At best, such normativism will give rise to unrealistic attitudes and demands. Normativism, however, can have far worse consequences. Associated with disappointment after disappointment and annoyance after annoyance, as a result of a series of failures in trying to implement a teaching in which someone believes — a failure, in fact, caused by those unrealistic attitudes and demands themselves — normativism can easily push a person towards a radical and unconstructive attitude. With the addition of feelings of defeat and despair (which often seep into the subconscious), normativism can send people to the brink of destructive actions.

Indeed, because of this, throughout the teachings of the Qur'an, there is the guarantee that excellence and superiority, including victory and success, will be bestowed by Allah upon those who are faithful and erudite (Q. 58:11).

"Faithful" means having a divine orientation in life, making God's blessing the aim of all their activities; and "erudite" means understanding teachings properly, and having a proper understanding of the environment in which they will act, socio-culturally and physically, like the knowledge that was bestowed by God upon Adam to perform the task of caliph on earth, and was a factor in his superiority over the angels (Q. 2:31). Faith alone is indeed enough to make people oriented towards virtue, and to have "good intentions". Faith, however, does not provide them with an ability to implement their intentions. So it is no guarantee of success. Conversely, knowledge alone may enable people to do something tangible. However, without the guidance of faith their knowledge will bring them greater misfortune than those who lack knowledge. Hence the Prophet said, "Whosoever expands his knowledge but does not augment the rules by which he lives adds nothing except his distance from Allah."

ISLAM IN INDONESIA: PROBLEMS OF DEVELOPMENT

In order to weather the present and face the future we think and work in the context of implementing Islamic teachings. Returning to the previous argument, for such implementation we need a proper understanding of Islamic teachings themselves, and of the environment in which we intend to implement them, namely Indonesia. It would probably be excessive if we were to emphasize that both our efforts to understand these teachings, as well as our efforts to understand our environment, are all a form of *ijtihād*, with all the value and meaning of *ijtihād*. So, too, we no longer need to emphasize that we are aware of the possibility of being right or wrong, proportional to the facilities we enjoy and limitations we face in our efforts to understand doctrines and our environment.

If the concept we have tried to outline above is correct, then every step towards implementing Islamic teachings in Indonesia has to take into account socio-cultural conditions, the main characteristics of which are growth, development, and plurality. There is as yet no socio-cultural pattern, which might be viewed as the permanent shape of Indonesianness, either as a system of values or an institution. So in this process of growth and development, it is hoped Indonesian Muslims will contribute their share and take responsibility proportional to their numerical strength.

Development as an idea is not foreign to Muslims. Part of the Islamic faith is the formula that "Everything changes except the Face of God" (Q. 28:88). Although Muslim scholars did not reach a conclusion about the law of entropy according to modern physics, they were aware that a characteristic of all existence besides the existence of God is change (*taghayyur*). In fact the law of change suggests that nothing is permanent, and this impermanence, in turn, indicates the existence of God the Creator who created everything — God being the only eternal form.

These ideas about change and development are reflected in various theories about how to implement religious teachings in society. This is associated with the problem of historical consciousness, namely the consciousness that everything to do with the ordering of human life bears some relationship to differences in time and place. The theory of *Ushūl al-Fiqh* about *nāsikh mansūkh* — namely that a teaching or determination, like a law, may be erased and replaced by a new and better one — indicates the existence of a strong historical consciousness in Islamic teachings. Although this theory, like all others, invites controversy and polemic, it is worthy of note given its broad and significant implications that the majority of Muslims embrace, especially since for those who support it there is a divine revelation which indicates that Allah did indeed erase a verse or cause it to be forgotten, in order that it might be replaced with another which was equal or better (see Q. 2:106).

Among Allah's qualities are those of the Most Good and Most True. So the path towards Allah's blessing is the path towards Truth, such that the path, itself, takes on qualities of truth (becoming "the right path") even though truth along the path is constantly moving and dynamic, and therefore transient, and the path is only right because it leads or points to the Absolute Truth. So the true definition of "path" itself indicates the presence of movement, because everything and everyone on the path and who travels it has to move towards a destination. This ethos of movement is very strong in Islam, and in the Holy Book it is associated with the basic idea and spirit of the Pilgrimage (Q. 4:97 and 100, 29:26). The basic idea and spirit of *jihād*, *ijtihād*, and *mujāhadah* (the root of which is *juhd*, meaning "a determined effort") is also closely connected to the ethos of movement and the dynamic path which knows no end. Thus it is promised in the Holy Book that Allah will show anyone who does something with absolute determination several (not just one!) paths to Him (Q. 29:69).

Ideas about growth and development involve ideas about phasing (*tadrīj*, the division or introduction of levels or degrees of growth). From the point of view of phasing, and in keeping with the paradigm of the dynamic path and the ethos of movement in Islamic teachings outlined above, there are no "once and for all" solutions to life's problems, which are always shifting and changing. A particular solution to a problem is only ever valid for its time and place, and is possible only if there has been an accurate "reading" of that time and place. This does not mean that we are encouraged to let ourselves go in uncontrolled relativism such that we no longer have a stance and lose the will to act. While every form of solution to a problem that we encounter and feel sure is right for its time and place must be implemented with dedication, we must also remain open to improvements and progress. Thus we may conform to the Prophet's depiction that the faithful are those who are today better than those yesterday, and those who tomorrow will be better than those today.

This is also the case with the implementation of Islam in Indonesia. It has already been shown how much our country is changing, developing, and growing dynamically and relatively quickly. To understand better how fast the relative tempo of change in our country is, perhaps the use of Alvin Toffler's theory about waves of development in human civilization will help. On one of his visits to Indonesia, Toffler and his wife met me at my home. During our quite lengthy discussion, the problem of waves in the development of civilization was discussed. Toffler said that the civil war in America was really a clash between two waves: the first wave (agricultural society) represented by the South, and the second wave (industrial society) represented by the North. His message was that every clash between waves will produce a crisis of no small consequence. The crisis may take the form of a war (civil), but may also be restricted to purely social, cultural, political, or even psychological crises. In any event, the problem and consequences of these crises cannot be played down, and must always be considered in every effort to do something to the society concerned.

In my discussion with Toffler I discovered, based on that conceptual framework, how extensive the crisis now being experienced by Indonesia is. As a nation in the process of industrialization, Indonesia is experiencing a clash between the first and second waves similar to America last century. It is evident every day in the form of negative socio-cultural tendencies such as dislocation, deprivation, uprooting, etc., and although it may not give rise to a civil war, the crisis in Indonesia may actually be more serious than that in America. The world is now entering the third wave — the information age — and its influence on Indonesia is also inevitable. So what is happening in Indonesia is, in fact, not just a clash of two waves, but of three waves simultaneously. And if we add into the equation the existence of societies who are part of our nation but who do no know about advanced farming practices, like our brothers and sisters living in the isolated interior of the large islands, then what is really happening is a clash between four waves, from a "pre-wave" to the third wave.

Hence the dimensions of the crisis which has emerged cannot be underestimated. And the application of Islam must mean the implementation of the Muslim community's obligatory responsibilities and contribution towards the growth and development of the nation, in keeping with what is demanded by their religion, taking into account the situation mentioned previously. Every position that ignores socio-cultural realities and the sociological and political development of the nation will make us want to jump to conclusions, forming unrealistic expectations about the immediate achievement of end results. So a consciousness of phasing also involves consciousness of a time dimension in every major effort or "struggle". And this consciousness is the foundation of the spiritual qualities of patience and determination, that is, an attitude of willingness to undergo suffering (temporarily) denying oneself momentary pleasures (including the pleasure of purely tactical victories) because of faith that in the long term one will obtain a result bringing great happiness (a strategic victory, so to speak). Thus in the Holy Book, the teaching that we should remind each other to be determined and patient is associated with a reminder about the importance of a consciousness of the meaning of time (Q. 103:1–3).

So we as Indonesian Muslims, believing in the universal dimensions of Islam, also believe in the existence of our special rights as a people to solve our problems here and now, in accordance with the socio-cultural development of our society and its demands. The solutions we present for our problems here, in connection with the obligation to carry out God's teachings, may well be different from the solutions presented by other peoples to their problems, for they cannot be imitated even though they are grounded in the same universal values, namely Islam. And the reverse may also occur: we cannot simply imitate what is done by other Muslim peoples in their implementation of Islam.

So far we have discussed the necessity to work as well as possible and strive for the highest possible success on earth by following God's laws and drawing lessons from the experience and knowledge of anyone anywhere. Axiomatically, we have talked about the problem of good deeds and knowledge, or knowledge and good deeds. But all this is insufficient. Although science is a better guarantee of the success of good deeds, it doesn't guarantee happiness in the long term, let alone in the afterlife. An appropriate parable would be the experiences of Adam and his wife who, although they were given knowledge as preparation for carrying out their task as Allah's caliphs on earth (Q. 2:31), were still unable to control their desires (forgetting ethical considerations) and transgressed God's prohibitions, so that they had to descend or fall (*hubūth*) from heaven and experience a life of misery. Only through Allah's teachings (*Kalimāt*) given to Adam and their proper application by him could he eventually be saved (Q. 2:37).

But Muslims draw as a lesson from the parable of Adam's fall that man is weak, and cannot be left alone to live life. He needs Allah's love and generosity, so that in going through life he can see ahead as far as possible, as far as life after death. Knowledge helps mankind to achieve successes in life. But these successes, no matter how big they are, compared with the entire continuum of existence and the meaning of life, are transient successes — they are short term. Man cannot become a prisoner of the here and now. He must remain alert, and in orienting his life towards God's blessings he must prepare himself for the future (Q. 59:18). Because of this, if necessary, he must dare to suffer temporarily and put off short-term pleasures, through asceticism and denying himself (*zuhd al-nafs*), but without torturing himself which is actually forbidden by Allah — in the interest of achieving long-term happiness. This is the "great struggle" (*jihād akbar*), which requires steadfastness, and is the basis of Allah's assessment for His blessing of eternal happiness (Q. 3:142).

Consequently, it is not sufficient merely to work as well as possible and to achieve success by considering and following God's laws through the use of knowledge to obtain His blessings as *al-Raḥmān*. We must also endeavour with full consciousness in order that knowledge and success do not deceive us and make us forget what is more eternal, namely the blessing of the happiness that is Allah's favour as *al-Raḥmān*. So to make our living environment complete, living actively on earth to create the greatest of civilizations has to be accompanied by the deepest understanding and appreciation of the existence of Allah in life itself, wherever and whenever we exist. We must constantly bring ourselves closer (*taqarrub*) to Allah and absorb as deeply as possible individual religious values like reciting prayers, surrender to God, patience, sincerity, obedience, and by real trust in Allah while making the greatest social commitment. Thus our success will be neither purely for our own pleasure nor solely for the present, but also for the welfare of society at large and in preparation for the future. A very beautiful illustration of this attitude to life can be read in the Holy Book, and translated it reads more or less:

> Only those who believe in our teachings, when they are reminded of them, fall down prostrate and celebrate the Praises of the Lord, and they are not proud. Their bodies are lifted from their beds to pray to their Lord in fear and hope, and they spend [through charities] part of the blessings We have bestowed on them. (Q. 32:15–16).

We realize this attitude of hope in Allah is an attitude full of praise for all the comforts and blessings bestowed on us, like the success of an enterprise, happiness, and ease in life, and so on. Comforts and blessings also take the form of the desire, the ability, and the opportunity to remember Him all the time and everywhere. This is the basis of spirituality which is very important for the growth of a sense of happiness within our deepest selves.

Our fear of Allah compels us to live with full consciousness, interest, and concern, living ascetically (denying ourselves and having no desire to chase only happiness). We realize this concern through an empathetic attitude to less fortunate parts of society, and we give shape to it in a social commitment to help free them from the chains (*raqabah*) of humiliation, and to raise them from the mud or dust (*matrabah*) of misery. We spend part of God's blessing upon us, and strengthen among one another determination in facing and overcoming life's problems, and mutually strengthening feelings of care and affection (*marhamah*) (Q. 90:11–18).

With an attitude to life like the one described here, we endeavour and hope more or less to be able to grasp and implement Allah's message in the Holy Book. It is all summarized in the *al-Fātihah* chapter as the Essence of the Book (*Umm al-Kitāb*), and further, according to religious scholars, is condensed into the recitation of the *basmalah.* We say *basmalah* each time we start work, so that we always remember that we must work with absolute responsibility to Allah as His caliphs on earth; we work in His name and for His blessing, and we work taking as our guide the aim of earning His blessing both as *al-Rahmān* and *al-Rahīm*, attaining success in worldly matters (*umūr al-dunyā*) and walking the right path in religious matters (*umūr al-dīn*). This is the basis of material and spiritual happiness in this world and the afterlife (*fi al-dunyā hasanah wa fi al ākhirah hasanah*), and salvation from eternal suffering (Q. 2:201). If God wills it.

CONCLUSION

This chapter has tried to indicate how difficult and complex our problems are. We will find real solutions to our problems in the realities of living and acculturating. What is meant by culture here is not just a body of knowledge, but a continuous process by which old values are questioned, tested, guarded, enhanced, and transformed — not embraced uncritically, and not dismissed out of hand. So there are no easy answers. Simply, what is needed is the right spiritual interest and motivation, and appropriate knowledge of the situation. Faith and knowledge, that's it. All that can be raised here are the key ideas, every aspect of which still requires further elaboration, wider knowledge, and a better grasp of the problem.

Our age being the modern age is unique in the history of mankind. Although not independent of previous ages, constituting an immediate continuation of the past, the modern age has a much greater and more intricate complexity. And this uniqueness makes the solutions to its problems unique and specific.

An Indonesian Christian figure, the late and respected Dr Walter Bonar Sidjabat, expressed a fear that Islam, the majority religion in Indonesia, would force its religious views on minority groups. We refer to his view because, for right or wrong, it is a reflection of non-Muslim views about Islam. We can understand and even feel sympathetic to his fear. However, we only wish to indicate that this fear is unfounded. We wish to stress that according to Islam and the Holy Book, all religions must be protected, and their followers must be given freedom to carry out their teachings.

We have enjoyed many benefits from modernity, both in physical life thanks to technology, and in socio-political life thanks to more humanitarian concepts and views. But we have also felt negative side effects from modernity. We wish to contribute to fostering the good aspects of modernity and reducing the negative aspects, in accordance with what is possible and within our abilities.

We also appreciate modern freedoms practised in states with strong democracies. With this freedom humans experiment with a range of ideas, and new discoveries in all fields are realized. Experimentation and creativity are prerequisites of growth, and all of this requires freedom. Now it is becoming increasingly clear that freedom cannot be unlimited.

The problems have not all sorted themselves out. America now appears as the uncontested world leader, and America, according to its leaders, has a commitment to act as well as possible, with total responsibility and restraint. Behind Americanism is the concept of astonishing freedom. Freedom is the keyword for the idea of modernity, and is the fortress of its legitimacy. Freedom, however, will only truly bring advantages if it is realized within a system which provides an opportunity for the checking of uncontrolled tendencies. America seems to have a particular weak spot in this regard. Uncontrolled tendencies in the name of freedom have produced many of America's social blights, the solutions to which are yet to appear. And these negative aspects may spread to the rest of the world.

We shan't be too hasty to pretend that we know how to overcome them. We are only taught by religion that man, for his salvation: firstly, must have a transcendental aim in his personal life based on faith; secondly, the demands of faith are expressed in charity for the social good; thirdly, there must be a positive freedom within society which facilitates caring for one another, and increasing truth and good among fellow citizens; and fourthly, there must be a collective awareness of the existence of a time dimension necessary for every endeavour to achieve success, and steadfastness and hope for the future is always needed.

Notes

This chapter is based on material in the introduction to one of the author's books, *Islam Doktrin dan Peradaban: Sebuah Telaah Kritis tentang Masalah Keimanan, Kemanusiaan dan Kemoderenan* [Islam Doctrine and Civilisation: A Critical Examination of Belief, Humanitarianism and Modernity] (Jakarta: Yayasan Wakaf Paramadina, 1992). It was written in January 1992 in Montreal and appears here for the first time in English, translated by Amelia Ceridwen Fyfield and adapted by Virginia Hooker.

The Economy

6

FINANCIAL ACTIVISM AMONG INDONESIAN MUSLIMS

Nur Ahmad Fadhil Lubis

This chapter describes the dynamics of the Islamic perspective on the economy within the context of Indonesia. It argues that in modern times, particularly during the New Order period and the reformation afterwards, a significant number of Muslim intellectuals have been developing ideas on an Islamic-inspired economic system, and some have been implemented together with the communities. Islamic economic discourse and activism are playing an important role in the economic recovery of Indonesia. It became one of the determinant factors in transforming the Muslims' creed and religiosity. This will also play a role in determining the type of relationship between religion (Islam) and state in Indonesia.

The perspective shall be discerned by looking into the increasing awareness and activism of Indonesian Muslims in economic and business matters, both at the conceptual-ideal level and in their implementation programmes. It starts with a brief introduction on Islam in Indonesia and the general issue of Islamicity in this developing nation-state. This is followed by a discussion of the economic challenges and Islamic ideals, as well as the efforts to transform certain Islamic values and principles into the national legislation. Some of these ideals have been put into practice and some programmes have been implemented, and this will be the focus of the next section. Lastly, I deliberate on the prospects of the resurgent activism.

ISLAMIC STATE OR ISLAMIC SOCIETY?

Among the most controversial issues at stake for Muslims, and for researchers of Islam alike, is the seemingly simple question: "What is Islam?" Muslims may differ on the exact definition, let alone on the details, but they seem to agree that Islam means "submission to Allah". One who submits to God (Allah) is a Muslim. One who does not is excluded from the community of the faithful. How far a Muslim submits himself or herself to the will of God depends on how he or she perceives the role and function of the religion in his or her life.

Islam came to Southeast Asia quite late compared to the expansion of Islam in the Middle East, Central Asia, and North Africa. It was brought by Muslim traders whose religiosity was shaped more by Sufi inclination. The legal-normative stance came later, and with it came another wave of puritanism and a modernist movement. Many studies show that there has been an increasing inclination of Indonesian Muslims over the last few decades to follow God's injunctions in all aspects of their lives. There are many formerly nominal Muslims who have become more aware and loyal to Islamic creeds and its norms of behaviour, not only in the field of ritual but also in socio-economic activities. Muslims in Indonesia gradually realize that their efforts to improve their worldly welfare is part of their religious duties. This will surely influence their position in the hereafter. Consequently, Muslims' efforts to strengthen their role and to improve their condition in Indonesian government, economy, and society are on the increase.

One of the crucial problems, which has caused debates and controversy, both among Muslim adherents as well as students of Islam, is the relationship between religion and state. This is an ongoing issue. Even if it is maintained only by a small fraction of Indonesian Muslims, many tend to hold the assumption that most Muslims want — some openly but most discreetly — to replace the present republic with an Islamic state. Subsequent developments in the country have remarkably changed the Muslim proportion and their perspectives on their nation-state.

Many authors have observed that the 1980s witnessed the beginning of another Islamic revival of unprecedented proportion in Indonesian society (Woodward 1996, p. 291). The impact of this deepening Islamization was apparent in all segments of society. However, it is powerfully evident and subsequently significant among the urban middle class (Ramage 1995, p. 101). The growth of the middle class in the 1970s and 1980s had been facilitated by an economic expansion and welfare improvement brought about by the New Order government.

Leading Muslim intellectuals during the Soeharto period have tried to explain, or more appropriately to reinterpret, that Islam can be *dibumikan* (grounded in the soil), *dipribumikan* (indigenized), or even *diindonesiakan* (indonesianized) so it may function better in the country and contribute more for the population. Islam is perceived more as a source of moral teachings and the motivator of moral behaviour which can inculcate values and meanings to its adherents, especially in responding to the ongoing rapid social changes.

Nurcholish Madjid, a well-known Islamic thinker and non-partisan Muslim leader, stated that the concept of "*negara Islam*" (Islamic state) was not actually known in Islamic history (Madjid 1983). With regard to the relationship of religion and politics as well as state, Cak Nur, as he is popularly known, prefers to separate the two. To him, politics, or more precisely the state, is one of mundane, material life whose dimension is rational and collective, while religion is another aspect of human life whose dimension is spiritual and personal. Thus, the concept of an Islamic state is a distortion of the appropriate relationship between Islam and the state. The idea of an Islamic state has been developed more as an apologetic attitude and defensive mechanism among Muslim leaders.

Abdurrahman Wahid, before becoming the fourth president of the Republic of Indonesia, has always said that in Islam, "the state is *al-hukmu*" (originally meaning both law and government). So, Islam does not have a specific form of state at all. In the perspective of *ahl al-sunnah wa al-jama'ah,* to which NU (Nahdlatul Ulama) belongs, a state is scrutinized and evaluated through its function, not through its formal existence, whether it is an Islamic state or not. It means that for Gus Dur, as Wahid is popularly known, as long as the Muslim communities may fully carry out their religious duties, the context and the format of their government is not the prime object of their concern (Wahid 1984, p. 35).

In this matter, Amien Rais, the present chairman of the People's Consultative Assembly (MPR), seems to have a different perspective. He recognized that there is no Qur'anic verse or prophetic tradition that commands Muslims to establish an "Islamic state". However, Islam has given clear-cut ethics and norms of behaviour by which Muslims must manage the whole of life, including state and government affairs. He maintains that Islam is entirely contradictory to secularism. So each and every good Muslim must strive to make his or her life, family, community, and nation governed by and based on those ethics and guidance (Rais 1987, p. 41).

Even though they may have described their perspectives differently, the young generation of leaders of Indonesian Muslims do not find the issues of national foundation and the formal form of the nation-state, which were considered crucial in the early years of independence, as significant and strategic as their predecessors. At present, it seems that what is more significant is the implementation of Islamic values and *shari'a* principles at the societal level, rather than delving into the muddy debates on the symbolic terms and formal forms of the state. In short, it is the realization that Islamic society (*masyarakat Islam*) is more important than the superficial recognition of an Islamic state. Recent discussion on it has been within the context of "civil society" discourse (Usman 2000).

It was interesting to find out, in the previous annual meeting of the MPR in 2000, that most of the large Muslim organizations did not approve the resolution to amend the Constitution's articles on religion by reintroducing the provisions of the 1945 Jakarta Charter. NU and Muhammadiyah, the two most important and biggest Muslim groups in the nation, did not support the demand. Fraksi Reformasi, whose members include PAN (Partai Amanat Nasional) and PK (Partai Keadilan) political parties, and Fraksi Kebangkitan Bangsa, of PKB (Partai Kebangkitan Bangsa), NU-based political party, refused to endorse the resolution. The demand was forwarded by PPP (Partai Persatuan Pembangunan) and some other small Islamic political parties (*Republika,* 23 August 2000). It is obvious that contemporary Indonesian Muslims do not find the demands of their previous leaders important. However, they are also under pressure to prove that they can be more "Islamic" by presenting more realistic programmes, including those of economic recovery and welfare improvement.

ECONOMIC CHALLENGES

Indonesia is the largest nation in the Southeast Asian region, besides being the most populous Muslim country in the world today. Nearly 90 per cent of its 200 million inhabitants are Muslims. Indonesia has been blessed by rich natural resources, and for the last few decades, before the plague of the present economic crisis, it was used as one of the success stories of Western-assisted development programmes, despite most of its population having to struggle even to survive subsistently (cf. Arndt and Hill 1999).

What has gone wrong with our country or, more precisely, with our economy? Many experts have come up with findings, and various factors have been identified. This multidimensional crisis, which is still going on in Indonesia, is aptly described by Hal Hill as "momentous and tragic" (Forrester 1999, p. 93). "Momentous" because nobody foresaw it, and "tragic" because most Indonesians are suffering a great deal, as they experience a catastrophic decline in their living standards. It is even more tragic for many ordinary Indonesians to see the culprits and the corrupt going free and enjoying the fruits of their crimes against the people. It is also ironic to find that after nearly four years, whilst its neighbours have been recovering, the crisis has no visible end in Indonesia.

All these explanations may be right, but for Muslims, as one reads in their mass media or often hears in their religious sermons, first and foremost it is because the people have gone against God's guidance and the Prophet's messages. Indonesian economic performance, which was still highly praised by the IMF (International Monetary Fund) and World Bank as late as the first half of 1997, even though the crisis had hit the people badly, was in reality a paper tiger. However strange and sudden the crumbling of such an "economic miracle" as Indonesia, for many Indonesian Muslims, it has proved that economic development that neglects the masses and goes against divine guidance will crumble eventually. Some Muslim preachers have depicted this crisis as a warning — some even called it a curse — from the Almighty about immorality, ungratefulness, and unfaithfulness to God's injunctions. The rampant practices of KKN (corruption, collusion, and nepotism) are really against Islamic principles.

The crisis has also heightened the suspicion of and opposition to Western theories of economics and modernization. It has been perceived that these theories and ideas lead to the emergence of the widening gap between the majority poor and a selected few rich, especially the capitalists. The country's political power-play also conspired to make the situation much worse. The crisis hit the population tremendously, much harder that the one which occurred in 1985–86. Then the rural economy could still act as a "shock absorber" (Forrester 1999, p. 99), but since then Indonesia's rural and small- and medium-scale economies have been significantly weakened. It is no exaggeration to say that these groups have been neglected, if not sacrificed, and forced to "subsidize" the modern, urban-based sector of economy.

The crisis is not so "momentous" for many Indonesian Muslims, however. One may recall some authors and experts warning of the danger of the top-down, undemocratic, and elitist development policies of the New Order government. Since the very beginning, many critical Muslim leaders have been silenced, and those who could be co-opted were used to rally Muslims' support. This is well known as a policy of bamboo-split, as mentioned by Syafi'i Ma'arif, the national chairman of Muhammadiyah, in his book: a bamboo is split by pushing down one half, and lifting the other. Actually even without this policy, the Muslims in Indonesia are already diversified, to the extent that if one talks about Muslims in Indonesia, a question may appropriately be asked: "Which Muslims?"

Let's go back to the economic challenge. Some Muslim leaders in the 1980s dedicated themselves to bringing about a shift in the New Order strategy of *pembangunan* (developmentalism). Amien Rais and Sri Bintang Pamungkas, just to mention a couple, argue that the vast majority of poor Muslims had not benefited from the government's development programmes, some had even been impoverished by government initiatives. Many Muslim batik producers and batik traders had to see their businesses taken over by large companies not owned by their fellow natives. Some further argued that certain minority groups grabbed most of the fruits of development, and it was very hard for ordinary Indonesians to get access to credit and other economic opportunities.

At the height of the Soeharto period, the call for concrete efforts to lift up the Muslim people from poverty and economic powerlessness was getting stronger. M. Dawam Rahardjo, a leading independent economist, published a book in 1987, entitled *Perspektif Deklarasi Makkah: Menuju Ekonomi Islam*. It is a collection of his articles, written for different forums, encouraging Muslims to return to Islamic principles in solving socio-economic problems. He points out the shortcomings of both the capitalist and socialist economic systems, and reiterates that Islamic economics is a viable alternative and a reliable solution, not only religiously but also economically (Rahardjo 1987).

These ideas have been prominent among many Muslim scholars who later became the rank-and-file of ICMI (Indonesian Association of Muslim Intellectuals), founded in 1990. Many activists associated with the Association encouraged Muslims to strive for fundamental changes in the current development strategies that did not address the question of mass poverty. ICMI and some other Muslim organizations took initiatives in identifying Islamic economic ideals and how to help the poor Muslim majority so that they could live humanely in their own country.

The idea of improving the welfare of the masses may be shared by all Muslim leaders, but their approach and strategies have been varied. Habibie, who was appointed as the chairman of ICMI and later became the third president of Indonesia, used to envision a capital-intensive, technological leap forward for Indonesia, and was not likely to endorse his own secretary in the association, Adi Sasono, who maintained a labour-intensive, agricultural, and agro-industrial development that would help the needy masses most. This signifies the different perspectives of and approaches to economic development that are held by Muslim activists in Indonesia.

The Muslims in Indonesia have to face enormous social transformation as the twenty-first century progresses. Industrialization and urbanization are reducing the rural population and changing the people's way of life at a rapid rate, while the expansion of modern national education and the accelerating wave of globalization are affecting the continuity of the traditional and conventional Islamic religiosity. On the other hand, the rapid changes have forced many to wonder about their fate in life, the increasing material wealth gives the opportunity for some segments of society to concentrate on spiritual well-being. More and more people with a general education question the validity and legitimacy of foreign-origin values and external destructive influences.

IN SEARCH OF "ISLAMIC ECONOMICS"?

For Muslims, Islam is a universal religion, which is revealed for the welfare and salvation of humanity in this world and the hereafter. Islam is considered a comprehensive way of life because it provides the guidance and principles upon which Muslims can regulate their lives. Islamic religion (*din al-Islam*) is usually divided into three aspects and each consists of several pillars: *iman* (faith), *Islam* (acts of submission to the will of God), and *ihsan* (spiritual virtue). Muslims' acts and activities are divided into two general categories: *'ibadat* (rituals) and *mu'amalat* (human interactions). The former is strictly regulated and no human invention is allowed, while in the latter humans have more freedom to control and innovate.

The prime objective of a Muslim's life is to achieve happiness both in this world and in the hereafter (*fi al-dunya hasanah wa fi al-akhirat hasanah*) by submitting oneself to the Creator (Q. 2:201). In human interaction (*mu'amalat*), it means obeying Allah's commands and refraining from breaking any of His prohibitions. So the basic stipulation in *mu'amalat* is everything is lawful except that which is ordained otherwise. It is the opposite of the principle maxim in *ibadat;* namely, everything is prohibited except that which has a valid religious basis. It is clear from the above that Muslims have a wide range in which they can develop their expertise and find alternatives to solve their economic needs, as long as it is not contradictory to Islamic basic principles.

What are the Islamic principles pertaining to economic activities? Muslim authors have come up with somewhat different lists, but most seem to agree on the first five principles of Islamic economics. They are *tawhid* (monotheism), *khilafah* (human vicegerency), *'adl* (justice), *ta'awun* (co-operation), and *maslahat* (benefit).

The economic activities of a Muslim must always be guided by these principles, which have been digested from the divine revelations and Prophetic sayings. Earning one's life income through lawful ventures and decent labour is not only a duty but also a great virtue. Dependence of any able person who makes no effort on somebody else for a livelihood is a religious sin, a social stigma, and a disgraceful humiliation. Every Muslim must strive to gain salvation in the hereafter, but she or he must not forget his/her welfare in this world (Q. 28:77).

Furthermore, Qur'an prescribes that trade and business are lawful, but usury is forbidden (Q. 2:275). Those who practice usury will be touched by evil and will be driven to madness, because they regard trade and usury as the same (Q 2:274–76). Whatever the individual earns through lawful means is his private possession. However, proprietors are constantly reminded of the fact that they are in reality mere agents appointed by God to administer their holdings. The Qur'an considers possession of wealth a trying test, and not a token of virtuous excellence, or privileged nobility, or a means of exploitation (Q. 6:165). To lead a balanced life is the essence of God's guidance. Make not your hand be tied to your neck (being too stingy), the Qur'an says, nor stretch it forth to its utmost reach (like a foolish spendthrift), lest you become rebuked and destitute. Verily the Lord does provide sustenance in abundance for whom He pleases, and He provides in a just manner, for He does know and regards all His servants (Q. 17:26–27, 29–30). In short, Islam enjoins its adherents to "be economic and balanced in life".

God sent His messenger, Muhammad, for the blessing and benefit of all mankind, even for the whole universe (Q. 21:107). The purposes and objectives of *shari'a* (God's divine guidance) are the preservation and promotion of good and the prevention and elimination of bad. These principles not only frame the Islamic worldview, but also constitute the foundation of all other legal rulings in Islam.

Human needs, in the Islamic perspective, are generally classified into three categories. The first is *daruriyat* (literally, necessities), which have five components, namely faith (*din*), life (*nafs*), intellect (*'aql*), posterity (*nasab/ nasal*), and basic wealth (*mal*). Wealth is, appropriately, the last on the list, since, according to al-Ghazali and many other scholars, it is not an end in itself. It is only a means, though an important and indispensable one, for realizing human well-being.

This list encompasses those aspects of human primary needs necessary for the proper functioning of religious and mundane affairs. Any rupture in them necessarily results in disorder and chaos in individual and communal life, and in a less than happy state in the life to come. The *daruriyat* are maintained by two means: on one hand, all the good things are enhanced and strengthened, while on the other, all harm that may be about to affect them is prevented (Hallaq 1997, p. 162; Chapra 1995, p. 7).

The second category is *hajjiyat* (literally, needs) which signify those things required to alleviate hardship so that one may live without distress or predicament. The admission of the *salam* contract which involves risk, and the abridgement of certain obligations of a ritual under circumstances of hardship and illness, are two examples of relaxing the law when the need to accommodate the exigencies of daily life arises.

The *tahsinat* (literally, improvement), the last category, refers to those aspects of the law such as the recommendation to add payment beyond the terms of a loan, giving charity beyond the obligatory amount of *zakat,* and other virtuous deeds. They are needed to the extent that without them life may be deficient and unsatisfactory. This shows that economic activities are not only supplementary and additional, but are strategic and decisive in a Muslim's life, both in the present world, and more importantly in the hereafter. The Prophet Muhammad warns his followers that poverty comes very close to making one an unbeliever.

The above shows that economic affairs of Muslims have been approached mainly from legal-normative perspectives. As such, Muslim scholars look for God's injunctions in the Qur'an and in Prophetic traditions so that they can decide the legal status of each action and event. When they cannot find a textual base for a case, the scholars later formulate other sources, namely consensus (*ijma'*) and analogy (*qiyas*). These other sources find no disagreement among Sunni schools.

To the above main criteria, *usul al-fiqh* has added other supplementary principles, the most important of which are: (a) *al-tamassuk bi al-asl,* the principle that originality and essentially all beneficial actions are legitimate, all harmful ones illegitimate; (b) *istishab al-hal,* laws are permanently valid unless there is evidence challenging their beneficial nature; (c) *al-masalih al-mursalah,* a benefit is deemed legitimate if the *shari'a* is not known to have established or denied it; (d) *sadd al-dzara'i,* the legitimacy of that which is instrumental is directly affected by the benefit or harm implicit in the final end to which it leads; (e) *istiqra' al-naqis,* a universal law may be derived from a particular law through ascending generalization, if no exception is known to challenge the generalization; (f) *al-istihsan,* a weaker *qiyas* may be preferred to a stronger one if it fulfils the general purposes of the *shari'a* better; and (g) *al-'urf wa al-'adah,* customs and established practices may be legitimate sources of law (Faruqi and Faruqi 1986, pp. 267–68). With this legal-normative perspective, the Muslims initiate their formulation and deliberation on economic matters.

What is "Islamic economics?" The topic of Islamic economics, or the economic system of Islam, or "*shari'a* economics" (Harahap 2000), is one of the thorniest in contemporary Muslim debate. No subject in recent Islamic writings has been more open to honest misunderstanding on the one hand, and deliberate misrepresentations, on the other. As a separate modern discipline, "Islamic economics" has appeared rather late in Indonesia. However, once born it has been growing rapidly.

LEGISLATION OF *SHARI'A* VALUES

As mentioned above, the problem of economics has been settled first and foremost by Muslims through a legal-normative approach. The study of *shari'a* (divine-origin Islamic norms of behaviour) and *fiqh* (Islamic jurisprudence) have been conceived as the knowledge par excellence in Islamic scholarship. It may not be an exaggeration to state that Islamic economics have more emphasis on its normative side, than on its descriptive empirical aspects. Further progress of Islamic economics actually calls for closer co-operation between Islamic economists and *shari'a* scholars, on the one hand, and between Islamic economists and their colleagues, including the non-Muslim among them, on the other. Let us consider how this has been dealt with in this perspective.

Islamic law has been developing differently from Anglo-Saxon and Continental Roman-origin legal systems. If Common Law has been based more on judge-made law and Roman-Continental has been concentrating on legal statutes, Islamic law has been progressing more as jurist-made law. It is the *ulama* (religious scholars) who derive and formulate legal rules out of legal sources (*masadir al-ahkam*). Consequently, legal opinions (*fatwa,* pl. *fatawa*) of the *ulama,* either individually or collectively, are influential in defining valid rules for all human conduct (see further Chapter 12).

Al-Qur'an, the first and most important source of Islamic law and teachings, contains many verses pertaining to economic matters. In 1978, *Mimbar Ulama*, the official journal of the MUI (Indonesian Council of Ulama) published an article written by a Muslim economist, entitled "*Ajaran Ekonomi dari al-Qur'an*" [Economic Teachings of the Qur'an]. The article identifies more than 200 verses in the Qur'an pertaining to various aspects of economy (Moehammad 1978).

Al-Qur'an does prescribe many rulings concerning economic matters. For example, it enjoins Muslims to work hard and rush for God's bounties after communal prayers, to be moderate in consumption, and not to do anything harmful to themselves and to others. The Qur'an also describes things pertaining to economics. It describes a good life and approved behaviour, contrasting them with a bad life and undesirable conduct. Human attitudes towards poverty, work, trade, saving, spending, and so on may differ, and these attitudes have different consequences for the individual as well as for society. Humanity is certain to be concerned about these consequences and hence they need to analyse, describe, and prescribe. These two aspects of Islamic guidance, namely the prescriptive aspects and the descriptive aspects, should be dealt with concurrently so that it can be translated into reliable policies and viable programmes.

In the Indonesian context, the prescriptive values of religiosity and belief in God has been an integral part of the Indonesian way of life. The 1945 Constitution, and all the constitutions ever enacted in Indonesia, contain the statement: "Blessed by God the Almighty and impelled by noble desires for a free national life, the Indonesian people do hereby proclaim their independence." While it is explicitly stated in the Preamble, Article 29 of the Constitution further stipulates that: firstly, the State shall be based upon Belief in God the Almighty; and secondly, the State shall guarantee the freedom of every inhabitant to adhere to his/her own religion and make observance in accordance with such religion and belief.

Some legal experts claim that the above provisions establish religion in a significant position and the previously held principle of "reception theory" has been abrogated for good. The theory was proposed by Professor C. Snouck Hurgronje and adopted by the Dutch colonial government, determined that Islamic law could only be enforced if it had been received by the people as a part of their *adat* (customary law). It meant that the rulings of Islamic law did not automatically regulate Muslim affairs, unless they were accepted as customary rules by the community.

Consequently, demands to legislate *shari'a* principles as part of the positive national laws have come to the surface from time to time, both in the Sukarno and Soeharto periods. The turning point occurred during the heated debate and fierce controversy over the draft of the marriage law in 1973. Many provisions in the draft, which are in contradiction with Islamic legal principles, drew angry protest and huge demonstrations from many segments of Islamic communities. Faced with the strong opposition and realizing that the issue had united various Muslim groups, the government gave in to most of the

Muslim demands, until Law no. 1/1974 concerning marriage was more in line with *shari'a* injunctions.

The promulgation of this marriage law has strengthened the position and function of (Islamic) religious courts (*pengadilan agama*), even though by then the decisions of these courts had still to be approved by the (secular) general courts (*pengadilan negeri*). The requirement to be endorsed by another court was erased much later when the law concerning Religious Courts (Act No. 7/1989) was promulgated. The following years have seen more and more Islamic legal ideas absorbed and transformed into national legal statutes, some of them directly related to economic affairs.

The most important new legislation is probably the laws on banking. The government of Indonesia always declined the proposition to establish any bank based on Islamic principles. Even when they adopted a very liberal policy on banking in the late 1980s, on which many conglomerates built their own banks, the request to open an "Islamic" bank was refused. The changing attitude of the ruling élite, especially President Soeharto himself, the growing demands of Muslim leaders, as well as external pressures, especially due to Indonesia's involvement in IDB (Islamic Development Bank), led to the enactment of the new Law on Banking in 1992. The law (No. 7/1992) stipulates that besides all the conventional services, a bank may be established on the principle of *bagi-hasil* (profit-loss sharing ventures). Even though the law does not mention any Islamic legal terms, this is surely a *shari'a* principle of *mudharabah* (profit-loss sharing) and *musharakah* (joint ventures). This was later confirmed by the Government Regulation (no. 72/1999) which clarifies what is meant by a profit-loss sharing bank: it is one whose operational system is based on the principles of *shari'a.* Later, this banking law was replaced by Law No. 23/1999, which has not only confirmed the *shari'a* principles but also extended it to other *shari'a*-based monetary transactions (section 10, article 2).

It is not only legislation pertaining to the banking system which has been affected by Islamic institutions. *Zakat* is one of the five pillars of Islam which obliges every able Muslim to pay a certain amount to help particular segments of the society. Efforts to functionalize and maximize the *zakat* in eradicating poverty and upgrading the welfare of the Muslim community were quite extensive during the second half of the Soeharto period. However, it took the reform movement (*reformasi*) to eradicate the phobia of a ruling government, and change a government entirely, so that a new law concerning *zakat* management was only enacted in 1999 (Law No. 38 of 1999). With this law, *zakat* is no longer a private affair of individual Muslims, it becomes the government's duty to regulate it so that it will contribute as much as possible to the development of the society. Subsequent discussions among Muslims on the ways to integrate this law on *zakat* with the existing tax laws, so that Muslim businessmen would not be overburdened with multiple taxation were quite intensive (*Republika,* 9 September 2000).

Another important Islamic institution that has been formally absorbed into the national legal system was *waqf* (pious foundations). The government of Indonesia since the Sukarno period issued several government regulations concerning the *wakaf* on land. The existing agrarian law also recognizes the existence and functions of *wakaf* among Muslims. Even though there is no reliable data on *wakaf* in Indonesia, any observer will find that *wakaf* plays an important role in fulfilling various social needs, including religious buildings, schools, clinics, cemeteries, etc. (Ali 1995).

These new trends of legislating Islamic norms have been strengthened by the MPR, which was the product of the 1999 general election, the most democratic held in Indonesia. In the general session of 2000, the MPR decided, that in the field of law, the government policy must be directed towards a comprehensive and integrated national legal system which recognizes and respects religious law (*hukum agama*) and customary law (*hukum adat*), as well as reforming the legacy of colonial laws and discriminative national laws, including gender injustices and unconformity to the reformation demands through legislation programmes (TAP MPR no. IV/1999).

Even though there has been an increasing transformation of Islamic injunctions into the national laws of Indonesia, there are additional issues of economic and worldly affairs that have not been covered by legal statutes. In these cases, Muslims refer to the legal opinions of the *ulama,* more often than not in the form of *ijtihad jama'i* (group deliberation). The MUI (Indonesian Council of Ulama) as well as many other Muslim organizations issue *fatwa* regularly. Indonesian Muslims usually look to the legal opinion of the organization to which they belong as members or sympathizers. In this matter, there have been significant differences in methods and outcomes of *ijtihad* between the NU and Muhammadiyah (Djamil 1995; Ka'bah 1999; Hooker 2003).

These differences have been remarkably visible concerning economic activities and modern banking. The NU inclines to differentiate the various products offered by banks — some are usurious and consequently unlawful, but others are not — so Muslims can engage in them without breaking religious prescription. As early as 1938, the NU, in its national congress, affirmed that bank interest benefits the customers and the society at large, and based on this it is allowed (*halal*). Despite the decision issued at the national level, the NU has never succeeded in convincing all of its religious scholars that interest in banking is permissible. Even its rank and file voice concerns from time to time (Addary 1972).

It has taken longer for Muhammadiyah to come up with a decision about the legal status of interest in the modern banking system. Its national congress in 1936 mentioned the lack of banking services for native Indonesians and petitioned the government to elaborate a banking policy that would assist the growth of Muslim businesses. *Riba* is forbidden, but bank interest was identified as *mutasyabihat* (a legal issue that is not yet clear and for which additional study is needed). In 1968, Muhammadiyah still did not come up with a definite opinion but with the provision that Muslims may use banking services, as they are needed based on the emergency condition (*darurat*), because there weren't any banks operating on Islamic bases. In 1993, the Muhammadiyah congress took a stand that Muslims had to strive to build banking and financial institutions based on Islamic teachings and that all types of interest are forbidden. Therefore, it is not surprising to find that Muhammadiyah leaders were among those who strongly supported the establishment of Islamic banks in Indonesia.

All Muslim scholars agree on the prohibition of *riba*, but they have differed as to whether this prohibition applies to interest in the modern banking system. Their differences come from the way they perceive the Qur'anic verses and the Prophet's sayings. If they look only at the literal statements in which *riba* has been formally prohibited, they tend to forbid it. When they emphasize the rationale for its prohibition, that is injustice, they naturally look into what is happening with modern banking practices. If they find interest brings about injustice, they forbid it, if not, it is lawful (Saeed 1990, p. 323ff.). Mohammad Hatta, Indonesia's first vice-president, tends to follow the second perspective. For him, the interest charged on consumptive credits is *riba,* but when it is used for productive purposes, it is not *riba,* so it is lawful. It is true that the Qur'anic verse that prohibits *riba* concludes with the statement: "Do not commit injustice and no injustice will be committed against you."

However, this position has been refuted by a neo-revivalist view revealing legal and economic arguments. It is interesting to make a comparison here. In many Muslim countries it is the modernists who embrace the lawfulness of bank interest, while the traditionalists maintain the prohibition of all kinds of interest. In Indonesia it is the NU, the traditionalists who hold the opinion that bank interest is not *riba,* while Muhammadiyah, the modernist organization, sustains the illegality of bank interest. Regardless of their positions on bank interest, both organizations, among others, strive to alleviate their member's economic circumstances.

ECONOMIC ACTIVISM

International conferences on Islamic economics have been held quite regularly, the first in Makkah (1976), the second in Islamabad (1983), the third in Kuala Lumpur (1992), and the fourth in the United Kingdom (2000). The theme of the 2000 conference was "Islamic Finance: Challenge and Opportunity in the Twenty-first Century". Indonesian delegates have been present at all these conferences, and the events have been widely covered by Muslim-based mass media in Indonesia. Many of the writings of leading Islamic economists abroad have been translated and published in Indonesia. Some have been invited to speak and give lectures at various conferences, seminars, and workshops on Islamic economic themes, which have been regular events for the last decade.

At the international level, there have been more than 200 financial-monetary institutions based on *shari'a* principles. More and more centres of learning have been established to teach and train professionals Islamic economics, and old, established universities, including Harvard University (USA) and Loughborough University (UK), have opened new programmes and offered courses on Islamic economics and related subjects.

Islamic economic discourse came quite late in Indonesia, but when it started in the mid-1980s, it progressed rapidly. Some leading universities in Indonesia, such as Universitas Indonesia (UI) Jakarta, Universitas Airlangga Surabaya, and Trisakti University Jakarta, have added new programmes on Islamic economics. Nearly all faculties of economics in both state and private centres of higher learning have at least offered courses on Islamic economics and/or business ethics. IAINs (State Institute of Islamic Studies), which have fourteen campuses all over the country have followed suit by opening diploma and degree (undergraduate and graduate) programmes in Islamic economics, Islamic finance, and Islamic business law. Conferences, seminars, workshops, and other scholarly activities have been organized regularly by various Muslim organizations and academic institutions (Zadjuli 2000).

The *shari'a*-based banks and other financial institutions, which have been introduced into Indonesia since 1992, have not shown expected or adequate growth (Arifin 1999, p. 133). They are still in their infancy. This is indicated by, among other things, their small contribution to the aggregate economic activities in general. By 2000, there were only 8 general banks,

77 BPRs (*shari'a*-based rural credit banks), compared to 208 conventional general banks, and 2231 BPRs in the country. However, there is another impressive trend. The number of BMT (Baitul Mal wat Tamwil — *shari'a*-based people's co-operatives) shows a rapid increase, starting with only one unit in 1992, there were 1,957 BMTs at the end of 1999. This is made more impressive by the fact that these small financial co-operatives are scattered over nearly all the provinces of Indonesia and they are mostly sponsored by local Muslim communities.

To see more of Indonesian Muslims' concern for their economic welfare and their conformity to Islamic values, it may be appropriate to look back at the emergence and contributions of several large Muslim organizations before independence. The first of these, SDI (Syarikat Dagang Islam, or Islamic Business Union), was founded in 1911. From its very name, it is quite obvious that economic and business interests were the main reasons for its foundation. Its aim was to unify Muslims and to help them defend themselves against, among others, Chinese competitors.

With a clearer mission of purifying Muslims' religiosity and improving their welfare, Muhammadiyah, which was founded in 1912, has been more effective. This organization, which was started in Java, spread all over the archipelago especially among the urban Muslim population and it is considered the most powerful current Muslim reformist movement in Southeast Asia (Esposito 1995, vol. III, p. 165). Muhammadiyah is an effective organization with a good record (*Republika*, 24 July 2000). It has a national board in Jakarta and Yogyakarta and at every level of regional administration — namely province, district/municipality, sub-district, and village — there is a board. Altogether, Muhammadiyah has 8,880 boards throughout the country, and it even has branches in some neighbouring countries (Singapore, Malaysia, and Thailand). Muhammadiyah manages and promotes many pious foundations and social service centres, the most important of which are schools (*madrasah*) (5,535 units), religious boarding schools (55 units), universities/colleges (132 units), hospital/health clinics (312 units), and orphanages (240 units).

K. H. Ahmad Dahlan, the founder of Muhammadiyah, was encouraged to establish the organization after realizing that many Islamic teachings, including those on social welfare and economic necessities, had been neglected and misunderstood. He was encouraged also by more effective social services and economic activities conducted by Christian missionaries. As an organization with a puritanism mission, Muhammadiyah has been steadfastly against usury and all usurious transactions. This has been a hindrance to Muhammadiyah members because they have to practise business in a system, which is based on usury. In dealing with this situation, Muhammadiyah preaches to the Muslim population that *riba* (usury) and any usurious transaction remain *haram* (forbidden), but due to the emergency condition (*dharurat*), a Muslim may make the best out of the existing banking services to fulfil his or her needs. The obligation to create and establish Islamic-based institutions is also maintained by all Muslims. Therefore, Muhammadiyah has encouraged their members to establish economic institutions, co-operative foundations, and other business ventures in accordance with Islamic prescriptions.

Founded in 1926, the NU (Nahdlatul Ulama) is the largest Islamic social organization in contemporary Indonesia. It embodies the solidarity of traditionalist *ulama* and their followers who adhere to one of the four recognized schools of Sunni Islam. The social basis of the NU has been and still largely is the *pesantrens* or traditional institutions of Islamic learning, in which *santri* (religious students) live and learn the Islamic way of life under the tutelage of *kiyais* (the leaders of *pesantrens*). The NU original charter of 1926 stated that among its purposes was to organize the *ummah* for the advancement of agriculture, trade, and industry lawful in Islamic terms (Esposito 1995, vol. III, p. 218).

The NU has adopted a lenient attitude towards local traditions and prevalent customs. Its leaders maintain many pre-Islamic traditions and try to "Islamize" them. This has been the case also with the NU attitude towards modern banking and certain types of interest. It tends to hold that modern banks' interest is not usury, and consequently it is lawful and Muslims can be involved in all banking activities. The NU, itself, established two banks in Jakarta in 1950, and a third one was founded in 1960. All three banks were operated on an interest basis. Though all these ventures eventually failed, they provided a precedent and good experience for NU's involvement in conventional banking.

In 1990, the NU set up an ambitious programme to establish BPR (People's Credit Banks) all over the country. Its leaders proclaimed a plan of establishing 2000 such units over twenty years. The plan was initiated by founding nine BPR in NU-concentrated areas. Each bank has assets of around Rp100 million, which is very small, but these funds were privately generated and they have been channelled to the smallest and neediest entrepreneurs. This is an alternative Muslim banking system to serve small enterprises and new entrepreneurs in which certain qualified interest is not considered *riba*, and consequently is not *haram*.

Although it also seeks to address the needs of small-scale Muslim economies, this initiative was different from that of BMI (Bank Muamalat

Indonesia). One of the differences has been the matter of interest. Even though the NU ventured banking programmes in the 1950s and 1960s, the later rural banks were closer to conventional banking practices, as they charged interest. The other difference is the fact that BMI and its affiliates try not to get involved with any interest-based or other un-Islamic institutions, the NU-sponsored enterprises find no problems to closely co-operating with Chinese, non-Muslim conglomerates. With this co-operation, the NU seems not to concentrate on establishing a major bank, but on founding a network of small, locally generated financial institutions (Woodward 1996, p. 114).

As the largest Muslim organization, the NU has always played a major role in the socio-political progress of the country, affecting the power balance both during the Soeharto regime and the transition. However, as rightly observed by authors like Forrester (1999, p. 179), NU's preoccupation with the material interests of the constituency and the suspicions of other factions of the anti-Soeharto movement prevented it from being an active participant in the movement that finally brought the New Order down for good. On the other hand, besides being more rural-based, loose organization, this same preoccupation and the nature of the relationship among its followers have prevented the NU from becoming a leading exponent of economic enlightenment and empowerment of the Muslim population in the country. No one denies, however, that without the NU's active participation, any programme to empower Muslims, or even the nation, economically, will not bear optimal results.

THE PROSPECTS

The exploration and formulation of Islamic economics can be discerned in a variety of approaches among Muslim scholars, and likewise Muslims' economic behaviour is influenced by many factors. The traditionally educated *ulama* have been merely restating — for some, also include reinterpreting — the position of *shari'a* on various questions. Their explanations may contain an implicit awareness of the social reality but their emphasis has been more on the legality of each situation. In their writings, juridical content is predominant. In a strict sense their contributions may not be classified as economics, but in the context of Islamic economics, their writings form the core materials. They have provided a strong toehold for the development of the subject. However, dominated by a legal-normative approach, their attitude has been mostly reactive and conservative. Also they incline to maintain the status quo. Most books read and studied in the Islamic traditional schools, from secondary to the highest levels, are mostly of this type and approach.

The writings of modernist activists are mainly conceptual and not empirically descriptive. They are conceptual because they provide an elaboration or analysis of the basic principles of Islamic economic teachings. Their analysis has usually been based on their ideal perception of Islamic teachings as reiterated in Islamic texts. However, their perception on the first base has been considered unreliable, especially by the traditional scholars. They tend to test each and everything with limited knowledge and visible bias, and this, according to Mannan, may destroy the basic foundation of Islamic economics (Mannan 1983, p. 56). Some Muslim economists, especially those who are trained in the Western tradition, even conclude that the only permanent aspect of Islamic teachings concerns ritual practices, while for other areas only basic principles are given.

Considering the above phenomena and trends, what is urgently hoped for is an actual contribution by Muslim scholars who are not only mastering Islamic teachings well, but are also really conversant with contemporary achievements of economics. By combining the valid prescription of Islam and the academic foundations and scholarly findings of economics, they can research and study Muslims in real-life situations. Subsequently they may be able to explain the empirical realities and offer prescriptions to improve them.

On the one hand, Islamic teachings on the economy, or Islamic economics, have been of a "utopian nature", to borrow Mannan's phrase (1989, p. 290). On the other hand, Islamic economics has been seen by lay Muslims as a "magic formula" that can cure each and every economic illness for good. Both have been a distraction to the real-life problems of Muslims here and now.

Apart from this scientific-academic prospect, one can conclude that economic activities are inseparable aspects of a Muslim's Islamicity. Islam has enjoined that a Muslim must prepare for his or her salvation in the hereafter, but without neglecting his or her condition in this world. To lead a good Islamic life, every Muslim must strive to fulfil all his or her necessities, including material needs. Motivated by one's intention to follow God's injunction, earning one's livelihood, and all economic activities are religiously sanctioned and rewarded.

What is needed most is Muslim economists who understand the guidance of Allah and His Messenger, and at the same time comprehend their real-life conditions and economic realities. It is exactly what the Muslims in Indonesia have been struggling for over several decades. Based on conditions now, Muslims are likely to have a better prospect in the future. Last but not least, every Muslim, besides praying for God's will, should be aware that this better prospect is also dependent upon Muslims themselves, as Allah has prescribed in the Qur'an that: "Verily, Allah shall not change a condition of a nation, until they change what is within themselves" (Q. 13:12).

References

Addary, Ali Hasan Ahmad. *Risalah Bunga Deposito dalam Islam*. Bandung: Al-Ma'arif, 1972.

Ahmad, Araby. *Etika Usahawan menurut Hukum Syara' Islam*. Banda Aceh: Badan Harta Agama Daerah Istimewa Aceh, n.d.

Ali, H. Mohammad Daud and Habibah Daud. *Lembaga-lembaga Islam di Indonesia*. Jakarta: RajaGrafindo Persada, 1995.

Antonio, Muhammad Syafi'i. *Bank Syari'ah: Wacana Ulama & Cendekiawan*. Jakarta: Tazkia Institute and Bank Indonesia, 1999.

———. *Bank Syari'ah: Suatu Pengenalan Umum*. Jakarta: Tazkia Institute and Bank Indonesia, 1999.

Arifin, Zainul. *Memahami Bank Syari'ah: Lingkup, Peluang, Tantangan dan Prospek*. Jakarta: AlvaBet, 1999.

Arndt, H. W. and Hal Hill, eds. *Southeast Asia's Economic Crisis: Origins, Lessons and the Way Forward*. Singapore: Institute of Southeast Asian Studies, 1999.

Chapra, M. Umer. *Islam and Economic Development*. Herndon: International Institute of Islamic Thought, 1989. The Indonesian version translated by Ikhwan Abidin Basri. *Islam dan Pembangunan Ekonomi*. Jakarta: Gema Insani Press, 2000.

———. *Islam and the Economic Challenge*. London: Islamic Foundation, 1995.

Chatib, Lukman. *Syari'at Islam bagi Pembangunan*. Bandung: Armico, 1983.

Djamil, Fathurrahman. *Metode Ijtihad Majlis Tarjih Muhammadiyah*. Jakarta: Logos, 1995.

Esposito, John L., chief editor. *The Oxford Encyclopedia of the Modern Islamic World*. Oxford: Oxford University Press, 1995.

Faridi, F. R., ed. *Essays in Islamic Economic Analysis*. Kuala Lumpur: S. Abdul Majeed, 1997.

Faruqi, Ismail and Lois Lamya Faruqi. *The Cultural Atlas of Islam*. New York: Macmillan Publishing Company, 1986.

Forrester, Geoff and R. J. May, eds. *The Fall of Soeharto*. Singapore: Select Books, 1999.

Hallaq, Wael. *A History of Islamic Legal Theories*. Oxford: Oxford University Press, 1997.

Hooker, M. B. *Indonesian Islam: Social Change Through Contemporary Fatawa*. St Leonards: Allen & Unwin, 2003.

Iqbal, Munawar. *Distributive Justice and Need Fulfilment in an Islamic Economy*. Islamabad: International Institute of Islamic Economics, 1986.

Ka'bah, Rifyal. *Hukum Islam di Indonesia*. Jakarta: Universitas Yarsi, 1999.
Kamal, Mustafa, ed. *Wawasan Islam dan Ekonomi: Sebuah Bunga Rampai*. Jakarta: Lembaga Penerbit Fakultas Ekonomi UI, 1997.
Madjid, Nurcholish. *Aspirasi Umat Islam Indonesia*. Jakarta: Leppenas, 1983.
Mannan, M. A. *Islamic Theory: Theory and Practice*. Delhi: Idarah'i Adabiyat-i Delli, 1980.
———. "Islamic Economics as a Social Science: Some Methodological Issues". *Journal of Research in Islamic Economics* 1, no. 1 (Summer 1983).
———. "Islamic Economics: the State of the Art". In *Toward Islamization of Disciplines: Proceedings and Selected Papers of the Third International Conference of Islamization of Knowledge*, pp. 295–316. Herndon: International Institute of Islamic Thought, 1989.
Moehammad, Goenawan. "Ajaran Ekonomi dari al-Qur'an". *Mimbar Ulama*, vol. III, no. 22 (August 1978): 38–55.
Mubyarto. *Sistem dan Moral Ekonomi Indonesia*. Jakarta: LP3ES, 1988.
———. *Ilmu Ekonomi, Ilmu Sosial dan Keadilan*. Jakarta: Yayasan Agro Ekonomika, 1980.
Muslehuddin, Muhammad. *Insurance and Islamic Law*. Delhi: Maktaba Islami, 1995. The Indonesian version translated by Burhan Wirasubrata. *Menggugat Asuransi Modern: Suatu Alternatif Baru dalam Perspektif Hukum Islam*. Jakarta: Lentera Basritama, 1999.
Muthahhari, Murtadha. *Al-Riba wa al-Ta'min*. Beirut: Dar al-Hadi, 1993. The Indonesian version translated by Irwan Kurniawan. *Pandangan Islam tentang Asuransi dan Riba*. Jakarta: Pustaka Hidayah, 1995.
Rahardjo, M. Dawam. *Etika Ekonomi dan Manajemen*. Yogyakarta: Tiara Wacana, 1990.
———. *Perspektif Deklarasi Makkah: Menuju Ekonomi Islam*. Bandung: Mizan 1987.
Rachbini, Didik. "Assalamu 'Alaikum: Kyai Masuk Bank". *Info Bank* no. 124 (April 1990), p. 7.
Rais, Amien. *Cakrawala Islam*. Bandung: Mizan, 1987.
Rais, Amien, et al. *Meretas Jalan Baru Ekonomi Muhammadiyah*. Yogyakarta: Tiara Wacana, 2000.
Ramage, Douglas E. *Politics in Indonesia: Democracy, Islam and the Ideology of Tolerance*. London: Routledge, 1995.
Sadzali, Munawir. "Religion and Society in the Modern World". Opening Remarks at the seminar "Religion and Society in the Modern World: Islam in Southeast Asia", LIPI, Jakarta, 29–31 May 1995.
Sadeq, Abulhasan M. et al., eds. *Development and Finance in Islam*. Petaling Jaya: International Islamic University Press, 1991.
Saeed. Abdullah. "Indonesian Islamic Banking in Historical and Legal Context". In *Indonesia: Law and Society*, edited by Timothy Lindsey. Annandale: The Federation Press, 1990.

Tim Asistensi Pembangungan LKS Bank Muamalat, eds. *Perbankan Syari'ah: Perspektif Praktisi*. Jakarta:Muamalat Institute, 1999.

Usman, Widodo, et al., eds. *Membongkar Mitos Masyarakat Madani*. Yogyakarta: Pustaka Pelajar, 2000.

Wahid, Abdurrahman. "Nahdhatul Ulama dan Islam di Indonesia". *Prisma*, no. 4 (April 1984).

Woodward, Mark R., ed. *Toward a New Paradigm: Recent Developments in Indonesian Islamic Thought*. Tempe: Arizona State University Press, 1996.

Ya'qub, Hamzah. *Industrialisasi dalam Pandangan Islam*. Jakarta: Bina Ilmu, 1979.

Zadjuli, Suroso Imam. "How to Develop an Islamic Economics Curriculums in Universities". A paper presented at the seminar and workshop, Islamic Economics Teaching at Universities, Jakarta, 19–20 July 2000.

7

ISLAMIC BANKING AND FINANCE

In Search of a Pragmatic Model

Abdullah Saeed

During the twentieth century, with the emergence and intensification of a global Islamic revivalist movement, calls were made to transform the existing political, legal, social, and economic institutions of Muslim societies into institutions that were more in line with Islamic norms and principles.[1] In this context, from the mid-twentieth century Islamic banking and finance were given a considerable boost at both the theoretical and practical levels. They have since constituted a discourse that reflects the aspirations of Muslims to be "authentic" and true to their tradition, while at the same time remaining part of the ongoing and rapid changes that are occurring in the world today. Hence, Muslims are faced with a problem. To what extent should they remain faithful to the ideals that are enunciated in the foundation texts of Islam? In other words, they find themselves needing to be pragmatic to keep up with the changes that are occurring in the world. An examination of some key aspects of Islamic banking and finance will thus shed light on the whole question of idealism versus pragmatism in the Islamic revivalism of the late twentieth and early twenty-first centuries.

Muslim economists who argue for an Islamic model of banking and finance constantly turn to the Qur'an and the Sunna, as well as past interpretations of these texts, to seek guidance.[2] From the 1950s onwards, economic and financial matters that were dealt with in classical *fiqh* works have been given a high degree of importance. Newly developed contracts and products for Islamic banking and finance are often justified on the basis of what classical jurists proposed or formulated. It is also common to find arguments for or against a particular contract or product based on arguments that were advanced by classical jurists such as Malik b. Anas (d. 179 AH), Sarakhsi (d. 483 AH), Ibn Rushd (d. 595 AH), or by other figures who on occasion wrote on economic issues, such as Abu Yusuf (d. 182 AH), Yahya b. Adam (d. 203 AH), and Ibn Khaldun (d. 808 AH). The precedents of the past 1,400 years have thus become an important part of how and what the Islamic banking and financial system should be. In constructing such a system, because of the diversity of approaches, interpretations, and understandings, Muslims in the late twentieth century naturally differed on how a contemporary Islamic banking and financial system should be conceptualized. Whereas some tended to be more closely bound by the actual practice of the past, others looked to a more "liberal" approach. Still others preferred a middle way, keeping an eye on the past while emphasizing current needs and aspirations.

PRINCIPLES OF ISLAMIC BANKING AND FINANCE

Of the principles of Islamic banking and finance that are largely agreed upon among Muslims today, the most important is the Qur'anic prohibition of *riba,* which, according to a significant number of Muslims, covers modern bank interest. One of the important points of emphasis in the Qur'an is that the disadvantaged should not be exploited through *riba*-based transactions. In this context, the Qur'an prohibits *riba* in no uncertain terms.[3] However, there is some debate today on the precise definition of *riba*, and on whether the term covers modern bank interest.[4] Despite this debate, Islamic economists and bankers have remained insistent that all forms of interest which are in practice today are indeed manifestations of *riba* and have no role in an Islamically acceptable financial system. They argue that the prohibition of interest is based on clear Qur'anic instructions and on the Sunna of the Prophet.

Apart from avoiding interest, Islamic banks are also required to avoid transactions that involve excessive speculative risk (*gharar*): that is, contracts in which a significant element of uncertainty exists, or similar transactions such as gambling.[5] In addition, Islamic financial institutions must continue to follow the rulings that are provided by the Qur'an and Sunna in relation to other prohibited contracts.[6]

To meet this objective of a *riba*-free banking and financial system, Muslim scholars have devised contracts and products, and have developed principles for engaging in productive ventures, in which capital can be combined with the skill of entrepreneurs to lead to socially beneficial incremental returns.[7] Risk plays an important role here. The possibility of putting one's money at no risk, while at the same time being entitled to a positive return, is rejected in Islamic law.[8] It is the combination of effort, capital, and risk that justifies the return on the money. Thus, the sharing of risk is emphasized in the literature on Islamic finance — as profit is shared, so is risk. This system is known as profit and loss sharing (PLS), in which the provider and the user of the funds share in the outcome of the venture, be it positive or negative.[9] Two types of contracts have been developed and utilized in Islamic banking: contracts that are based on PLS, and contracts that are akin to "sales" or are based on predetermined returns. The former includes *mudaraba* and *musharaka*, the two contracts on which Islamic banking was to be based (as argued in the literature of the 1950s and 1960s), whereas the latter covers contracts such as *murabaha*, *ijara*, and *istisna'*, on which Islamic banking is largely based today.

In accordance with these principles and contracts, Islamic banking emerged from the 1960s, and continued to grow and expand in the 1980s and 1990s. In 1985 it was estimated that Islamic banks held deposits of US$5 billion, and by the mid-1990s this figure had grown to US$60 billion. In 2000 the figure was reckoned to be US$100 billion, excluding the economies of Iran, Pakistan, and Sudan, which are considered to be operating along "Islamic" lines, but with varying degrees of commitment to the spirit of the principles. As we move further into the twenty-first century, the role of Islamic banks in Muslim communities will become increasingly important as more institutions are established — from village banks to major international development banks — in competition with conventional banks, but with significant co-operation with them as well. However, such growth and development have not had a smooth ride. In the process, pragmatic adjustments in the understanding of the principles had to be made to ensure their ability to function in a largely conventional banking and finance environment.

ISLAMIC BANKING FROM IDEALISM TO PRAGMATISM

In looking at the principles of Islamic finance, one cannot fail to observe that the early "idealistic" vision of the 1960s has significantly changed in practice.[10]

Idealist, liberal, and pragmatic approaches to Islamic banking and finance can be identified and placed in a continuum. The idealist approach seeks to maintain the vision that was described in the Islamic banking literature of the 1950s and 1960s, and to remain faithful to the letter and spirit of relevant contracts that were developed in the *shari'a* in the classical period. At the opposite end of the continuum are those scholars who argue that the term *riba* does not include modern bank interest.[11] This approach is the most "liberal"; indeed, it even makes a case for there being no need for separate Islamic banks. In this view, provided that they adopt ethical principles, conventional banks should be able to provide financial services to Muslims. Between these two extremes lies the pragmatic approach, which is realistic enough to see that the idealist model of Islamic banking and finance has significant problems in terms of feasibility and practicality, but which at the same time maintains the interpretation of *riba* as interest.

Within the pragmatic approach there are many voices, some tending towards the "soft" end and others towards the "strict" end of this pragmatism. The majority of Islamic bankers can be classified as pragmatists who lie between the "soft" and "strict" ends, and who are prepared to balance practicalities with the demands of the relevant classical Islamic legal principles. When these principles clash with the demands of modern banking and finance, there is a need for some flexibility in their interpretation and application. The result has been that these bankers and their *shari'a* advisers have opted for a more pragmatic form of Islamic banking and finance. This has been achieved through a creative process of the interpretation and reinterpretation of relevant texts and principles, and through the use of an eclectic approach to the laws and sources of Islamic law. The practical and feasible are given priority over the idealistic and impractical, even though this may lead to a somewhat questionable outcome in the event of a moving away from an interest-based financial system towards a so-called Islamic system. This chapter will explore four examples of such pragmatism.

PRAGMATIC UNDERSTANDING OF *RIBA*

In theory, Islamic economists, bankers, and *shari'a* experts who support the idea of Islamic banking and finance generally uphold the view that "interest" in all forms, nominal or real, fixed or variable, simple or compound, must be understood as *riba*, and should be prohibited.[12] This view was adopted at the expense of the views that were propounded by the more liberal thinkers of the modern period such as Abdullah Yusuf Ali,[13] Fazlur Rahman,[14]

Muhammad Asad,[15] and Doualibi.[16] The vast majority of contributors to Islamic banking and finance in the 1950s, 1960s, and early 1970s argued that *riba* should be interpreted as interest. Agreeing with this, the Council of Islamic Ideology of Pakistan claims that "there is complete unanimity among all schools of thought in Islam that the term *riba* stands for interest in all its types and forms".[17] Muhammad Umar Chapra, who is a theorist of Islamic banking, states that *riba* "has the same meaning and import as interest".[18] Mohammad Uzair asserts that interest in all of its forms is synonymous with *riba*, and claims that there is a consensus on the issue.[19] Further broadening the meaning and interpretation of *riba*, Islamic bankers and their *shari'a* advisers appear to have also accepted in the early stages of Islamic banking and finance, at least in theory, the legal maxim of classical Islamic law that "every loan which begets an advantage is *riba*".[20] This maxim broadens the concept of *riba* to cover the prohibition of any loan or debt in which an "advantage" or "benefit" is assigned to the creditor, not necessarily in the form of a clearly spelt out "increase", that is, interest, over and above the principal. However, this rather idealistic and all-encompassing interpretation of *riba*, which attempts to remain faithful to the letter and spirit of the relevant texts and principles of *shari'a*, has been gradually weakened and tightened in practice. This weakening has taken a number of forms.

Riba (interpreted as "interest") has been increasingly seen by Islamic bankers and their *shari'a* advisers as primarily a *legal* and not *economic* concept.[21] Though "interest" was understood by the Muslim economists who developed models of Islamic banking and finance as primarily an economic concept and secondarily a legal concept, the pragmatists chose the legal view because it allows bankers to utilize contracts that would otherwise not be available to them in the process of the changeover from an interest-based banking system to an "Islamic" system. The pragmatists tend to interpret *riba* as occurring largely in the context of financial transactions: that is, as a contractual obligation by the borrower to pay an *increase* in a loan transaction.[22] For them, Islamic law prohibits the giving of any positive return to the provider of capital in a purely financial transaction, such as when an entrepreneur receives funds from a bank for utilization at his or her own discretion. Interest is such a positive return, and must be prohibited. This is governed by the requirements of the contract of loan (*qard*). If the contract changes, for instance from being a loan to being a "sale" (*bay'*), then the return, which in reality may not appear to be much different to fixed interest in certain cases, will be permissible. An example of this is the mark-up in *murabaha*, which from a *legal* point of view is not a purely financial transaction, and therefore a positive return (mark-up) is considered permissible.

However, a number of leading Islamic economists have rejected this view of *riba* as a largely *legal* problem. The Pakistani experiment in Islamic banking and finance, which came to be seen as interest-based banking under the guise of Islamic banking, led a number of Islamic economists to question the practices on which that model of "Islamic" banking functioned. The main targets of the criticism were the mark-up and profit margin techniques in trade and rent, which formed the backbone of Islamic banking and finance in practice. Many Islamic economists argued that there was no substantial difference between what was practised under the banner of Islamic banking and what had been the norm under the interest-based system; the difference existed only in name. Some critics openly declared that the cost of credit in this so-called Islamic financing, for instance the mark-up in price, was substantially the same as interest, with only minor differences.[23] For Ziauddin Ahmad, one of the prominent theoreticians of the Islamic banking movement, "the replacement of interest by a technique such as 'mark-up' does not represent any substantive change."[24] Considering the implications of the mark-up system, Muhammad Nejatullah Siddiqi, who was one of the prominent contributors to the development of Islamic banking, argued that "for all practical purposes this [mark-up system] will be as good for the bank as lending on a fixed rate of interest."[25] Recognizing the same implication of the mark-up system, the Council of Islamic Ideology of Pakistan was highly critical:

> There is a genuine fear among Islamic circles that if interest is largely substituted by "mark up" under the PLS operations, it would represent a change just in name rather than in substance. PLS under the mark-up system was in fact the perpetuation of the old system of interest under a new name.[26]

From the perspective of the pragmatists, the views of these critics appear to have been too idealistic and out of step with the demands that are made on Islamic banks by the current financial and economic environment, and such views have been largely ignored in Islamic banking practice.

The dilution of the interpretation of *riba* as interest continued with the acceptance by the Islamic banks of the idea that demanding an increase, or a so-called fine, was permissible in the case of a debtor who did not pay the agreed amount of the debt that was owed to the bank as scheduled. The Islamic banking literature holds that when a debtor is late in paying, the creditor cannot demand an increase from the debtor, which is in line with the Qur'anic command to give the debtor time without charging any additional amount in lieu of that time. Much of the pre-Islamic *riba* appears to have been associated with such increases. Islamic bankers, however, found that a number of their debtors were not paying what was owed to the bank on time. As the capital was considered to have an opportunity cost, any delay in repayment of a debt was regarded as a recoverable loss on the part of the bank, at least in situations where the debtor simply opted not to pay the debt on time. Hence, the imposition of a "fine" as compensation for the loss that is suffered by a bank is now considered to be justified. In its contract of *murabaha*, the Faisal Islamic Bank of Egypt notes that:

> Since the bank does not deal with interest, any delay in paying the instalments when they are due as agreed upon causes serious harm to the bank, which requires compensation. This is on the basis of the *shari'ah* rule that no harm should be inflicted on any party [to the contract], which is the basis of transactions.[27]

To safeguard the integrity of the instrument, some practitioners have argued that the compensation should not be determined by the bank itself but by its religious supervisory board, or in consultation with a neutral third party.[28]

Another adjustment in the interpretation of *riba* has occurred in the discarding of the legal maxim which states that "every loan that begets an advantage is *riba*". According to this maxim, Islamic banks should not make use of arrangements such as the placement of funds by a conventional bank with an Islamic bank on an interest-free basis on condition that the latter should place funds with the former on a similar basis.[29] According to the legal maxim, the Islamic bank should not use such a facility because the transactions lead to the accrual of an "advantage" in kind. However, to facilitate this arrangement, the pragmatists ignore the maxim and allow interbank mutual arrangements, in which the Islamic bank places funds with the conventional bank for a certain period on an interest-free basis on the understanding that the conventional bank does the same.[30] Though there is no explicit charge or payment of interest, the "cost" of placing the funds is recovered in the reciprocal arrangement. Such placement of funds to facilitate borrowing and lending on an "interest-free" basis is now standard practice in Islamic banking and finance.

A further adjustment in the interpretation of *riba* occurs when an Islamic bank allocates so-called rewards to depositors or receives such "rewards" from institutions like a central bank or a national development agency.[31] Strictly speaking, a depositor of the bank who is not placing funds in a profit and loss sharing (PLS) account (that is, at risk) is not entitled to any return on those funds. In practice, however, many depositors are not interested in risking their money by placing it in a PLS account. They may wish instead to keep their funds intact in the form of a savings deposit or a current account deposit. In some Islamic banks, these funds constitute a significant portion of deposits, and are naturally utilized by the bank in its investment activities. To cater for the needs of these depositors, several Islamic banks have begun to provide "rewards". The banks argue that as long as there is no contractual obligation between the depositor and the bank to give a specific reward or benefit to the depositor, they can provide such "rewards" at their discretion.[32] Indeed, this argument can technically be made on the basis of Islamic law, because some Hadith suggest that when paying a debt a debtor can repay more than the loan amount.

The practice of giving "rewards" has become institutionalized in Islamic banking, though it is somewhat questionable from the *shari'a* perspective. It is therefore natural for the depositors of Islamic banks to expect such "rewards", even though they may not be placing their funds at risk as envisaged in the early literature on Islamic banking and finance. More importantly, in some countries Islamic banks themselves place large amounts of funds with institutions such as the central bank on the understanding that "rewards" will be given. This is evident in Indonesia for example, where an Islamic bank can place its surplus funds with the central bank upon the expectation that the central bank will give a certain percentage, say 3 per cent, as a "reward". This practice may even extend to a contract between an Islamic bank and a government, and may involve millions of dollars. In some countries, such as Malaysia, this concept of "reward" appears to have become the basis of *some* of the so-called interest-free Islamic bonds that are issued by public authorities.

PRAGMATIC UNDERSTANDING OF "PROFIT"

In the literature on Islamic banking and finance in the 1950s and 1960s, "profit" was understood to be profit that resulted from a *real* profit and loss sharing (PLS) venture, and not interest by another name. In Islamic law as well as in the literature on Islamic banking and finance, the concept of profit is closely associated with an uncertain positive return that is the result of engaging in a PLS venture or a sale transaction. In practice, however, some of what came to be known as "profit" in Islamic banking was close to being fixed interest.[33]

In Islamic banking and finance, *murabaha* transactions, for instance, have replaced what in traditional banks amounted to loans on the basis of fixed interest for the purpose of acquiring consumer goods, or in some cases capital goods. When the client needs such a loan they request that the Islamic bank "purchase" the goods from a third party and sell them to the client at a "profit". Hence, the bank and the client enter into an agreement under which the bank supplies the goods, either through its own subsidiaries or another third party supplier, at an agreed price and profit (mark-up). The client pays the agreed "price" (the total cost to the bank plus mark-up) over an agreed period. In calculating this mark-up, the bank takes into consideration the duration and schedule of the repayment of the resulting debt: the shorter the time the less the mark-up, and conversely, the longer the time the higher the mark-up. This is determined in consultation with the client before the price of the sale by the bank is finalized. Once agreed on, there cannot be any change in the sale price, which is perhaps the most important difference between fixed interest and mark-up based financing.

One key point of contention among Muslim jurists is whether it is permissible for the mark-up in contracts such as *murabaha* to be related to the length of time that is given for repayment.[34] Disagreements among classical jurists exist on the issue: some vehemently argue that it cannot be,[35] whilst others argue that charging extra for the time is consistent with the customary practice of merchants, and should therefore be permissible.[36] Whatever the validity of the extra mark-up, the Council of Islamic Ideology of Pakistan stated that doubts might arise in relation to the increase that the seller receives in the case of deferred payment sales, and that such an increase may resemble *riba*.[37] In some respects, therefore, mark-up in contracts such as *murabaha* comes very close to the interest that it is supposed to replace.

Another pragmatic adjustment is the importance that is given to "time" in the calculation of profit in various contracts. Time enters into the calculation of profit/return, not only in *murabaha,* but also in a number of other areas: profits on *mudaraba* and *musharaka,* profits on investment deposits and rent, and housing finance. Time is so important that, for example, the Faisal Islamic Bank of Egypt specifies in its contract of *musharaka* that the client must pay the bank's share of the profits, plus capital, on the date that is specified in the contract. In case there is any delay, the client's share of profits, given as a management fee, may decrease.[38] In the same way, if the client pays the sum owing before maturity, the share of profits that is given as a management fee may increase.[39] If time is so important in the calculation of profit/return, then the position of the Council of Islamic Ideology of Pakistan that is referred to above with respect to time and mark-up is perhaps too problematic for Islamic bankers. The "mark-up" and the variation that is based on time are *legally* valid, according to some jurists at least, and are vital to the continued business of the Islamic banks. Hence, pragmatism is given priority over idealism.

A further issue that dilutes the concept of profit is the consideration that is given to interest rates in the calculation of profit or mark-up in sale-based operations. Highlighting this, the Chief Executive of the Qatar Islamic Bank said that "rates of interest are taken into account when the mark-up on *murabaha* transactions is determined" and suggested that this was "being practical and facing the facts of life".[40]

A question that is currently being debated in the literature is whether profit can be predetermined. The question has not been resolved, but Islamic banks and fund managers at least appear to accept the view that such a predetermined return is unacceptable. One view, though a minority one, is that there is nothing wrong in determining profit in advance as long as this determination takes place between the two parties by choice and consent. However, it must be said that Islamic banks or their religious supervisory boards have not yet accepted that the profit from an investment project, for example, can be determined in advance. It is possible that such a shift may occur as more and more emphasis is put on developing a variety of investment products with less risk and more predictable returns. If this occurs, then the differences between the fixed interest based financing of the traditional banks and the practice of Islamic banks will be further diminished.

PRAGMATIC SHIFT TO SALE-BASED BANKING

A further pragmatic shift in Islamic banking and finance is the almost complete move from supposedly PLS banking to a sales-based system. The literature of the 1950s and 1960s was clear that Islamic banking and finance should be based on PLS. Early on, in an attempt to comply with the theoretical writings, a number of Islamic banks attempted to utilize the concept of PLS in their investment operations, but often with disastrous results for the bank as "partners" mismanaged the funds, which led to the loss of the capital that was contributed by the bank. Apart from the relationship between the bank and the depositor, in which a form of PLS that is based on *mudaraba* is institutionalized, Islamic banks in the vast majority of cases now avoid PLS as the most important basis for their investment activities. Instead, such activities operate largely on the basis of contracts that are considered "mark-up based", such as *murabaha*, *salam*, *ijara*, or *istisna'*.

For the bulk of their investment operations, Islamic banks have opted for these mark-up based, relatively safe contracts, which are similar, in some respects, to lending on the basis of fixed interest. So successful has this been that mark-up based contracts now account for over 75 per cent of investment operations of a large number of Islamic banks, despite the concerns of some idealists that such contracts can be covert ways of dealing on the basis of interest. Simultaneously, the use of less secure and more risky contracts such as *mudaraba* and *musharaka* has been dramatically reduced to only a small share of assets on the investment side.

PRAGMATIC APPROACH TO INVESTMENT IN COMPANIES

One of the main areas in which this pragmatism has manifested itself is investment in the stocks of leading companies.[41] The strict adherence to *fiqh* rules on investment, partnership, and shareholding precludes investment by Islamic banks in companies whose business in one way or another involves a significant *haram* (prohibited) element, such as dealing in *riba* or the production, purchase, and sale of prohibited goods or services. However, in the modern period, investment in the stocks of publicly listed companies became a major part of investment for banks and investment funds. Islamic banks and fund managers could not ignore this lucrative investment avenue. Efforts to find a solution to the problem posed by *fiqh* began earnestly when Islamic banks moved on from the initial stages of institution building. The religious supervisory boards of Islamic banks, as well as the relevant committees of the Islamic Fiqh Academy in Jeddah and of the Islamic Development Bank, organized seminars and workshops to explore this important issue.

One of the issues for debate was whether it was permissible to invest in companies whose business involved a prohibited activity.[42] As most publicly listed companies in developed countries rely heavily on interest-based finance for their activities and interest-based investments to generate income from surplus funds, the payment and receipt of interest are part of the normal life of these companies. However, as interest is considered to be *riba* and therefore prohibited, there is a significant problem in investing in these businesses, even though they may be engaged in the production of *halal* (permissible) goods or services. Scholars were divided into two camps: one declaring that investment in the stocks of such companies was unambiguously prohibited and unlawful for Muslims according to *fiqh*, and the other maintaining that such investment was lawful provided certain conditions were met.[43] The latter attitude was more pragmatic, taking the position that such investment was a worldwide practice and difficult for Muslims to avoid. The important question was on what basis the activity should take place: the means, justification, and criteria had to be found.

Relying on concepts such as "necessity", "public interest", and "general need", and on analogy (*qiyas*), proponents of permissibility attempted to provide a legal justification for involvement in such investment.[44] As it was difficult to find clearly spelt out legal arguments in favour of such a position in classical sources, its supporters had to rely on the rather arbitrary interpretation of legal maxims to serve their purpose. If interest was *riba*, then its prohibition in the Qur'an was explicit. The Prophet's reported "curse" on anyone who becomes involved in *riba* was also clear in its meaning and import. Hence, any involvement, from the point of view of the Qur'an and Sunna as well as *fiqh*, should have been prohibited. However, as with other aspects of Islamic banking and finance, the pragmatists found a way of justifying their position, even if it meant discarding classical positions on such matters, and they triumphed. Many Islamic banks today do not object to investing in companies that are involved in receiving or paying interest as long as certain conditions are met.

Given that this position goes against clearly spelt out prohibitions in both the Qur'an and Sunna, the pragmatists could not give it a blanket permission. They had to introduce concepts such as the "cleansing" of the profits on investment from the prohibited element, that is, the estimated interest component, and setting a maximum limit to the involvement of a firm in interest-based dealings. Based on these conditions the Dow Jones Index, for example, has established its Islamic arm, the *Dow Jones Islamic Market Index*, and Islamic banks have established their own funds to invest in such companies.[45] In line with the criteria that were developed for this purpose, the Albaraka group, one of the leading Islamic banking and finance establishments, states that the Islamic Market Index excludes the following from its investment portfolio:

1. Firms whose business includes alcohol, pork-related products, banks, entertainment, tobacco and cigarettes, and arms and defence.
2. Companies with total debt to total asset ratios that are equal to or greater than 33 per cent.
3. Companies with accounts receivable to total asset ratios that are equal to or greater than 45 per cent.[46]

What we have here is a clear case of a pragmatic decision, justified by need and based on concepts that are somewhat unfamiliar to Islamic law, such as the "cleansing" of *haram* elements.

CONCLUSION

The pragmatism of Islamic bankers is driven by a number of factors, the most important of which appear to be as follows. First, Islamic banks function in an environment in which they are competing with interest-based institutions, and therefore the feeling among many Islamic bankers and financiers is that they have to provide the same types of services and investment mechanisms to their clients. This perceived need is at the forefront of the pragmatic nature of what is happening in Islamic banking and finance. Second, many Islamic bankers, financiers, and economists are graduates of modern "Western" economics, regardless of whether they studied at a Western university or a university in a Muslim country, and their experience at times leads them to think that in order to survive, Islamic finance must follow Western practice to some extent. Third, most Muslim government policies on banking, finance, and economic matters rely largely on Western approaches and models, and view any deviations with suspicion. Fourth, most Islamic countries from the nineteenth century onwards discarded Islamic law except in matters related to family law, and any attempt to return to pre-modern Islamic law is faced by significant challenges. Finally, Islamic finance has to function in a global environment, which means interacting with the interest-based system and its institutions, including banks, insurance companies, stock exchanges, and foreign exchange.

To function in this environment, Islamic bankers and their *shari'a* advisers have had to be creative and pragmatic in their approach to the development of their operations. Although Islamic finance has its roots in the rather idealistic literature of the 1950s and 1960s, it has undergone a process of redefining the acceptable, which has been made possible by the flexibility that is available in interpreting *shari'a* texts, as well as by the need to keep pace with the global economic and financial environment. The pragmatic approach has facilitated the development of a viable "Islamic" banking and finance sector. However unpalatable the pragmatic approach may be to idealists, it has provided Islamic banking practitioners with much needed flexibility in designing what they consider to be *halal* products for their Muslim clientele. Such developments are likely to continue in the future.

Notes

1. Abdullah Saeed, *Islamic Banking and Interest* (Leiden: E. J. Brill, 1999), pp. 5–10.
2. Muhammad Nejatullah Siddiqi, *Banking without Interest* (Islamic Foundation, Leicester, 1983); Mohammed Uzair, *Interest-Free Banking* (Karachi: Royal Book Company, 1978).
3. Qur'an 2:279. The prohibition of *riba* is mentioned in four different contexts in the Qur'an. The first emphasizes that *riba* deprives the wealth of Allah's blessing (Q. 30:39). The second condemns *riba* by equating it with the wrongful appropriation of property (Q. 4:161). The third asks Muslims to avoid *riba* (Q. 3:130). The fourth establishes a clear distinction between *riba* and trade, urging believers to take only the principal sum and to forgo even this should the borrower be unable to repay (Q. 2:275–80).
4. Saeed, *Islamic Banking and Interest*, pp. 41–50.
5. Nabil Saleh, *Unlawful Gain and Legitimate Profit in Islamic Law* (Cambridge: Cambridge University Press, 1986), pp. 62–66.
6. See, for example, Ahmad Hidayat Buang, *Studies in the Islamic Law of Contracts: the Prohibition of Gharar* (Kuala Lumpur: International Law Book Services, 2000).
7. See, for instance, Muhammad Nejatullah Siddiqi, *Partnership and Profit-Sharing in Islamic Law* (Leicester: Islamic Foundation, 1987).
8. Frank E. Vogel and Samuel L Hayes, III, *Islamic Law and Finance* (The Hague: Kluwer Law International, 1998), pp. 87–93.
9. Saeed, *Islamic Banking and Interest*, pp. 51–s75.
10. Studies that critically examine the practice of Islamic banking are few. For one such study, see ibid.
11. For some of these views, see Ala' Eddin Kharofa, *Nationalism, Secularism, Apostasy and Usury in Islam* (Kuala Lampur: A. S. Noordeen, 1994), pp. 128–36.
12. Abu al-A'la Mawdudi, *Towards Understanding the Qur'an*, translated by Zafar Ishaq Ansari. Vol. I (Leicester: Islamic Foundation, 1988), p. 213.
13. A. Yusuf Ali (trans.), *The Holy Qur'an* (Lahore: Sh. Muhammad Ashraf, 1975), p. 111.
14. Fazlur Rahman, "Riba and Interest", *Islamic Studies* (March 1964), pp. 1–43; Fazlur Rahman, "Islam: Challenges and Opportunities", in *Islam: Past Influence and Present Challenge*, edited by Welch and Cachia (Edinburgh: Edinburgh University Press, 1979), p. 326.
15. Muhammad, Asad, *The Message of the Qur'an* (Gibraltar: Dar al-Andalus, 1984), p. 633.
16. Saleh, *Unlawful Gain and Legitimate Profit*, p. 29.
17. Council of Islamic Ideology (CII), *Consolidated Recommendations on the Islamic Economic System* (Islamabad: Council of Islamic Ideology, 1983), p. 7.
18. M. Umer Chapra, *Towards a Just Monetary System* (Leicester: Islamic Foundation, 1985), p. 57.

19. Mohammad Uzair, "Impact of Interest Free Banking", *Journal of Islamic Banking and Finance*, Autumn 1984, p. 40.
20. See, for example, the use of this legal maxim in a *fatwa* that was issued by the religious supervisory board of the Jordan Islamic Bank (JIB). JIB, *al-Fatawa al-Shar'iyyah*, vol. 1 (Amman: JIB, 1984), p. 65.
21. Volker Nienhaus, "Islamic Economics, Finance and Banking: Theory and Practice", *Journal of Islamic Banking and Finance*, Spring 1986, p. 44.
22. Ibid.
23. Nawazish Ali Zaidi, "Islamic Banking in Pakistan", *Journal of Islamic Banking and Finance*, Summer 1988, pp. 29. One of the differences is that in sale-based transactions such as *murabaha*, if the debtor does not pay on time, then the creditor, that is the bank, cannot impose any extra charge on the original sale transaction.
24. Ziauddin Ahmad, "The Present State of Islamic Finance Movement", *Journal of Islamic Banking and Finance*, Autumn 1985, pp. 23–24.
25. Muhammad Nejatullah Siddiqi, *Issues in Islamic Banking: Selected Papers* (Leicester: Islamic Foundation, 1983), p. 139.
26. CII, *Consolidated Recommendations*, pp. 97, 121.
27. Faisal Islamic Bank of Egypt (FIBE), *'Aqd Bay' al-Murabaha*, n.d.
28. Ibid.
29. Saeed, *Islamic Banking and Interest*, pp. 116–16.
30. Ibid., p. 117.
31. Ibid., p. 112.
32. Ibid.
33. See, for instance, the profit in *murabaha* transactions. For a detailed discussion, see ibid., pp. 76–95.
34. Ibid., pp. 80–82.
35. See, for example: Malik b. Anas, *Muwatta' Imam Malik: Riwayat Muhammad b. al-Hasan al-Shaybani*, 'Abd al-Wahhab 'Abd al-Latif, ed. (Cairo: al-Majlis al-A'la li al-Shu'un al-Islamiyyah, 1979), p. 271; Syed H. A. R al-Kaff, *Does Islam Assign any Value/Weight to Time Factor in Economic and Financial Transactions?* (Karachi: Islamic Research Academy, 1986), p. 12ff.
36. Shawqi Isma'il Shihata, *Nazariyyat al-Muhasabah al-Maliyyah min Manzurin Islami* (Cairo: Dar al-Zahra' li al-I'lam al-'Arabi, 1987), p. 107.
37. CII, *Consolidated Recommendations*, p. 36.
38. FIBE, *Contract of Musharaka*. n.d.
39. Ibid.
40. Quasim M. Quasim, "Islamic Banking: New Opportunities for Cooperation between Western and Islamic Financial Institutions", in *Islamic Banking and Finance* (London: Butterworths, 1986), p. 25.
41. Nizam Yaquby, "Participation and Trading in Equities of Companies which [sic] Main Business is Primarily Lawful but Fraught with some Prohibited Transactions" Unpublished paper presented at Fourth Harvard

Islamic Finance Forum, Harvard University, 30 September–1 October 2000.
42. Ibid.
43. Ibid.
44. Ibid.
45. See, for example, the Albaraka Dow Jones Islamic Index Fund, <http://www.altawfeek.com/abdjiffunddetails.htm>.
46. Ibid.

References

Ahmad, Ziauddin. "The Present State of Islamic Finance Movement". *Journal of Islamic Banking and Finance* (Autumn 1985).

Ali, A. Yusuf, trans. *The Holy Qur'an.* Lahore: Sh. Muhammad Ashraf, 1975.

al-Kaff, Syed H. A. R. *Does Islam Assign any Value/Weight to Time Factor in Economic and Financial Transactions?* Karachi: Islamic Research Academy, 1986.

Asad, Muhammad. *The Message of the Qur'an.* Gibraltar: Dar al-Andalus, 1984.

Buang, Ahmad Hidayat. *Studies in the Islamic Law of Contracts: the Prohibition of Gharar.* Kuala Lumpur: International Law Book Services, 2000.

Chapra, M. Umer. *Towards a Just Monetary System.* Leicester: Islamic Foundation, 1985.

Council of Islamic Ideology. *Consolidated Recommendations on the Islamic Economic System.* Islamabad: Council of Islamic Ideology, 1983.

Faisal Islamic Bank of Egypt (FIBE). *'Aqd Bay' al-Murabaha.* n.d.

———. *Contract of Musharaka.* n.d.

Jordan Islamic Bank. *al-Fatawa al-Shar'iyyah.* Amman: JIB, 1984.

Kharofa, Ala' Eddin. *Nationalism, Secularism, Apostasy and Usury in Islam.* Kuala Lumpur: A.S. Noordeen, 1994.

Malik b. Anas. *Muwatta' Imam Malik: Riwayat Muhammad b. al-Hasan al-Shaybani,* edited by 'Abd al-Wahhab 'Abd al-Latif. Cairo: al-Majlis al-A'la li al-Shu'un al-Islamiyyah, 1979.

Mawdudi, Abu al-A'la. *Towards Understanding the Qur'an.* Translated by Zafar Ishaq Ansari. Leicester: Islamic Foundation, 1988.

Mohammed Uzair. *Interest-Free Banking.* Karachi: Royal Book Company, 1978.

Nienhaus, Volker. "Islamic Economics, Finance and Banking: Theory and Practice". *Journal of Islamic Banking and Finance* (Spring 1986).

Quasim, Quasim M. "Islamic Banking: New Opportunities for Cooperation between Western and Islamic Financial Institutions". In *Islamic Banking and Finance* London: Butterworths, 1986.

Rahman, Fazlur. "Riba and Interest". *Islamic Studies* (March 1964).

———. "Islam: Challenges and Opportunities". In *Islam: Past Influence and Present Challenge,* edited by Welch and Cachia. Edinburgh: Edinburgh University Press, 1979.

Saeed, Abdullah. *Islamic Banking and Interest.* Leiden: E. J. Brill, 1999.
Saleh, Nabil. *Unlawful Gain and Legitimate Profit in Islamic Law.* Cambridge: Cambridge University Press, 1986.
Shihata, Shawqi Isma'il. *Nazariyyat al-Muhasabah al-Maliyyah min Manzurin Islami.* Cairo: Dar al-Zahra' li al-I'lam al-'Arabi, 1987.
Siddiqi, Muhammad Nejatullah. *Banking without Interest.* Leicester: Islamic Foundation, 1983*a*.
———. *Issues in Islamic Banking: Selected Papers.* Leicester: Islamic Foundation, 1983*b*.
———. *Partnership and Profit-Sharing in Islamic Law*, Leicester: Islamic Foundation, 1987.
Uzair, Mohammad. "Impact of Interest Free Banking". *Journal of Islamic Banking and Finance* (Autumn 1984).
Vogel, Frank E., and Samuel L. Hayes, III. *Islamic Law and Finance.* The Hague: Kluwer Law International, 1998.
Yaquby, Nizam. "Participation and Trading in Equities of Companies which [sic] Main Business is Primarily Lawful but Fraught with some Prohibited Transactions". Unpublished paper presented at Fourth Harvard Islamic Finance Forum, Harvard University, 30 September–1 October 2000.
Zaidi, Nawazish Ali. "Islamic Banking in Pakistan". *Journal of Islamic Banking and Finance* (Summer 1988).

The Nation-State

8

POLITICAL ISLAM IN POST-SOEHARTO INDONESIA

Azyumardi Azra

The dawn of the new millennium has brought not only euphoria to citizens of the world, but also hopes of better political and economic lives for Muslims. By the same token, the new millennium brings increasing anxiety among Muslims as tendencies, which have gained momentum over the last decade, intensify.

As Liddle and Mujani (2000) rightly argue, one of the most evident tendencies in the post-Cold War period up until the new millennium was the rapid growth of democracies, or at least there was a strong tendency that increasing numbers of nation-states are becoming more democratic. This tendency, as both scholars further point out, seems not to be taking place in dominant or predominant Muslim states in the Islamic world as a whole. As a result, the old question regarding Islam and democracy: whether or not Islam could play a more positive role in the new wave of democracy, once again becomes a subject of heated discussion both from within Muslim communities and without (cf. Esposito and Voll 1996; Eickelman and Piscatori 1996).

The discussions and debates on the relationship between Islam and democracy have once again come to the fore in Indonesia in the aftermath of the fall of Soeharto. This has much to do with the rise of "political Islam" which appears to be one of the most visible political developments in post-Soeharto Indonesia. It can be clearly observed in several tendencies. First, the establishment of a great number of "Islamic parties" which mostly adopt Islam as their basis replacing Pancasila that used to be the sole basis of any organization; second, the increasing demands from certain groups among Muslims for the official adoption and implementation of *shari'a*; and third, the proliferation of Muslim groups considered by many as radicals, such as Lasykar Jihad (Jihad Troops), Front Pembela Islam (FPI, or Islamic Defence Front), Hizb al-Tahrir (Party of Liberation), and Angkatan Mujahidin Indonesia (the Jihad Fighter Group of Indonesia) (cf. Bamualim et al. 2000). The three developments — by no means exhaustive — appear to some to represent the return of the idea of the Islamic state in Indonesia, and this could supposedly bring the future of democracy and pluralism in Indonesia into question. I would argue, however, that despite the seeming recent tendencies among Indonesian Muslims to cling to political and formal Islam, it remains difficult to imagine that Indonesia would and could be transformed into an Islamic state. The three new tendencies could be very alarming for those who are concerned with the future of democracy in this country, but one should not overestimate them since there is also a number of factors that are working in Indonesian society which make the realization of an Islamic state in Indonesia only a remote possibility.

This chapter discusses these complex developments. One of the most important questions to answer is the feasibility and viability of the idea of the Islamic state in Indonesia. Not least important is, of course, the discussion of the future of democracy in Indonesia in relation to all the recent tendencies towards political and formal Islam.

CALIPHATE VERSUS MODERN NATION-STATE

Before proceeding, it should be made clear that any discussion of Muslim politics should avoid sweeping generalizations. In fact, there is no single Muslim politics and Muslims are not a monolithic phenomenon. Hefner has persuasively argued that there is no single, civilization-wide pattern of Muslim politics, but a variety of competing organizations and ideals. In his opinion, the modern era's nation making and market globalization have, if anything, only increased the pluralism and contestation of politics in the Muslim world. As a result, the most significant "clash of cultures" is not that between distinct civilizations, but rival political traditions within the same Islamic country (Hefner 1999, p. 41).

The contest and rivalry among a number of Islamic political traditions are even becoming increasingly complex with the contemporary Islamic revival. The so-called revival of religion — including Islam — that has swept many parts of the globe over the last two decades at least rekindles the old debates on the relationship between Islam and politics. Both at the theoretical and practical levels, Muslim intellectuals, *ulama*, and leaders have engaged in such issues as the compatibility or incompatibility of Islam and contemporary ideas and practices of democracy, civil society, and human rights. Again, there is no single answer to these questions. One sure thing is that the majority of Muslims have accepted — albeit tacitly — the modern form of nation-state. One can be certain, however, that there are a great number of differences among Muslims, for instance, regarding the type and level of democracy that would and could be implemented in their respective countries.

While Islamic revival is continually gaining momentum, there are signs that many secular nation-states in the Muslim world have failed to deliver their promises. This failure has not only eroded the credibility of secular regimes in the eyes of an ever-growing number of Muslims, but has also created scepticism about the viability of modern nation-states. This is evident from attempts carried out by certain Muslim movements regarded by many as radical, such as the Hizb al-Tahrir, Gama'ah Tafkir wa al-Hijrah, and other splinter groups of the Ikhwan al-Muslimun, to replace secular regimes and nation-states with the classic model of the "Islamic state", better known as the caliphate (*al-khilafah*), or in contemporary discourse among these movements, the "universal caliphate". The proponents of the universal caliphate believe that this kind of Islamic political entity led by a single caliph is the only solution to Muslim disunity and powerlessness *vis-à-vis* the Western powers (Dekmejian 1995; Abu-Rabi' 1996; Lawrence 1998).

The contemporary revival of the idea of a single and universal caliphate, undoubtedly, is problematic. I would argue that it is mostly based on historical and religious romanticism as well as misconceptions of not only the very meaning of the caliphate but also of the historical development of the caliphate itself in the post-Prophet Muhammad period. Supporters of the caliphate have confused and have failed to distinguish between the original and genuine caliphate during the Rightly Guided Caliphs (*al-khulafa' al-rashidun*) and the despotic monarchies of the Umayyads, the Abbasids, and the Ottomans. While at least the first two caliphs, Abu Bakr and Umar ibn al-Khattab, were elected on their merits, the subsequent "caliphs" in the post-*al-khulafa' al-rashidun* period were essentially kings (*muluk*) with all their uncontested rights and privileges over other Muslims. Therefore, modern "thinkers" of the caliphate such as Jamal al-Din al-Afghani, 'Abd al-Rahman al-Kawakibi, Rashid Rida, Sayyid Qutb, and Abu al-A'la al-Mawdudi have all refused to recognize the credibility and legitimacy of those Muslim kings as "caliphs" (cf. Azra 1996, p. 153ff.). One should be aware, however, that these thinkers proposed different, if not conflicting, ideas on some main themes of the caliphate. Al-Kawakibi and Rida, for instance, insisted that the caliph should be an Arab of the Quraysh tribe. Al-Mawdudi, on the other hand, strongly refuses this idea; to him the caliph should be democratically elected among all Muslims based on merit by a special electing body called "*ahl al-halli wa al-'aqd*", or Majlis al-Shura. According to al-Mawdudi, the lofty position of the caliph must not be reserved for an Arab, since Arabs have no special privileges over other non-Arab Muslims (cf. Thaib 1995, pp. 79–80).

Despite all conceptual and practical problems surrounding the feasibility and viability of the caliphate today, the idea seems to have continually attracted certain elements of Muslims throughout the world. In Southeast Asia, particularly in Indonesia, the idea of the caliphate has been put into circulation by such organizations as Hizb al-Tahrir and Jamaah Tarbiyah since the 1990s at least. It is important to note that during the Soeharto New Order era, these movements were very careful not to invite the regime to take firm actions against their activities. As a result, they survived the harsh Soeharto rule and have made themselves more pronounced in the post-Soeharto period (Azra 2001, pp. 45–46).

There is no doubt that the Indonesian Hizb al-Tahrir, established in Jordan in 1952 by Shaykh Taqi al-Din al-Nabhani, has become more prominent since the fall of Soeharto. Calling for the establishment of the universal *khilafah*, the movement held a *khilafah* conference in Jakarta in early 2000. The conference was reportedly attended by only a limited audience. Despite its seeming radicalism, the Hizb al-Tahrir apparently uses peaceful means to achieve its main agenda of establishing the *khilafah*.

The Indonesian Hizb al-Tahrir makes itself even more visible with its demonstrations, protesting against policies of the Indonesian Government, such as the planned trade relations between Indonesia and Israel. The Hizb al-Tahrir also took the streets when President Megawati's government increased the price of fuel in 2002. Arguably their largest demonstration was against the United States in the aftermath of the September 11 attacks on the World Trade Center in New York and the Pentagon in Washington, D.C. The Hizb al-Tahrir's staunch anti-Americanism is no surprise, since its leaders firmly believe that the United States is the mastermind behind the so-called Western conspiracy to destroy Islam and the Muslims (Azra 2002).

Despite its increased visibility, however, it is doubtful that the Hizb al-Tahrir's appeal for the establishment of the *khilafah* wins significant support from Indonesian mainstream Muslims. The majority of Indonesian Muslims, represented by large organizations such as the NU (Nahdlatul Ulama) and Muhammadiyah, and Muslim political parties, almost completely disregard the issue. In short, public discourse on *khilafah* is conspicuously absent; which indicates that mainstream Muslims are simply not interested in the *khilafah*, let alone support its establishment in Indonesia.

THE INDONESIAN CASE: PANCASILA

As mentioned earlier, polemics and debates among Indonesian and foreign observers on the relationship between Islam and politics, and Islam and democracy, in the nation-state of Indonesia have once again come to the fore in Indonesia in the aftermath of the fall of Soeharto. Many believe that the rise of political Islam represented by so many "Islamic parties" would bring serious political repercussions to the future of the Indonesian state which has been based on Pancasila.

In this regard, it is worth pointing out that despite the fact that the first pillar of Pancasila is the belief in the One Supreme God, many foreign observers view this Indonesian basis of state as basically secular. This argument is further supported by the fact that Indonesia does not adopt any religion — particularly Islam, as the religion most Indonesians adhere to — as the official religion of the state.

On the other hand, the majority of Muslims would love to argue that Indonesia is neither a secular nor a theocratic state. For them Pancasila is in accord with Islamic belief and teachings. For instance, the first pillar of Pancasila, in their opinion, is simply another reformulation of the Islamic belief in the One Supreme God (*tawhid*). The case is also the same with the other four pillars of Pancasila: just and civilized humanity; unity of Indonesia; democracy which is guided by the inner wisdom of its leaders; and social justice for the entire people of Indonesia (cf. Taher 1997, pp. 1–16).

In spite of Muslim acceptance of Pancasila, one should admit, however, that some Muslim groups in the past attempted to replace Pancasila with Islam as the basis of the Indonesian state. In the 1950s, the Masjumi Party, for instance, struggled in the national parliament to replace Pancasila with Islam. Then came the Darul Islam (Islamic State) rebellions under the leadership of Kartosuwirjo in West Java, and Daud Bereueh in Aceh which attempted to establish the Indonesian Islamic State (NII, or Negara Islam Indonesia). But as we already know, all these efforts — legal and illegal — failed. It is important to note that among non-Muslim groups, mainly Christians and secular circles, suspicions remain that Muslims will continue their struggle to establish an Islamic state in Indonesia at the expense of other groups of citizens (cf. Azra 2000*c*).

As a result, the Indonesian regimes of both Sukarno and Soeharto took harsh measures not only against any potential Muslim group that subscribed to the idea of an Islamic state, but also against any dangerous manifestation of political Islam. Thus, from the last years of President Sukarno in the late 1950s to the early 1960s and much of the Soeharto era was marked by the demise of political Islam. For more than forty years, therefore, Islamic political forces were subjects of state repression and manipulation. The New Order regime of Soeharto, in particular, provided no room for political Islam to breathe. Soeharto, in fact, carried out systematic depoliticization of Islam, the climax of which was the forced implementation of Pancasila as the sole ideological basis of any organization (see Effendy 1998).

The opposition to the forced implementation of Pancasila as the sole ideological basis of any organization came, of course, not only from many Muslim organizations; most, if not all, Christian organizations opposed the move even more bitterly. But given their history, Muslims became the main subject of suspicion. Potential Islamic political forces, therefore, remained under tight control even after their adoption of Pancasila.

The retreat of political Islam during much of the New Order period, however, provided a momentum for the rejuvenation of cultural Islam. This began with Soeharto's more accommodating and reconciliatory attitude towards Islam and Muslims in the period after Muslims' acceptance of Pancasila. Conflict, mutual suspicion and hostility between President Soeharto and most Muslim groups diminished significantly. Some argued Soeharto's more conciliatory gestures were because he had been successful in co-opting Muslims. But at the same time, for personal reasons Soeharto seemed to have developed a genuine leaning towards Islam, creating closer links with Muslims. As a result, one can argue that Soeharto had indeed been co-opted by Muslims.

The fact that Soeharto's newly found leaning to Islam had led to the reflowering of cultural Islam is evident, for instance, from his support for the enactment of the 1989 Law of Islamic Courts; and the 1989 Law of National Education which recognizes the existence of Islamic education on par with "secular" education. Then followed the establishment of ICMI (Ikatan Cendekiawan Muslim se-Indonesia, or Indonesian Association of Muslim Intellectuals) chaired by B. J. Habibie, then Minister of Research and Technology, and the founding of Islamic banks (Bank Muamalat Indonesia or BMI, and Bank Perkreditan Rakyat Syariah or BPR-Syariah).

Soeharto undoubtedly miscalculated and underestimated the far-reaching implications of so-called cultural Islam. He was not unlike Snouck Hurgronje, the most prominent Islamic Advisor of the Dutch Netherlands Indies government, who advised the Dutch to allow "Islam as cultural phenomenon" to express itself more freely at the expense of political Islam which must be suppressed by any means necessary. In the final analysis, Soeharto had slowly been seemingly contained and even dictated to by the growing political repercussions of the cultural Islam. There was much public discussion as to whether Soeharto's new-found Islamic leaning was in order for him to co-opt Islam or, conversely, that it was Soeharto who had been co-opted by Muslims.

The most widely discussed example of the political repercussions of "cultural Islam" is, of course, ICMI. Even though it is formally an association of "Muslim intellectuals" only, there is no doubt that it has played a significant political role since its establishment in 1990. By way of Habibie — often called the "super minister" — ICMI allegedly engineered the increase in the number of Muslim ministers at the expense of the Christians in the last two Soeharto Cabinets. It was also assumed ICMI played a significant role in high-ranking government appointments such as provincial governors. The result of these revelations was what some observers called the "honeymoon" between Soeharto and Islam.

Having considered the role of Habibie in ICMI political manoeuvres, it is not surprising that many Muslims considered Habibie and ICMI as representatives of Islam and Muslims. Habibie's personal piety only added to this sentiment. Therefore, when Soeharto resigned from the presidency on 21 May 1998 following the monetary, economic, and political crises that Indonesia experienced from the end of 1997, he was replaced by Habibie who was defended by some Muslim groups from his opponents who questioned the legitimacy of his assumption of the presidency in such an unorthodox way.

Even though President Habibie lifted the forced implementation of Pancasila as the sole ideological basis of any organization, it has admittedly won a bad name. A lot of resentment remains, not only against the forced implementation of Pancasila, but also against its monopolistic interpretation by the Soeharto regime. As a result, Pancasila has been markedly absent from public discourse since the time of Habibie's interregnum and his successor President Abdurrahman Wahid, and even during the period of President Megawati Sukarnoputri who replaced Wahid when he was impeached by the MPR (People's Consultative Assembly) on 23 June 2001. At the same time, however, there is no significant public discourse between Pancasila and any other ideology. There are, of course, smaller groups who appeal to the mainstream Muslims for the possible reintroduction of the

Jakarta Charter into the Preamble of the 1945 Constitution — thus allowing the possible transformation of Indonesia into an Islamic state; but again, as we see below, there is no solid support for this appeal. All this indicates that Pancasila is still regarded as the most acceptable common platform for plural Indonesia.

THE RISE AND FALL OF ISLAMIC PARTIES

The Habibie presidency lasted for only fifteen months. Despite his relatively short interregnum, one of his most significant contributions was the liberalization of Indonesian politics. Following his appointment, Habibie not only freed most of the political prisoners, abolished restrictions to press freedom, lifted the forced implementation of Pancasila as the sole ideology, but he also abandoned the three-party system of Indonesian politics represented by GOLKAR, PPP (Partai Persatuan Pembangunan), and PDI (Partai Demokrasi Indonesia). This last policy, as one might expect, has led to the rise of a great number of "Islamic political parties". The abolition of the 1985 Mass Organization Law that made it obligatory for all organizations to adopt Pancasila as the sole ideology has only encouraged political Islam. Without such a legal obligation, it was reasonable to expect that many Muslims would seek a return to Islam for their political parties (Azra 2000*a*).

The extent of political euphoria among Muslims can be clearly seen in the proliferation of Islamic parties. There were some 40 "Islamic parties" among the 141 parties that formally registered with the Ministry of Justice in the lead-up to the June 1999 general election. After a selection by the Team of Eleven (Tim 11), the committee entrusted with selecting the political parties that would contest the election, forty-eight parties — of which around twenty were Islamic — were found eligible to take part (Salim 2000, pp. 7–8). This was far more than the ten Islamic parties that had participated in the 1955 general election.

There have been a lot of discussions about what "Islamic parties" are. I would propose that there are at least two major elements that identify a party as "Islamic". First, in their documentation, many such parties have officially adopted Islam as their ideological basis. Examples include the United Development Party (Partai Persatuan Pembangunan or PPP); the Moon and Crescent Party (Partai Bulan Bintang or PBB); the United Party (Partai Persatuan or PP); the Indonesian Islamic Political Party of Masyumi (Partai Politik Islam Indonesia Masyumi or PPIIM); the Indonesian Islamic Association Party (Partai Syarekat Islam Indonesia or PSII); the Indonesian

Islamic Association Party of 1905 (Partai Syarekat Islam Indonesia 1905 or PSII 1905); the Islamic Nation Party (Partai Umat Islam or PUI); and the New Masyumi Party (Partai Masyumi Baru). One party, KAMI, adopts the Qur'an and the Sunna of the Prophet Muhammad as its basis. Taken together, there are ten parties adopting Islam or the original sources of Islamic teachings, instead of Pancasila, as their sole ideological basis. This group of Islamic parties, as Fealy proposes, might also be best categorized as "formalist Islamic parties" since those parties formally have Islam or the Qur'an and the Sunna as their sole ideological basis (Fealy 2000, p. 3).

The second group of "Islamic parties" are Muslim parties that have retained Pancasila as their basis but, at the same time, employ obvious Islamic symbols such as Arabic scripts, the star and crescent, the *ka'bah* (cube-shaped building in Mecca which is the direction Muslims face when they pray), and other symbols that are widely associated with Islam. While these parties seems to be "pluralist parties" adopting Pancasila, they are in fact Muslim-based parties for, in some cases, they are supported mostly by members of non-political Muslim organizations such as the NU and Muhammadiyah. The parties included in this group are the National Awakening Party (Partai Kebangkitan Bangsa or PKB) supported by the NU; the National Mandate Party (Partai Amanat Nasional or PAN), whose members are mostly from a Muhammadiyah background; the Fathers of the Orphans Party (Partai Abul Yatama); the New Indonesia Party (Partai Indonesia Baru or PIB); the Uni-Indonesia Solidarity Party (Partai Solidaritas Uni Indonesia or Partai SUNI); the Peace-Loving Party (Partai Cinta Damai or PCD); the Democratic Islam Party (Partai Islam Demokrasi or PID); and the Indonesian Muslim Nation Party (Partai Umat Muslimin Indonesia or PUMI). To this group, one could add two "splinter" parties among the NU members — Partai Nahdlatul Ummat (PNU or Nation Awakening Party) and Partai Kebangkitan Ummat (PKU or Nation Awakening Party), both of which have Pancasila and Islam as their ideological bases. According to Fealy, this group might be best described as "pluralist Islamic parties" (Fealy 2000, p. 4).

Several months before the June 1999 elections, I predicted that the prospect of the Islamic/Muslim parties was very doubtful (Azra 2000*a*). The prediction was primarily based on three arguments. First, these parties have only caused acute political fragmentation, schisms, and conflicts among both Muslim leadership and the masses. They have created confusion and tensions among the Muslims at the grass-root level. As a result, there have been cases of open fighting among fanatic supporters of the Islamic parties, even among members of the NU who support different parties.

Second, the Islamic/Muslim parties have mostly been trapped in the romanticism of Islamic politics and the fact that Muslims represent 87 per cent of the Indonesian population rather than in political realism. Many Muslim political leaders expected that all of the 87 per cent of Indonesian Muslims would automatically support them, and would cast their votes for their parties in the election.

Third, they seemed to have underestimated both the PDI-P (Indonesian Democratic Party of Struggle) and GOLKAR. Many Muslim political leaders believed that Megawati's PDI-P would not get many votes for several reasons: Megawati's gender, her unproven capability, and her seeming influence mostly coming from the charisma of her father, Sukarno; and the predominance of non-Muslim and secular figures in the PDI-P leadership. All these proved to be wrong. They did not prevent Megawati's PDI-P from winning the election, in spite of appeals from many Muslim *ulama* and leaders that Indonesians not cast their votes for PDI-P. On the other hand, GOLKAR had also been underestimated because of its past strong connection with the Soeharto regime. Since the fall of Soeharto, GOLKAR has come under continued attacks as the status-quo party which should be disbanded. The fact is, while the majority of the Islamic parties have struggled to establish branches in many parts of Indonesia, GOLKAR was able to keep most of its political machine intact. As a result, to the surprise of many, GOLKAR came second in the election.

All of these arguments could explain why Islamic parties were defeated in the June 1999 election. Together, all twenty Islamic parties got only 37.1 per cent of the total votes. This is a significant decrease compared with the result of the 1955 election, when Islamic parties won 43.9 per cent of the total national votes. In contrast, PDI-P and GOLKAR got more than half of the total votes, 33.76 per cent and 22.46 per cent respectively. Worse still, of the twenty Islamic parties, only four met the required minimum threshold of 2 per cent of parliamentary seats (ten seats); they are PPP, PKB, PAN, and PBB.

The fact that Islamic parties gained only a small share of the vote in the 1999 election worried many Muslims, who believed that it marked the end of political Islam. However, certain external factors such as PDI-P's complacency and insensitivity to Muslims' aspirations had provided the stimulus for the fragmented Islamic parties to unite and establish their own political front, initially called *fraksi Islam* (the Islamic faction) and later known as *poros tengah* (the middle axis). The growing unresolved conflicts among the supporters of Habibie and Megawati had created an opportunity for *poros tengah* to propose Abdurrahman Wahid as its presidential candidate in the MPR General Session in October 1999.

Considering the fragmentation of the Islamic parties, the election of Abdurrahman Wahid as the fourth president of the Republic of Indonesia, I would argue, was more a result of "political expediency" than of real strength of the Islamic/Muslim political parties. As one might expect, before long President Wahid proved to be a disappointment for the Islamic parties. He showed that he was elected more for his personal credentials than anything else. Through his controversial statements and policies he soon created open conflicts with *poros tengah*. His erratic attitude and unorthodox management style, which produced the so-called Buloggate I and Bruneigate scandals and the declaration of martial law, finally led to his impeachment in the Special Session of the MPR in June 2001 when he was replaced by Vice-President Megawati Sukarnoputri.

Now, with this dismal picture, what is the prospect of Islamic parties, or even political Islam? How viable is the idea of stronger and formal connections between Islam and the Indonesian nation-state?

First of all, the result of the 1999 election once again confirmed that Islamic parties have never been very popular among Indonesian Muslims. One of the most important reasons for this is that most of the Muslim population are leaning more towards what I call "substantive Islam" rather than towards "formalistic Islam" (Azra 2000*a*). Though there is a continued tendency among Muslims to undergo some kind of "*santrinization*", this seems to have more to do with ritualistic or cultural Islam at best rather than with political Islam or Islamic parties. The tendency among Muslims to become more devout (*santri*), at least formally, has therefore not necessarily been translated into a more Islamic political orientation. To put it more simply, belief and rituals are one thing, and political behaviour is another.

Therefore, at the level of political behaviour and political praxis, there are no convincing signs of Muslims, as represented by Islamic parties, supporting the idea of formal Islamic politics. Again, this attitude is hardly surprising, since no one among the prominent Muslim political leaders even subscribes to the idea or aims to establish an Islamic state in Indonesia at the expense of Pancasila. Prominent Muslim political leaders such as Abdurrahman Wahid, Amien Rais, Yusril Ihza Mahendra, Deliar Noer, Ahmad Sumargono, Muhaimin Iskandar, Nur Mahmudi Ismail, A. M. Fatwa, Salahuddin Wahid, amongst others have declared openly that they and their political parties do not aim to establish an Indonesian Islamic state (Salim 2000, p. 10). To this list one might also add the leaders of the largest Muslim social-religious organizations, such as K. H. Hasyim Muzadi (general chairman of NU) and Ahmad Syafii Maarif (national leader of Muhammadiyah), who also dismiss the idea of establishing an Islamic state in Indonesia.

The prominent leader Amien Rais, former leader of Muhammadiyah who is now the Speaker of the MPR, long before the euphoria associated with the rise of political Islam, considered the idea of an Islamic state as having no precedent in Islamic history. Therefore, he argues, there is no religious obligation for Muslims to establish one. Nur Mahmudi Ismail, president of the Justice Party (Partai Keadilan or PK) which is considered to represent the new spirit of Islamic contemporary political revival, also maintains that the most important element in Islam is the substance, not the label or formalism. Therefore, he accepted Pancasila as the sole foundation of the Indonesian state. He recognizes that his party is indeed based on Islam, but this does not necessarily mean that it would lead to the struggle of establishing an Islamic state (Salim 2000, p. 10).

As I argued elsewhere, the adoption of Islamic formalism and symbolism, represented by Islamic/Muslim parties in post-Soeharto Indonesian politics, is not largely motivated by "Islamic ideology" but by a power struggle or, to put it more bluntly, by a lust for power among Muslim political leaders. More than anything else, political pragmatism is the most important feature of political behaviour of most Muslim political leaders. Therefore, the so-called Islamic ideology in many cases has no clear relevance with political realities and development.

One of the most obvious indications of this tendency can be seen in the current split within Islamic/Muslim parties. Such a split is of course not unique to Islamic/Muslim parties, since non-Islamic parties such as PDI-P and GOLKAR are also afflicted by this sorry situation. However, given the Islamic teaching on Islamic solidarity (*al-ukhuwah al-Islamiyyah*), the split of Islamic parties for many people could be unexpected.

The current split within Islamic parties can be observed clearly in the PBB; the intense conflicts between Yusril Ihza Mahendra and Hartono Mardjono resulted in the expulsion of the latter from PBB. Hartono finally established his own party, PII (Partai Islam Indonesia), in mid-March 2002.

More intense conflicts and splits have taken place within the PKB and PPP. The root cause of the split within PKB was Matori Abdul Djalil's unsupportive attitude to the embattled and later impeached President Abdurrahman Wahid. Joining the Special Session of the MPR in June 2001 that unseated President Wahid, who is also the founder of the PKB, Matori was expelled from the PKB; but he claimed the he remained the legal general chairman of the party. Abdurrahman Wahid, on the other hand, appointed Alwi Shihab as the caretaker of the PKB. Attempts to reconcile the two camps failed; and each camp finally held its Extraordinary Congress in early 2002.

A split also afflicted the PPP. The main cause was the decision of the PPP national leadership under Hamzah Haz, who also occupies the position as Vice-President of the Republic of Indonesia, to postpone its national congress from 2002 to 2004. Certain elements within PPP opposed this decision on the basis that it is simply a move by Hamzah Haz to maintain his power in PPP in order to pursue his own agenda in the General Election of 2004. The dissenting elements within PPP finally split from the Hamzah Haz's PPP and declared the establishment of the PPP-Reformasi (Reform PPP) under the leadership of Zainuddin M. Z., the most popular *da'i* (preacher) dubbed as the "*kiyai sejuta ummat*" (preacher of a million Muslims) in contemporary Indonesia.

It is important to mention that, in addition to the split in these parties, new parties are being founded in anticipation of the 2004 General Election. Many of them are new Islamic parties. According to the Ministry of Justice and Human Rights, more than 300 parties have registered. One might wonder how the National Election Commission can limit the number of the parties to a more reasonable number so that they will not be counter-productive to the healthy growth of democracy in Indonesia.

CONCLUSION

The failure of Islamic parties, again, is a clear indication of formal Islam's lack of appeal to Indonesian Muslims. It is not dissimilar to the growing appeals from some Muslim groups for the aplication of *shari'a*, Islamic law, in Indonesia. The application of *shari'a* is, of course, not a new idea. It can be traced back to the days of Indonesian independence during which Indonesian leaders formulated the Indonesian Constitution, better known as the 1945 Constitution. In the initial stages of its formulation, Muslim leaders introduced to its Preamble the phrase, "the Indonesian state is based on the belief in the One, Supreme God with the obligation of the adherents of Islam to implement the *shari'a*." This stipulation is known in Indonesia as "the seven words" of the Piagam Jakarta (Jakarta Charter).

Before long, however, this stipulation was dropped because of objections by Christian leaders and secular nationalists. They argued that the national Constitution should not give preferential treatment to any religious group. Furthermore, the Constitution should maintain the integration of national plurality. For these reasons, Muslim leaders agreed to omit the "seven words" of the Jakarta Charter (Taher 1997, pp. 38–39). However, the debate on the "seven words" continued and Muslim leaders once again brought their case to the Constituent Assembly in 1959. The debate only ended with a decree issued by President Sukarno on 5 July 1959 stating the return of Indonesia to the 1945 Constitution. This means that the Piagam Jakarta, the basis of the application of *shari'a*, should be abandoned.

It is clear that the issue of the application of *shari'a* is far from being resolved. It came up again in both the post-Sukarno and post-Soeharto eras. The 1966 and 1967 sessions of the MPR, following the fall of Sukarno, were tense with rumours of Muslim proposals to bring the Piagam Jakarta under consideration. But as one might expect, this aspiration was suppressed by the army-backed Soeharto regime. In the period post-Soeharto, some of the newly founded Islamic parties once again demanded the legalization of the Jakarta Charter as an integral part of the Preamble of the 1945 Constitution (Salim 2000, pp. 13–14).

The appeal for the application of *shari'a* gained momentum during the Habibie presidency with the adoption of Islamic law in Aceh, as an integral part of the proposed solution to the unrest in the province. The main reasons behind this move were: firstly, that the majority of the population of Aceh province — as well as Indonesia as a whole — are Muslims; secondly, that *shari'a* would be able to resolve the breakdown of law and order in the post-Soeharto era; and thirdly, that only *shari'a* could overcome the increase of social ills in Indonesian society such as drug abuse and crime.

The adoption of Islamic law in Aceh was finally approved by the central government when President Megawati signed the Law of Negeri Aceh Darussalam in early 2002. The enactment of the law created mixed feelings both in Aceh and at the national level. Many were seceptical that Islamic law could be implemented since constraints existed both within *shari'a* itself as well as in the Acehnese society.

The most significant move for the application of *shari'a* took place in the period surrounding the 2000 Annual Session of the MPR. Some Islamic parties, particularly the PPP, openly declared their intention to reintroduce the Piagam Jakarta in the session, thus allowing the application of Islamic law. It is important to note that the move was strongly opposed by the majority of MPR members, and the issue of the application of *shari'a*, once again, failed in the Indonesia's highest political institution. The issue was not on the agenda of the MPR Special Session of 2001; and, therefore, it is doubtful whether it will reappear on the agenda in the future.

Despite the ill-fated response, the aspiration of Islamic law appears to continue to attract certain Muslim groups. In late October 2000, some Muslims in South Sulawesi province also appealed for *shari'a* to be implemented in their region. In fact some groups formed a Special Committee for the Preparation of the Implementation of Shari'a in South Sulawesi Province, but to date they have made little progress. In addition, the districts of Cianjur and Tasikmalaya in West Java also attempted to implement *shari'a.* There is no clear comprehensive concept of how the implementation could work. In these districts the implementation seems ad hoc and partial, in which *shari'a* is treated simply like an elixir to combat all kinds of social ills.

Despite scepticism and the problematic implementation of *shari'a*, one significant recent trend is that the proponents of *shari'a* try to achieve their aims by taking advantage of the decentralization process that is now occurring in Indonesia as a whole. This approach is taken by the proponents of the implementation of *shari'a* because of their failure at the national level through the DPR and MPR. Whether this new approach, that is through province and district, would be successful remains to be seen. But one thing is quite clear: that the move through province and district will create more complications in the autonomy and decentralization processes.

The case is the same with the worrisome phenomenon of the Lasykar Jihad and other similar groups, which also seem to seek the application of Islamic law. Worse still, in the name of Islamic law they attack nightclubs, discotheques, and houses allegedly used for prostitution. These radical groups have also been very active in mass demonstrations against the United States when they conducted military operations in Afghanistan in the aftermath of the September 11 tragedy. The slow and undecisive response of the Megawati government to both U.S. policy as well as to these groups has attracted criticism. Thus, when the government finally took harsh measures to put an end to the mass demonstrations held by these groups against the United States, the image of Indonesian Islam had been tarnished.

I believe that the rise of these radical groups reflects the failure of the government to enforce the law, thus providing them with an excuse or *raison d'etre* to take law into their own hands. Therefore, as long as the government is weak and indecisive, the groups hold sway to do what they call "*amar ma'ruf nahi munkar*" — enjoin good, prohibit evil in their own way, or to hold rallies and demonstrations against any group, either in Indonesia or abroad, that they consider has disregarded Islam and Muslims.

In conclusion, there are key factors to be addressed in regard to the issues of the appeal from certain Muslim groups for the implementation of *shari'a*; and the increased radicalism among splinter groups. They are: firstly, the restrengthening of the state and good governance; secondly, the enhancement of democracy and civil society; thirdly, the reinforcement of law and order; and lastly, the speedy recovery of the national economy. Otherwise, Indonesia will continue to face the problems outlined above.

References

Abu-Rabi', Ibrahim M. *Intellectual Origins of Islamic Resurgence in the Modern Arab World.* Albany, NY: State University of New York Press, 1996.

Azra, Azyumardi. *Pergolakan Politik Islam: Dari Fundamentalisme, Modernisme hingga Post-Modernisme.* Jakarta: Paramadina, 1996.

———. *Islam Substantif: Agar Umat Tidak Jadi Buih.* Bandung: Mizan, 2000*a*.

———. "The Islamic Factor in Post-Soeharto Indonesia". In *Indonesia in Transition: Social Aspects of Reformasi and Crisis*, edited by Chris Manning and Peter van Dierman. Singapore: RSPAS-ANU and ISEAS, 2000*b*.

———. "Islam and Christianity in Indonesia: The Roots of Conflict and Hostility". Paper presented at the international conference on Religion and Culture in Asia-Pacific: Violence or Healing?, RMIT University, Melbourne, 22–25 October, 2000*c*.

———. "Globalization of Indonesian Muslim Discourse: Contemporary Religio-Intellectual Connections between Indonesia and the Middle East". In *Islam in the Era of Globalization: Muslim Attitudes towards Modernity and Identity*, edited by J. H. Meuleman. Leiden and Jakarta: INIS, 2001.

———. "Indonesian Islam in a World Context". Paper presented at the conference on Islam in Modern Indonesia, The Asia Foundation and USINDO, Washington, D.C., 7 February 2002.

Bamualim, Chaider S. et al. *Laporan Penelitian Radikalisme Agama dan Perubahan Sosial di Indonesia*, Jakarta: Pusat Bahasa dan Budaya IAIN Jakarta and Badan Perencanaan Pembangunan Daerah Pemerintah DKI Jakarta, 2000.

Dekmejian, R. Hrair. *Islam in Revolution: Fundamentalism in the Arab World.* 2nd ed. Syracuse, NY: Syracuse University Press, 1995.

Effendy, Bahtiar. *Islam dan Negara: Transformasi Pemikiran dan Praktik Politik Islam di Indonesia.* Jakarta: Paramadina, 1998.

Eickelman, Dale F. and James Piscatori. *Muslim Politics.* Princeton: Princeton University Press, 1996.

Esposito, John L. and John O. Voll. *Islam and Democracy.* New York: Oxford University Press, 1996.

Fealy, Greg. "Islamic Politics: A Rising or Declining Force?". Paper presented at conference on Rethinking Indonesia, Melbourne, 4–5 March 2000.

Hefner, Robert W. "Islam and Nation in the Post-Soeharto Era". In *The Politics of Post-Soeharto Indonesia*, edited by Adam Schwarz and Jonathan Paris. New York: Council on Foreign Relations, 1999.

Lawrence, Bruce B. *Shattering the Myth: Islam beyond Violence.* Princeton: Princeton University Press, 1998.

Liddle, William and Saiful Mujani. "Islam, Kultur Politik, dan Demokrasi: Sebuah Telaah Komparatif Awal". Unpublished paper, 2000.

Salim, Arskal. "The Idea of Islamic State in Indonesia". Paper presented at the University of Wisconsin-Madison and Northern Illinois University Student Conference on Southeast Asia, DeKalb, Illinois, 3–4 March 2000.

———. "Shari'a in Indonesia's Current Transition: An Update". In *Shari'a and Politics in Modern Indonesia,* edited by Arskal Salim and Azyumardi Azra. Singapore: Institute of Southeast Asian Studies, 2003.

Taher, Tarmizi. *Aspiring for the Middle Path: Religious Harmony in Indonesia.* Jakarta: Center for the Study of Islam and Society (Censis), IAIN Jakarta, 1997.

Thaib, Lukman. *The Islamic Polity and Leadership.* Petaling Jaya, Malaysia: Delt Publishing, 1995.

9

THE EXPERIENCE OF THE ISLAMIC REPUBLIC OF IRAN

Gholamali Khoshroo

At the conceptual level, the universality of Islam and the plurality of nations seem irreconcilable. However, in practice one can find different ways and means to build bridges between the two. The main concern of this chapter is the compatibility of Islam and the nation-state, with particular attention given to the Iranian experience of an Islamic Republic.

The chapter is in two parts. The first part will focus on the significance of Islam and its relevance to politics, the notion of the nation-state and its role in international relations, and the ways in which Islam has coped with the concept of the nation-state. The second part will focus on the experience of the Islamic Republic of Iran, its doctrine of combining the sovereignty of God with that of humanity, and the issue of the independence of the nation-state *vis-à-vis* the unity of the Islamic world. For this purpose, particular attention will be paid to the Constitution of the Islamic Republic of Iran.

THE SIGNIFICANCE OF ISLAM IN WORLD POLITICS

Islam is a universal religion that invites humanity into the unity of God so that it can satisfy its material and spiritual needs.[1] Hence, the unity of God has wide philosophical, social, and political dimensions. Islam also places strong emphasis on the unity of believers and urges them to refrain from conflict and discord.[2] Communities of believers constitute the Islamic *ummah*, which has a meaning far beyond the definition of tribe, nation, or state. The unity of the Islamic *ummah*, per se, is a manifestation of society's belief in unity, whilst conflict and animosity are the natural result of following Satan. In fact, the invitation to "unity of God in belief, and the unity of believers in practice" can play an active political role in domestic as well as international affairs.[3]

From the Islamic perspective, religion and politics are not separate or independent arenas. According to one interpretation, politics is considered a part of religion, and religion completely overlaps politics. Even if one resists acceptance of such an interpretation, it is still hard to deny that Islam as a comprehensive religion provides a legitimate basis for politics.[4] A quick consideration of the political and social developments that have taken place in the Islamic world in the last fifty years shows that a kind of "back to basics movement" is building. This movement emerges at times in the form of a political philosophy or a political system, or even as a complete new model.[5]

As it is both the most recent and most active monotheistic religion, Islam plays a major role in the political and cultural arenas. About fifty-five Islamic countries with more than 1.2 billion people are forming a new identity with which to resist domineering Westernization and increasing modernization. This nascent Muslim identity is saving Islamic nations from being dissolved in the Westernization process, and it empowers them to take more active roles in world politics. Combined with Muslim unity, the universal calling, and the "back to basics" movements, it reflects the principles of political Islam and the engagement with power and politics. Such developments have been labelled as "fundamentalism" by some Western observers, and have been seen as threatening Western interests and creating a movement towards a clash of civilizations. However, I will introduce a new perspective that will allow a better understanding of such phenomena.

THE NATION-STATE

In comparison to Islam, which has been practised for more than fourteen centuries, nation-states are rather new. The concept of the nation-state gradually emerged in the West between the sixteenth and seventeenth centuries CE, not long after the collapse of the Holy Roman Empire. The nation-state, which is smaller than an Empire but bigger than a city-state, relies on an exclusive supremacy within defined borders. Thus, "territorial sovereignty" and the independence of the state *vis-à-vis* other states constitute the basic characteristics of the nation-state.

For the sake of our discussion, we can separate the notion of the nation from that of the state. The nation has three main components: people, territory, and sentiments. The state represents the will of the people, provides security and stability within its own boundaries, and protects the nation from external threats.

If the state reflects the exclusive right to the means of force and coercion, then the nation — comprising various individuals who share common values, culture, and history — legitimizes the very existence of the state and its claim to power. Historically, the gradual decline of the Church's political power in Europe contributed to the shift in the source of legitimacy from the Church to the people. A gradual transition took place, from the supremacy of religious authority to a secular concept of international relations, and this paved the way for the formation of nation-states and the rise of democratic legitimacy. The growth of nationalism and the expansion of citizens' rights became the main factors in consolidating the new nation-states.

Nationalism and the territorial state are rather new to the Muslim world, and both are products of colonization and decolonization in the nineteenth and twentieth centuries.[6] At the conceptual level, nationalism, as a distinctive form of political identity, runs counter to the Islamic ideal of the *ummah*, and is a source of controversy in Muslim countries. The notion of the *ummah* renders Islam the most genuine and unified political affiliation, and it supersedes national boundaries. Political practices and intellectual endeavours to resolve this profound contradiction between the *ummah* and the nation-state has divided the Muslim world into three main classes:[7] countries in which nationhood overshadows Islam and is the primary political identity (Turkey, Pahlavi Iran, and Tunisia); those in which the Islamic *ummah* is expected to supersede national identity; and those in which there is harmony between nationhood and the idea of the Islamic *ummah*.

STRIKING A BALANCE IN IRAN

The Islamic Republic of Iran supports the third approach, and seeks to strike a balance between the confines of the nation-state and the comprehensive calling of the Islamic *ummah*. Iran, in contrast to many Muslim countries, was not colonized, though at times it was heavily under the influence of

Western powers. The 1979 Islamic Revolution was directed against this influence, and at the same time reasserted Islamic ideals and the people's will. Accordingly, the Revolution's prime aim was independence, freedom, and establishing an Islamic republic.

Emphasizing independence, the Revolution heavily relied on Iranian history and identity. Moreover, it gave a pivotal role to the people. Freedom, as another pillar of the Revolution, aimed to liberate the people from suppression and domination in line with Islamic tenets and teachings. Therefore, the Islamic Revolution neither denied Iran's past, nor did it negate certain aspects of Western civilization, such as freedom and political participation.

Any negation of either the modern or the historical aspects of Iranian society will disturb this balance. Hence, President Khatami's policy of enhancing civil society and promoting civilizational dialogue, though a new emphasis, is consistent with the objectives of the Revolution. This approach represents the three basic dimensions of the system: being Iranian, remaining Islamic, and having a republic. In a very broad perspective, each of these dimensions belongs to a specific type of civilization (Iran, Islam, and the West), and in a balanced interaction between the dimensions lie the cultural and political foundations of Iranian society.

The process of globalization gained momentum in the twentieth century, and at the same time the ideological gap polarized the world. By the end of the century, despite diminishing ideological differences in the socialist and capitalist worlds, not only was the existing gap between the industrial and developing countries still apparent, but the political, military, technical, and communications imbalances had also steadily increased.[8] The idea of portraying deep-rooted and very ancient civilizations such as the Indian, Chinese, and Islamic cultures as a threat to Western civilization[9] forms a cover to disguise the existing structural imbalances. Such an approach, instead of using the end of ideological disputes as favourable ground for enhancing civilized relations between the West and the rest, tends to create new enemies for Western civilization.

The benefits of dialogue among civilizations are the critical appraisal of past hostile relations and the establishment of new relationships based on justice, objectivity, independence, wisdom, and moral codes. In this context, dialogue should not merely be confined to the relations between nations and civilizations: it should be rooted in their culture and reflect the way that civilizations look at themselves as well as others. If the idea of dialogue among civilizations is removed from the "game of power", then more peaceful and constructive relations will emerge.[10]

As already mentioned, the Islamic Republic of Iran is based on a combination of Islam, republicanism, and nationalism. Although these elements might seem to be incompatible, the Constitution of Iran achieves a workable balance by sensible mechanisms and a defined structure.

Creating a Balance between the Sovereignty of God and Human Sovereignty

According to the Islamic tenets that lay the foundation for Article 56 of the Constitution,[11] God has sovereignty over the world and humanity, but His sovereignty over the world is different from that which he has over humanity. In the former, God's sovereignty is immutable because the universe is without a will. In the latter, God's sovereignty includes the giving of will and reason to human beings. Consequently, humanity must understand and accept the duty of making its own social and political destiny according to its own acts, will, and reason.

On this basis, human beings are held accountable for their own actions because of their free will and ability to reason. This notion of sovereignty lays the foundation for the political system in Iran. In accordance with Article 56 of the Constitution:

> God Almighty has absolute sovereignty over the world and humanity, and He has made humanity the master of its own social destiny. No one can divest humanity of its divine right or apply it in the service of interests of a particular individual or group. The nation shall exercise this God-given right in a manner set forth in the following Articles.

At the same time, people's rights are secured through participation in national as well as local elections, such as those of parliament and the presidency. In Article 6, the Constitution stipulates the manner in which the people's sovereignty is recognized:

> In the Islamic Republic of Iran the Affairs of State shall be managed by relying on public opinion through elections, such as the election of a President, representatives of the Majlis-e-Shura-e Islami, members of councils and the like, or through referenda in cases set forth in other articles of this law.

Creating a Balance between Freedom and Independence

The freedom of individuals and the independence of the country are not always compatible. The Constitution attaches the utmost significance to these two freedoms, and safeguards them in a manner that neither can be used as a pretext for eliminating the other. Article 9 stipulates that:

> In the Islamic Republic of Iran, freedom, independence, unity and the territorial integrity of the country shall be inseparable from each other. It shall be the duty of the government and every single member of the nation to safeguard them. No individual, group or authority shall be allowed, on the pretext of enjoying freedom, to violate in any manner whatsoever the political, cultural, economic, and military independence and territorial integrity of Iran. No authority shall be allowed to violate legal freedoms and liberties on the pretext of safeguarding national independence and territorial integrity, even by enacting laws and regulations.

Combining the Unity of the *Ummah* with the Integrity of the Nation-State

The Islamic Republic of Iran, as an independent nation-state, seeks to strengthen the unity and friendship of all Muslim nations. This ideal is reflected in Article 11, which states that:

> According to the stipulation of the Qur'anic verse, *(verily, this your nation is one nation, and I am your Lord, so serve me)* all Muslims are one and the government of the Islamic Republic of Iran shall be under obligation to lay its general policy on the basis of the coalition and unity of Muslim nations and strive perpetually to achieve political, economic, and cultural unity of the Muslim world.

According to the Constitution, the territorial integrity of Iran does not contradict the support for the Muslim *ummah*. Article 152 stipulates that:

> The foreign policy of the Islamic Republic of Iran shall be based on the negation of exercising or accepting any form of domination whatsoever, safeguarding all-embracing independence and territorial integrity, defence of the rights of all Muslims, non-alignment with domineering powers, and peaceful and reciprocal relations with non-belligerent states.

Incorporating Islamic Ideals and the Necessities of Time and Place

The general principles of Islam are comprehensively reflected in the Qur'an and the Sunna (the teachings and behaviour of the prophet). Nevertheless, to deal with certain contemporary social and political issues, Shi'ism created a third source of deducing rules that are consistent with the Qur'an and the Sunna, that is, the *ijtihād*. Those scholars who are capable of making independent legal and religious judgements in accordance with new circumstances are designated as *mujtihid*.[12]

In the Constitution, the concept of historical context is considered vital in law making and leadership. The Council of Guardians, whose tasks are to examine the consistency of all legislation with Islamic ordinances and the Constitution, must be conscious of contemporary circumstances. Article 91 stipulates that:

> With a view to safeguarding the rules of Islam and the Constitution, and to see that the approvals of the Majlis are not inconsistent with them, a council known as the Council of Guardians shall be established composed of the following: Six Faqihs, just and acquainted with the needs of the time and the issues of the day. These individuals shall be appointed by the Leader. Six jurists, specialising in various branches of law, elected by the Majlis from among Muslim jurists proposed to the Majlis by the Head of the Judiciary.

In the Islamic Republic of Iran all laws must be consistent with Islam, but in the interpretation of Islam and in its application the needs and necessities of time and place must be carefully considered. When the Council of Guardians considers that a particular piece of legislation is inconsistent with Islam but the Parliament insists on it, the matter is referred to a higher body, not to study the consistency of the legislation with Islam, but rather to ascertain its necessity to the system. If its necessity is substantial, then a rule will be passed and the legislation will become law. Thus, Article 112 stipulates that:

> The Majma-e-Tashkhis-e-Nezam (Expediency Council) shall be convened at the order of the leader to determine such expedience in cases where the Council of Guardians finds an approval of the Majlis against the principles of Sharia or the Constitution, and the Majlis, in view of the expedience of the system, is unable to satisfy the Council of Guardians.

For example, the Foreign Investment Bill was passed by the parliament but has been rejected by the Council of Guardians for both inconsistency with Islam and the Constitution. However, the Parliament did not accept the modification of the Council of Guardians so the Bill was then considered in the Expediency Council. This council looked at it from different perspectives; it examined whether this Bill is a necessary step for Iranian economy and employment. It seems that Iran's joining the World Trade Organization (WTO) will be another legislative battle that eventually will be resolved by the Expediency Council.

In conclusion, the universality of Islam should be studied in light of the plurality in Islamic societies. The Islamic Republic of Iran, through striking a delicate balance among various elements, has sought to ensure the sovereignty of God and the sovereignty of humanity, the freedom of individuals, and the independence of the country in sympathy with the Islamic *ummah* and the integrity of the nation-state, as well as the ideals of Islam and the demands of time and place. From a sociological point of view, the Islamic Republic of Iran is facing a great challenge in the new millennium. That challenge is neither Islam nor democracy alone. It is in continuing to strike a balance between Islam and democracy. The extent to which that endeavour is successful will depend on the will of the people and the blessing of God.

Notes

1. Qur'an, *Surah Yusuf*, 40: "The command is for none but Allah, he has commanded that you worship none but Him; that is the straight [true] religion."
2. Qur'an, *Surah Al-Anbiya*, 92: "Truly this, your ummah is one ummah [religion] and I am your Lord, therefore worship me."
3. Qur'an, *Surah Al-Imran*, 103: "And hold fast, all of you together to the rope of Allah and not be divided among yourselves."
4. Qur'an, *Surah Al-Hadid*, 25: "Indeed we have sent our messengers with clear proofs, and revealed with them the Scripture and the Balance [Justice] that mankind may keep up justice."
5. James P. Piscatori, *Islam in a World of Nation-States* (Cambridge: Cambridge University Press, 1986), pp. 144–50.
6. John L. Esposito, *The Oxford History of Islam* (Oxford: Oxford University Press, 1999), pp. 650–56.
7. Piscatori, *Islam in a World of Nation-States*, pp. 77–81.
8. Ali A. Mazrui, *Cultural Forces in World Politics* (London: James Curry Ltd, 1990), pp. 1–10.
9. Samuel P. Huntington, *The Clash of Civilizations and the Remaking of World Order* (New York: Simon & Schuster 1996), pp. 40–55.
10. Mohammad Khatami, *Islam, Dialogue and Civil Society* (Canberra: The Australian National University, 2000), pp. 2–5.
11. The Constitution of the Islamic Republic of Iran.
12. Tabatabai, *Allmah Sayyid Muhammad Husayn Shi'a* (Qum, 1981).

References

Esposito, John L. *The Oxford History of Islam*. Oxford: Oxford University Press, 1999.

Huntington, Samuel P. *The Clash of Civilizations and the Remaking of the World Order.* New York: Simon & Schuster, 1996.
Khatami, Mohammad. *Islam, Dialogue and Civil Society.* Canberra Centre for Arab and Islamic Studies: The Australian National University, 2000.
Mazrui, Ali A. *Cultural Forces in World Politics.* London: James Curry Ltd, 1990.
Piscatori, James P. *Islam in a World of Nation-States.* Cambridge: Cambridge University Press, 1986.
Tabatabai. *Allmah Sayyid Muhammad Husayn Shi'a.* Qum, 1981.
The Constitution of the Islamic Republic of Iran.

Muslim Women

10

MUSLIM WOMEN AND HUMAN RIGHTS IN THE MIDDLE EAST AND SOUTH ASIA

Occupying Different Spaces

Samina Yasmeen[1]

Social movements are not new phenomena. Human beings have long organized themselves into non-hierarchical groups that bypass political structures to bring about desired change. In the early nineteenth century, a number of religious, feminist, nationalist, and class movements attempted to change the prevailing conditions and notions of social organization. This process gained momentum in the twentieth century, with the number and activities of such movements markedly increasing by the 1960s. Since then, the notion of social movements has gradually evolved. "New" or contemporary social movements are seen as distinct from political parties and interest groups. These movements are characterized by loose and often non-hierarchical networks of disparate individuals, groups, or organizations that focus on specific issues or activities. The process creates or modifies the "collective or shared identity" that aims at bringing about or opposing social change at a systemic or non-systemic level. By their very nature, these movements are oriented more towards civil society than the state, and they have an inherent suspicion of bureaucracies.[2] Nevertheless, they can still engage with state structures, and their influence can be local, national, regional, or international. There is little exclusivity in membership: being a member of one movement does not exclude participation in several other movements.

Globalization and easier communication across national boundaries have enabled social movements to proliferate. Such movements focus on many issues: for instance, women's rights, the rights of the child, the rights of indigenous people, environmental issues, and sustainable development. Membership changes with time, as does the significance that is attached to the "agenda of social change" by members. It is obvious that these movements have emerged as significant international actors: non-governmental organizations (NGOs) have been given observer status at a number of international forums, including the United Nations. Women in many countries actively participate in these movements. However, the question is whether Muslim women from the Middle East and South Asia are also participating in such movements or are silent observers. This chapter will answer that question with respect to the participation of Muslim women in human rights movements.

Participation in social movements can be seen in terms of recently developed understandings of citizenship. Like women across the globe, women in the Middle East and South Asia are gradually expanding their areas of operation beyond the family sphere. This process is paralleled by the emergence of a number of organizations that deal specifically with the rights of women. The language and approach that are used by these women can be understood in terms of a spectrum of ideas. At one end of the spectrum, women from these areas subscribe to secular ideas of human rights. They couch their arguments in terms of the evolving global regime of women's rights. At the other end of the spectrum are the views of feminists who think about the issue of women's rights in terms of Islamic teachings. They generally subscribe to absolutist interpretations of Islam that bring their views and language into conflict with secular points of view. Women who combine their Islamic and secular identities to various degrees occupy the middle of the spectrum. The multiplicity of these views will remain a reality for Middle Eastern and South Asian societies, which is a fact that needs to be accepted when looking at the role of Muslim women today.

The first part of this chapter deals with the socio-economic context in which Muslim women from the region are operating. The second part discusses the multiple views on women's rights in the region, and draws detailed examples from Pakistan.

MUSLIM WOMEN AND EXPANDING SPHERES OF CITIZENSHIP

The notion of citizenship has traditionally been approached from three different directions.[3] The legalistic approach has restricted the concept to a relationship between an individual and a state, which is generally viewed as finding expression in political acts that include voting in elections and membership in political organizations. The spatial approach to the concept identifies citizenship in terms of an individual's relationship with a multitude of spheres within a nation-state. T. H. Marshall first acknowledged this broader notion of citizenship in his seminal work *Citizenship and Social Class*, in which he categorized civil, political, social, and economic spheres. The third view of citizenship is expressed in terms of rights and duties. This notion is sometimes elevated to the status of a value: the knowledge of one's citizenship rights and the willingness to volunteer for activities, is viewed as the criteria for identifying a "good" or "competent" citizen. Thomas Janoski synthesized these approaches into a broader definition of citizenship as "passive and active membership of individuals in a nation-state with certain universalistic rights and obligations at a specified level of equality".[4] This notion of citizenship is closely connected to his concept of civil society with four interactive and overlapping components: "the state sphere, the private sphere, the market sphere and the public sphere".[5] In other words, citizenship can find expression in one or all of these interrelated spheres.

Janoski's integrated approach provides a useful starting point for assessing the relationship of different groups to the state and society of which they are a part. It also provides a context for understanding the nature of social movements. One could argue that these movements emerge when citizens cease to operate solely in the family sphere. Instead, they expand the area of their operation to include other spheres. In doing so they identify the causes of the processes and actors that hamper or impede their participation in various spheres of citizenship. They also prescribe solutions to these problems, and struggle to change the cultural notions of what is appropriate and inappropriate.

Women in the Middle East and South Asia live in cultures that are dominated by notions of patriarchy.[6] Men are identified as the head of their households. They are viewed and presented as the breadwinners of the family. In contrast, women are identified and presented as the nurturers. They bear children, raise families, and operate predominantly within the family sphere. Such clear identification of roles creates the possibility and reality of men acquiring the right or the ability to determine the nature of interaction between members of the family and society at large.

Such hierarchical structures notwithstanding, the data on women who live in these regions suggests that they have gradually expanded their spheres of operation beyond the family.[7] One of the major indicators of this change is the improvement in the rates of female literacy. Between 1985 and 1998, literacy rates increased for women over fifteen years of age in all of the countries of the region (Table 10.1). A similar trend was apparent among girls who were enrolled in primary and tertiary educational institutions (Table 10.2). Women in these countries also demonstrated an increase in the Economic Activity Rate (EAR). Between 1985 and 1999, for instance, the EAR increased by 29 per cent, 40 per cent, 60 per cent, and 26 per cent for women over fifteen years of age in Kuwait, Qatar, Jordan, and Pakistan respectively. Bangladesh was the only country where the rate declined (by 1 per cent) during the same period (Table 10.3).

Some variations existed in the nature and effects of increased activity by these women in the spheres of citizenship. Female adult literacy levels, for instance, were generally higher in the Middle East than in South Asia.[8] The same situation existed in terms of the average estimated income for women (Figure 10.1). However, as shown in Table 10.3, more South Asian women participated in the economic sphere than did their counterparts in the Middle East.

Given this participation beyond the family sphere, it is not surprising that women from the Middle East and South Asia have increasingly become active in social movements. They deal with and raise awareness about multiple issues, including environmental degradation, sustainable development, the need for democratization and reducing the risk of conflicts and wars. These women are also active participants in feminist movements. This is primarily a result of the increasing awareness of the implicit and explicit disparity in the socio-economic status of women in these countries. Women are still less educated in these countries than are men (Table 10.4). The proportion of women who participate in the economic sphere is also considerably less than that of men.[9] This inequality is apparent in the extremely low percentage of women who are employed as administrators, managers, professionals, and technical workers. It is also obvious in the level of political participation by women (Table 10.5).

Against the backdrop of this inequality, the number of groups and organizations that deal with the question of women's rights has multiplied. South Asia and the Middle East are providing fertile ground for active and vibrant women's movements.[10] This phenomenon, it is important to

TABLE 10.1
Increase in the Female Literacy Rate (1985–98)

Country	Rate (%) 1998	Index (1985 = 100) 1998
Bahrain	81.2	122
Bangladesh	28.6	143
Egypt	41.8	143
Iran	67.4	143
Iraq	43.2	159
Jordan	82.6	130
Kuwait	78.5	117
Lebanon	79.1	116
Oman	57.5	217
Pakistan	28.9	168
Qatar	81.7	114
Saudi Arabia	64.4	155
Turkey	75	123
UAE	77.1	118
Yemen	22.7	266

Source: United Nations Development Program, *Human Development Report 2000* (New York: United Nations, 2000).

TABLE 10.2
Increase in Primary School and Tertiary Level Enrolment: 1985 as Index Year

	Primary School Enrolment	Tertiary Level Enrolment		
Country	1997 (%)	Indexed Increase (1997)	1997 per 100,000 women	Indexed Increase 1994–97
Bahrain	98.8	99	1,975	135
Bangladesh	69.6	149	129	71
Egypt	90.6	122	1,467	141
Iran	89.2	120	1,311	533
Iraq	69.6	80		
Jordan	N.A.	N.A.	N.A.	N.A.
Kuwait	64		2,214	129
Lebanon	74.9	99	2,604	N.A.
Oman	66.7	105	662	1,226
Pakistan	N.A.	N.A.	220	153
Qatar	84.5	88	3,278	116
Saudi Arabia	58	137	1,529	190
Turkey	98.1	101	1,636	263
UAE	81.3	103	1,722	200
Yemen	N.A.	N.A.	105	N.A.

Source: United Nations Development Program, *Human Development Report 2000* (New York: United Nations, 2000).

TABLE 10.3
Increase in Female Economic Activity Rate as a Percentage of the Male Economic Activity Rate (1985–99): Women Over 15 Years of Age

Country	Rate (%) 1999	Index (100 = 1985) 1999	As % of Male Rate (1999)
Bahrain	32.1	135	37
Bangladesh	65.8	99	76
Egypt	34.5	118	44
Iran	28.3	136	36
Iraq	N.A.	N.A.	N.A.
Jordan	25.8	160	33
Kuwait	40.7	129	52
Lebanon	29.1	132	38
Oman	18.6	175	24
Pakistan	35	126	41
Qatar	35.9	140	40
Saudi Arabia	20.7	166	26
Turkey	49.3	111	60
UAE	32	129	37
Yemen	30.1	108	36

Source: United Nations Development Program, *Human Development Report 2000* (New York: United Nations, 2000), pp. 210–13.

FIGURE 10.1
Estimated Earned Income PPP
(in US$)

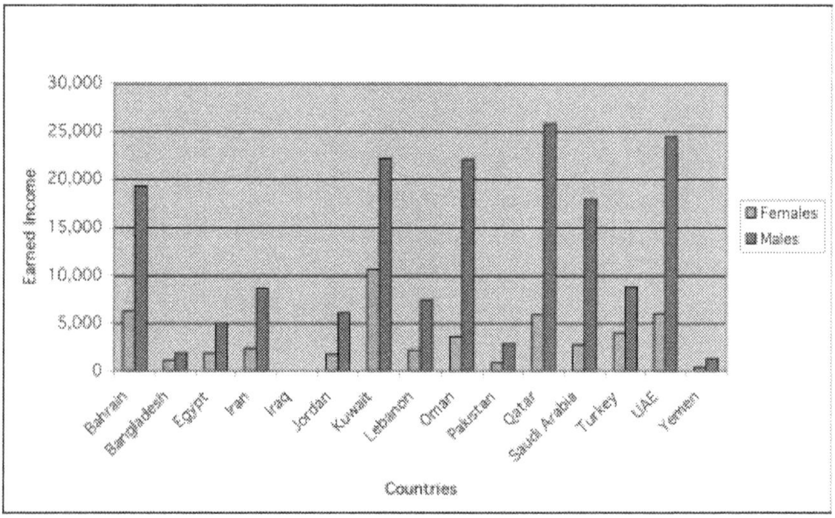

Source: United Nations Development Program, *Human Development Report 2001* (New York: United Nations, 2001), pp. 210–13.

TABLE 10.4
Gender-based Adult Literacy Rates, 15 Years and Above: 1999

Country	Females	Males
Bahrain	82.2	90.5
Bangladesh	29.3	51.7
Egypt	42.8	66.1
Iran	68.7	82.7
Jordan	83.4	94.5
Kuwait	79.4	84
Lebanon	79.8	91.8
Oman	59.6	79.1
Pakistan	30	58.9
Qatar	82.6	80.1
Saudi Arabia	65.9	83.5
Turkey	75.9	93.2
UAE	78	73.8
Yemen	23.9	66.6

Source: United Nations Development Program, *Human Development Report 2001* (New York: United Nations, 2001), pp. 210–13.

TABLE 10.5
Gender Empowerment Measures as a Percentage of the Total for the Latest Available Year

Country	Seats in Parliament	Female Legislators, Senior Officials and Managers	Female Professional and Technical Workers
Bahrain	—	9	20
Bangladesh	9.1	5	35
Egypt	2.4	11	29
Iran	3.4	—	—
Jordan	2.5	—	—
Kuwait	0	—	—
Lebanon	2.3	—	—
Oman	—	—	—
Pakistan	—	8	25
Qatar	—	—	—
Saudi Arabia	—	—	—
Turkey	4.2	9	36
UAE	0	—	—
Yemen	0.7	—	—

Source: United Nations Development Program, *Human Development Report 2001* (New York: United Nations, 2001), pp. 214–17.

emphasize, is not new. The history of feminism in these countries dates back to the early twentieth century. However, the intensity with which the issue is being addressed today indicates that Muslim women in the region are becoming active agents of change in their respective societies. The question that arises is whether the participants in these movements approach the issue of women's rights from similar perspectives.

FEMINIST MOVEMENTS: DIVERSITY AMIDST UNITY

Social movements, by their very nature, lend themselves to pluralism.[11] They are also influenced by a combination of socio-economic, political, and ideological factors. For instance, the socio-economic status of the members and the conditions that pertain in a specific locality, often determines the manner in which members of a movement approach an issue. The prevalence or absence of democracy as well as other political alignments, and the flow of ideas at regional or global levels can also influence the process. While all members of a social movement may accept the need for changing or avoiding a condition, they may disagree on the causes of and solutions to the problem. Hence, the language that is used to address a particular problem or issue can vary. This can cause divisions or plurality in any social movement. Such has been the case in the feminist movements of the Middle East and South Asia. They differ among themselves in terms of the diagnosis, prescription, and practical responses to prevailing gender-based discrimination. This diversity is heightened by the predominant role that is played by Islam in these societies.

Over a number of centuries, the teachings of Islam have interacted with and influenced local cultures in Middle Eastern and South Asian societies. It is often difficult to distinguish between religious and cultural practices, many of which are justified in the name of Islam.[12] At the same time, some Islamic teachings transmute into what could be identified as "un-Islamic" practices.[13] In the contemporary world, this phenomenon is further influenced by Islamic revivalism. Against the background of a lack of democratization, difficult socio-economic conditions, and perceptions of anti-Islamic bias in the West, Islam has slowly moved to the centre of political and cultural debates. However, there is a diversity of opinion between those who subscribe to absolutist interpretations of Islam and those who argue for restricting the religion to the private domain. Feminist movements in the Middle East and South Asia operate against the background of this division, and are also being influenced by it. They differ among themselves in explaining the causes of and solutions to the problem of gender-based discrimination. This plurality can be best understood in terms of spaces that are occupied by different groups and organizations along a spectrum ranging from secularism to Islamic modernism and then to Islamic traditionalism.

At the secular end of the spectrum, feminist organizations and groups subscribe to universal notions of human rights. They posit that all human beings are born with certain inalienable rights, including the right to life and rights to social, economic, political, and psychological well-being.[14] As in other parts of the world, they argue, women who live in the Middle East and South Asia do not enjoy these rights to the fullest. Instead, in line with arguments that are presented by feminists across the globe, they explain the prevalence of gender-based discrimination in terms of patriarchy. Cultural norms, that place men above women in all spheres of life, create conditions in which women cannot realize their human rights. This process, in their opinion, starts with the birth of the girl-child, who is always treated as less significant than a boy-child and denied equal access to family resources. A girl-child has less access to food than do her male siblings. Her access to education is also compromised in favour of boys. These structural barriers ultimately create a situation that limits women's access to the economic sphere. In fact, through the emphasis of their role as nurturers and the restriction of their areas of operation to the family sphere, women are actively prevented from participating in the economic sphere. Even when women do enter the economic sphere and participate in the marketplace, social and structural barriers prevent them from achieving positions of leadership. Effectively, women are reduced to a position of relative inferiority in these societies, and are denied their human rights.

The secular prescriptions to change this situation centre round altering the cultural and socio-economic context in which Muslim women operate in Middle Eastern and South Asian states.[15] This, in turn, requires an acceptance and acknowledgement of the universality of human rights. Individual human beings, irrespective of their gender, race, and religion, are placed at the centre of this approach. Within the context of this broader picture, secular feminists argue that the existence of gender-based discrimination in various spheres of citizenship needs to be identified, acknowledged, and targeted. The ultimate aim of the process is to acknowledge that "women's rights are human rights" and create conditions in which these rights can be realized. The process, therefore, involves both *awareness raising* and *action-oriented* approaches.

In line with this prescription, secular feminists have focused on micro-level issues including the rights of the girl-child to education, access to the workplace, family planning, women's health, domestic violence, child custody, honour killings, sexual harassment in the workplace, the trafficking of women, and a host of laws that discriminate against women.[16] At another level, they have also targeted macro-level issues, including the right of women to political participation in its diverse forms. Women for Women's Human Rights (WWHR) in Turkey, Women's Action Forum in Pakistan, and the Revolutionary Association of the Women of Afghanistan (RAWA) are examples of organizations that deal with such issues. WWHR, for instance, has developed a training programme on "Women's Human Rights and Legal Literacy which aims to provide women and women's organizations at local levels with tools and strategies to confront structures of inequality and the effects of marginalization".[17] Similarly, the Women's Action Forum (WAF) campaign for the reservation of a certain proportion of parliamentary seats for women.[18] To this end they have organized seminars, and meetings, and conducted dialogue with members of various political groups. RAWA has dealt with a significantly different situation. Operating through the twenty years of destruction that were caused by the Soviet occupation of Afghanistan, the subsequent civil war and Taliban rule, its members have incessantly raised questions of women's rights. The organization has opposed Islamic fundamentalist tendencies, and argued for democracy and secularism. Its bilingual magazine *Payam-e-Zan* (Women's Message) is published to convey these ideas which are at the forefront of demands for women's rights to the newly established interim administration in Afghanistan.[19]

While raising issues and taking practical steps towards working for women's rights, secular feminists have not always engaged state structures. There is a rich tradition of these organizations working independently of state structures by raising funds locally. As the international regime of women's rights has evolved, these groups and organizations have also enlisted the help of willing foreign donors to undertake a number of projects for women. However, there are also examples of secular movements that have received patronage from state structures. In some cases, this has occurred due to the personal commitment of influential leaders to women's rights. In other instances, the international agenda has paved the way for the co-operation of these organizations with state structures. The Beijing Conference, for example, enabled secular feminists to work closely with the Pakistani Government. Later on, the military government, led by General Musharraf, established a National Commission for Pakistani women in September 2000, which identified the eradication of violence against women as one of its first tasks. A number of secular feminists supported the idea of the commission.[20] At the micro level, women's groups have worked with law enforcement agencies to improve the condition of Women's Police Stations in Pakistan.[21]

However, the adherence of secular feminists to liberal ideas as well as their links to foreign donors has sometimes pitted them against state structures. Such a conflict surfaced in Pakistan during 1998 and 1999 when the Nawaz Sharif regime tried to take control of local NGOs. It specifically targeted known secular feminists in the country and raised questions about their alliances with external actors. This occurred against the background of the Pakistani Government's push for the fifteenth amendment to the Constitution, which would have given it the autocratic right to revise any law in the name of Islam. The Women's Action Forum reacted to this situation by withdrawing from the committee that was set up by the government to implement the Beijing Plan of Action.[22] The issue of honour killings created a similar conflict between Pakistani legislators and secular feminists. After the murder of a young woman named Samia Sarwar in March 1999, these groups pressed for legislation to outlaw honour killings, but failed to receive support from parliamentarians.[23] They then argued that the male-dominated legislature was unsympathetic to the plight of women.[24] Such conflicts have also occurred during relatively "liberal" regimes that have not always been willing to work for the rights of women. In her two terms as Prime Minister, for instance, Benazir Bhutto did little to advance either formal or substantive equality for Pakistani women.

The relationship between secular feminists and culture also presents a mixed picture. In different ways, feminist movements have targeted the cultural practices and social norms that are present in the Muslim societies of the Middle East and South Asia. Feminists in Kuwait, for instance, have attempted to change cultural and political norms while mainly operating within a space that is provided by those norms. This was apparent in 1992 when the Kuwait Democratic Forum (KDF) took up the issue of women's right to vote. Generally, between sixty and seventy women attended these meetings at the headquarters. Instead of insisting on being present in the same room as male members, these women watched the proceedings at the headquarters on a closed circuit television network. It was only later that they claimed their right to participate in the discussions when seated in the public space.[25] In contrast, some Turkish feminists maintained that their right to substantive equality encompassed sexual equality. Hence, the feminist monthly *Pazartesi* regularly published a column in which women discussed their sexual fantasies and illicit relationships. However, such disclosures were viewed as promoting pornography, for which the journal was sued.[26] In Egypt, Nawal El-Saadawi, who founded of the Arab Women's Solidarity Association, is also known for targeting cultural practices through hard-hitting literature.[27] Such variations notwithstanding, the fact remains that secular feminists have introduced a new language of resistance and change in Middle Eastern and South Asian societies. In the process they have established networks and alliances with groups across the world that share their ideas.

At the opposite end of the spectrum, Muslim feminists contest the ideas of their secular counterparts.[28] They acknowledge that human beings are born with inalienable rights, but maintain that these rights are already enshrined in Islamic teachings. That the rights of women are often compromised in Middle Eastern and South Asian societies is also accepted. However, the root causes of this denial are traced back to the failure of Muslims to establish truly Islamic states. This, in turn, is linked to a combination of domestic and international factors. In a terminology that is reminiscent of neo-Marxist analysis[29] some Islamic feminists argue that rulers of Muslim states are caught in exploitative but mutually self-serving relationships with non-Muslim Western states. Undemocratic and authoritarian regimes survive due to the direct and indirect support of the West. While living lives of luxury, these rulers fail to deliver economic benefits to ordinary citizens. Working within the phenomenon of globalization, they also fail to protect the cultural norms of their respective societies. Consequently, the Islamic ethos of these societies has been gradually eroded. This has deeply affected the family unit which, according to Islamic teachings, forms the basis of human existence. Hence, the process has resulted in conditions under which the rights of *both* Muslim men and women are being compromised.

The prescriptions of Islamic feminists centre around changing both the politics and the existing cultures of these societies. At the macro level, this includes supporting and working for the idea of establishing truly Islamic states. Although differences exist between Islamic feminists about the exact nature of such states, they are seen as providing the conditions in which the rights of all human beings will be protected. At the micro level, such prescriptions include acknowledging the salience of the family unit. The family is portrayed by Islamic feminists as the "fundamental unit of society", in which the rights and duties of all members are clearly spelt out.[30] The rights of women, like those of men, are not defined in terms of the rights of individuals. Instead, their rights are seen as complementary to those of men. This notion of complementary interests leads Islamic feminists to argue that the home provides the main sphere of operation for women.[31] As nurturers, women must take care of their families and bring up their children, who will contribute to society as good citizens. They must also accept that men are "responsible for the running of the affairs of the family".[32] Such an acceptance of gender-specific roles carries the promise of women realizing the rights that are granted to them by Islam. It also questions the laws that are enshrined in Islamic teachings yet run counter to women's rights.

The emphasis on the centrality of the family unit and gender-specific roles determines the parameters within which Muslim women must operate. According to the Islamic feminists who occupy the traditional end of the spectrum, women are not restricted to the family sphere, but the nature of their activity outside of that sphere must be determined by their role as nurturers in society. They can participate in the market sphere, but must focus on certain professions to the exclusion of others. The teaching and medical professions, for instance, are considered suitable for women. However, a difference of opinion exists with reference to the political sphere. While some Islamic feminists have supported the notion of active political participation, others have presented it as an area that is best left to the men in their respective societies. Still others have subscribed to the idea of participating both directly and indirectly in supporting male family members who are engaged in the struggle to change political structures locally and globally.[33] In some extreme cases, this position also includes the idea of women participating in such activities.

Against the background of these diagnostic and prescriptive frames, Islamic feminists in the Middle East and South Asia have used the language of religion to bring about change in their respective societies.[34] The women's group in the Jamaat-I-Islami of Pakistan, for instance, has been actively promoting an Islamic model of education for girls. A number of professional women (including lawyers, doctors, and academics) have also been articulating their views about the rights and duties of Muslim women. In this context, they acknowledge the pressing need to combat sexual harassment in the workplace.[35] A similar phenomenon is present in Egypt, where professional Islamic feminists have tried to emphasize the need to follow Islamic teachings. They have advocated the right of women to political participation. For instance, in 2000 Jihan El-Halafawi, an Islamic feminist, decided to run for parliamentary election as a member of the Muslim Brotherhood.[36] In Iran, such feminists form part of a vibrant women's movement. They regularly identify areas of discrimination against women and work for its elimination on Islamic grounds. They have successfully argued against the practice of temporary and early marriages, and against child custody laws as well as punishment by stoning.[37]

The support of Islamic feminists' for selective participation in all spheres of citizenship has been paralleled by an emphasis on following the traditional Islamic dress code. Wearing the *hijab* stands out in this context.[38] Islamic feminists who subscribe to orthodox and traditional interpretations of the

Qur'an and the Sunna argue that Muslim women are required to cover their heads. Others even present a case for covering the face. These formal expressions of an Islamic identity are supposed to guarantee that women can freely operate in the public sphere. This is also presented as a practical manifestation and guarantor of equality between men and women. Such claims stand in marked contrast to the emphasis on the element of choice by secular feminists.

The extreme contrasts between secular and Islamic feminists do not represent the totality of women's participation in social movements in Islamic Middle East and South Asia. In fact, the space between these two extremes is occupied by women who try to negotiate between their Islamic identity and the reality of living in a globalized era.[39] To some extent, this mediation reflects the relative importance that different women's groups assign to religion in their overall view of the world, but it also grows out of the relative freedom that is associated with the middle space. By avoiding close identification with either extreme, Muslim women acquire a flexibility that enables them to explore new ways of promoting women's rights, which makes the middle space a vibrant and diverse place.

In some regions, Islamic identity provides the starting point for defining this middle space. In others, liberal notions of human rights guide the ways in which Islamic identity is adapted to present conditions. An example is the Al-Huda movement in Pakistan, which started in the early 1990s when Dr Farhat Hashmi began to give lectures on Islam at the official residence of Pakistan's President, Farooq Leghari. She also gave *dars* (religious lectures) in the houses of women from the élite class in Islamabad. Later she established the Al-Huda academy in Islamabad for women from the élite classes to learn about Qur'anic *tafsir* (detailed interpretation of the Holy Qur'an). Once the enrolment increased, Dr Hashmi also started giving lectures in five-star hotels of the two other major cities of Pakistan, Lahore, and Karachi. This resulted in the formal establishment of an Al-Huda centre in Lahore.[40]

Al-Huda women now formally enrol in a teaching programme that relies heavily on the writings of Maulana Mawdudi of the Jamaat-I-Islami, who subscribes to a traditional-orthodox interpretation of Islam.[41] However, an emphasis on their relevance to the modern world makes these teachings meaningful to women from the élite classes. Most of these women have been previously exposed to Western liberal thinking with little knowledge of Islam. Hence, they willingly "convert" to an ideology that draws upon the ideas of Islamic feminists but is also sensitive to the needs of the "modern woman". Once they graduate from the academy, these women are encouraged to spread the word by establishing study circles where they can give *dars*. These chain programmes are now creating a group of educated, often professional women from the élite class who operate freely in the market, state, and social spheres. They do not necessarily adhere to the traditional Islamic dress code, but they do place more emphasis on their Islamic identity than was the case in the past. They are effectively occupying the Islamic end of the middle space.

Other examples of the mediation between Islamic and secular identities exist across the Islamic world. Within Pakistan, for instance, some women have organized groups that address the issue of family planning, using international regimes of population control as starting points. They call attention to the danger that is posed to women's health by multiple pregnancies and the developmental costs for Pakistan from unrestricted population growth.[42] However, instead of presenting these ideas in Western liberal terms, they draw on a combination of Islamic ideas and economic necessities to explain the need for family planning to women from rural and urban areas.[43]

The creative mix of secular and Islamic feminism is also present in Saudi Arabia, where women have sought a role in the public space. The decision of some Saudi women to drive cars in November 1990 constituted part of this attempt. Their actions directly challenged the idea that women were not allowed to enter the public space unaccompanied. They were suspended from their jobs, but the push for a greater role for women in the public space has not halted. Women are actively participating in the market sphere. Instead of insisting on complete visibility, they are using intermediaries or *mahram* to conduct negotiations on their behalf. In Jeddah and Riyadh alone, more than 6,000 commercial licences have been granted to women who, despite being invisible, are now participating in the public sphere.[44] These actions, it can be argued, constitute a social movement that aims slowly to increase the space that is available for women. A similar strand of feminism can be found in Iran, where women are increasingly subscribing to liberal-Islamic ideas that distinguish between the sacred texts and the science of religion. While the texts are considered immutable, their interpretation is not. Such a dynamic view of religion enables liberal Islamists to argue for policies and ideas that take into account the changed realities of the modern world. It also enables them to question the state's right to legislate in all spheres of human activity.[45] Reflecting these ideas, Iranian feminists such as Samira Makhmalbaf are using the print media and cinema as a means of resistance and a vehicle for changing the existing cultural and social norms. Her movie *The Apple* is a case in point, in which she portrays the plight of two young girls who are kept locked up by their father for fear of their purity being spoilt.[46]

The creative combination of Islamic and secular identities has, on occasion, attracted secular feminists to the middle space as well. They have established networks that acknowledge the diversity of the Muslim world and, at the same time, work to "increase the autonomy of women affected by Muslim laws by encouraging them to reflect, analyse, and reformulate the identity imposed on them through the application of Muslim laws".[47] In Pakistan, for instance, a young woman, Saima Waheed, married a man of her choice. Her father registered a case against her on grounds that the marriage had taken place without the consent of the *wali*, the head of the household. Secular feminists contested the case on behalf of the young woman, and used examples from Islamic history to support their position that women are allowed to choose their spouses.[48]

The vibrancy of the middle space notwithstanding, the fact remains that its members predominantly come from the élite upper and upper-middle classes. However, increased access to education and the market sphere is also creating opportunities for women from lower economic classes. Some of these women are beginning to participate in or initiate projects that directly deal with the welfare of women who belong to non-élite classes. Nevertheless, these groups, are in minority and receive little publicity.

CONCLUDING REMARKS

During the last decade, Islam's role in the international system has come under increasing scrutiny. A number of analysts are investigating the implications of Islamic revivalism for the global balance of power. Others are focusing on the manner in which Islam influences or determines the evolving international regimes that deal with a variety of issues. The relationship between Islam and human rights, and specifically the rights of women, falls into this category of analysis. There is a great diversity of approaches to the issue of women's rights in the Middle East and South Asia. This plurality can be understood in terms of a spectrum of ideas in which secular and Islamic feminism occupy the extreme ends. Women who mediate their Islamic and secular identities to find new ways for protecting women's human rights occupy the middle space. Contrary to widespread misconception, women in this space use Islamic revivalism to their advantage instead of being repressed. Hence, the middle space has become more vibrant than the two extremes, which has prompted some secular groups to occasionally move into the space to fight for women's rights. Those at the Islamic traditionalist end of the spectrum have also used the middle space to communicate their messages of socio-cultural change.

This middle space needs attention from local and international donors who are interested in bringing about a change in the status of women. The relative creativity with which the groups therein address the issue of women's rights should be encouraged and supported. Their sheer diversity improves the chances of achieving substantial improvements in the status of women's rights, but they need support as agents of change who stand for moderation instead of extremism in any form. In a world where fundamentalisms have created division, the need for such moderation can hardly be overemphasized.

Notes

1. The author thanks Begum Sarfraz Iqbal and James Trevelyan for their suggestions and comments. Many thanks are also due to Kate Croker, Erum Burki, Begum Khurram Burki, and Kabilan Krishnasamy for their help with finding relevant information.
2. Kate Nash, *Contemporary Political Sociology: Globalisation, Politics and Power* (London: Blackwell Publishers, 2000), pp. 100–105.
3. For different interpretations of citizenship, see T. K. Oommen, *Citizenship, Nationality and Ethnicity: Reconciling Competing Identities* (London: Polity Press, 1997); Ronald Beiner, *Theorizing Citizenship* (New York: State University of New York Press, 1995); and David Prior, John Stewart, and Kieron Walsh, *Citizenship-Rights, Community and Participation* (London: Pitman Publishing, 1995).
4. Thomas Janoski, *Citizenship and Civil Society: A Framework of Rights and Obligations in Liberal, Traditional and Social Democratic Regimes* (Cambridge: Cambridge University Press, 1998), p. 9.
5. Ibid., pp. 12–13.
6. Farhad Kazemi, "Gender, Islam and Politics", *Social Research* 67, no. 2 (Summer 2000): 453–74.
7. See, for example, Valentine Moghadam, *Women, Work, and Economic Reform in the Middle East and North Africa* (Boulder, CO: Lynne Rienner, 1998).
8. See Table 10.1.
9. See Table 10.3.
10. Elizabeth Fernea, "The Challenges For Middle Eastern Women in the 21st Century", *Middle East Journal* 54, no. 2 (Spring 2000): 187–88.
11. These ideas reflect the discussion of "frames" that was developed by David Snow. See Kate Nash, *Contemporary Political Sociology*, pp. 124–27.
12. See, for instance, Azizah Al-Hibri, "Reviving Human Rights in the Muslim World", *Harvard International Review* 20, no. 3 (1998): 50–53.
13. See, for example, Lisa Beyer, "The Women of Islam", *Time*, 25 November 2001, pp. 50–55.

14. See, for instance, Nasreen Azhar, "Human Rights: A Women's Perspective", in *Unveiling the Issues: Pakistani Women's Perspectives on Social, Political and Ideological Issues*, edited by Nighat Saeed Khan and Apiya Shehrbano Zia (Lahore: ASR Publications, 1995).
15. For instance, *Auratun key Haqooq* [Women's Rights] (Lahore: Democratic Commission for Human Development, n.d.).
16. Ain o Salish Kendro (ASK) in Bangladesh provides free legal aid, mediation and counselling services, and monitors and documents campaigns on human rights and women's rights issues. See the South Asian Women's NETwork website, <http://www.umiacs.umd.edu/users/sawweb/sawnet>. Similarly, the Islamabad Women's Welfare Agency (IWWA) works in the areas of legal assistance, psychological counselling, awareness raising, research and publications, health, education and human resource development. A larger organization, Association Against Sexual Harassment (AASHA), focuses on sexual harassment in the workplace. See also, Nazish Brohi, *Summary Report on Harassment of Women at the Workplace* (Karachi: Working Women's Support Center, December 2000).
17. See Women for Women's Human Rights (WWHR), <http://www.undp.uz/GID/eng/TURKEY/NGO/wwhr_tr.html>.
18. Personal interviews with members of WAF in 1997; see also, "WAF for Restoration of Women's Seats", *The News*, 23 January 1994; and "WAF Demands Equal Rights for Women", *The News*, 21 April 1998.
19. See the website of RAWA, which was established in 1977 as an independent political/social organization. RAWA stands for a "separation of religious and political processes in Afghanistan". It argues that "only a secular government can prevent the religion of Islam from being used as a retrogressive tool in the hands of fanatics". <http://rawa.fancymarketing.net/index.html>.
20. Susannah Price, "Boost for Pakistan's Women", *BBC News Online*, 2 September 2000.
21. See, for example, Talath Naqvi, "Wanted Charity for Women's Police Stations", *The News*, 1 February 2000.
22. "WAF Withdraws from Body on Beijing Plan", *Dawn*, 22 January 1998.
23. Aziz Siddiqui, "A Vote for the 'Honour' Killers", *Dawn*, 8 August 1999. See also Asma Jahangir and Hina Jilani, *Lawyer to Lawyer Network*, May 1999, <http://www.lchr.org/121/pakistan0599.htm>.
24. The military regime that is led by General Musharraf declared honour killings as murder that is punishable under the law: *Dawn*, 22 April 2000.
25. Mary Ann Tetreault, "Civil Society in Kuwait: Protected Spaces and Women's Rights", *Middle East Journal* 47, no. 2 (Spring 1993): 285–86.
26. Yesim Arat, "From Emancipation to Liberation: The Changing Role of Women in Turkey's Public Realm", *Journal of International Affairs* 54, no. 1 (Fall 2000): 117.

27. The Associated Press, "Egyptian feminist opens women's conference", <http://www.cnn.com>, 3 January 2002.
28. For a general discussion on the views and actions of Islamic feminists, see Fernea, "The Challenges For Middle Eastern Women", pp. 185–93.
29. Interestingly, the Islamists do not acknowledge this similarity. See, for example, Mohammad Atta ullah Siddiqui, "Taraqqi pasand Islam ya Islam pasand taraqqi" [Progressive Islam or Islamic Progress?] *Khawateen*, January 2002, pp. 28–29.
30. See, for instance, the text of a speech that was made by Fatemeh Hashemi, World Congress of Families II, Geneva, 14–17 November 1999, <http://www.worldcongress.org/gen99-speakers/gen99_hashemi.htm>.
31. See, for example, Fakar-ul-Islam, "Islam mein Khawateen key Siasi Haqooq" [Political Rights of Women in Islam], translation of an article by Barabara Stowesser, *Aaeen* (Urdu weekly), December 2001, pp. 20–23.
32. See, for instance, "Women in Islam: Rights and Obligations, Jamaat-i-Islami", <http://www.jamaat.org/Islam/WomaRights.html>.
33. See, for example, Bashirul-Haq, "Naiki" [Good deeds], *Nabat-e-Aisha*, September/October 2001, pp. 127–28.
34. The language that is used by these feminists is similar to that which is used by Islamic feminists in Sudan. See Sondra Hale, "Gender, Religious Identity and Political Mobilization in Sudan", in *Identity Politics and Women: Cultural Reassertions and Feminism in International Perspective*, edited by Valentine Moghadam (Colorado: Westview Press, 1994).
35. Jamaat-I-Islami Pakistan, <http://www.jamaat.org/qa/gender.html>.
36. "Muslim Brotherhood Put Forth a New Image", 24 September 2000, <http://arabia.com/egypt/article>.
37. Robin Wright, "Iran's New Revolution", *Foreign Affairs* 79, no. 1 (January/February 2000): 133–45.
38. Jamaat-I-Islami Pakistan, <http://www.jamaat.org/qa/gender.html>; see also "Aurutun key leaye ziadah bareek libas ki mumaniat" [Prohibition Against Women Wearing Sheer Dresses], *Aaeen*, December 2001, p. 5; and Saif Ulah Rabbani, *Hijab ki Barakat: Noe Muslim Khawateen key Mushahedaat* [The Value of *Hijab*: Observations of Converted Muslim Women] (Lahore: Adara-e-Mutbuaat-e-Khawateen, 2000).
39. This trend is not limited to the Middle East and South Asia. Muslim immigrant women who live in liberal democracies also belong to this group. See, for instance, Azizah Al-Hibri, "Reviving Human Rights", pp. 50–53.
40. Personal interviews with women who had participated in Al-Huda's programmes or had attended the *dars* of Dr Farhat Hashmi, January 2001.
41. Al-Huda International, *Prospectus* (Lahore: Institute of Islamic Education for Women, n.d.).
42. Personal interview with a woman who was actively involved in promoting family planning practices in villages around Islamabad, January 2001.

43. Interestingly, some Islamic clergy have also portrayed family planning as Islamic in nature. See, for example, "Jordan's Clergy Say Family Planning Not Anti-Islamic", <http://www.unfpa.org/news/atwork/thaislam.htm>.
44. Ambika Patni, "Behind the Veil", *Harvard International Review* 21, no. 1 (Winter 1998–99): 15–16; see also, "Putting Saudi Women to Work", *The Economist* 26 (September 1998): 48.
45. See, for example, Robin Wright, "Iran's New Revolution", *Foreign Affairs* 79, no. 1, (January/February 2000), pp. 133–45.
46. Ibid., pp. 139–42.
47. A major example of such a network is Women Living Under Muslim Laws, the membership of which is drawn from more than eighteen countries.
48. The Lahore High Court handed down a ruling in 1999 that upheld a woman's right to marry freely, but called for amendments to the family laws on the basis of Islamic norms to enforce the parental authority to discourage "love marriages". *Women of Pakistan: Struggling Against Violence Diary 2002.*

References

Aaeen. "Aurutun key leaye ziadah bareek libas ki mumaniat" [Prohibition Against Women Wearing Sheer Dresses]. December 2001, p. 5.

Al-Hibri, Azizah. "Reviving Human Rights in the Muslim World". *Harvard International Review* 20, no. 3 (1998): 50–53.

Al-Huda International. *Prospectus*. Lahore: Institute of Islamic Education for Women, n.d.

Arat, Yesim. "From Emancipation to Liberation: The Changing Role of Women in Turkey's Public Realm". *Journal of International Affairs 54*, no. 1 (Fall 2000): 107–23.

Associated Press (The). "Egyptian Feminist Opens Women's Conference". <http://www.cnn.com>, 3 January 2002.

Azhar, Nasreen. "Human Rights: A Women's Perspective". In *Unveiling the Issues: Pakistani Women's Perspectives on Social, Political and Ideological Issues*, edited by Nighat Saeed Khan and Apiya Shehrbano Zia. Lahore: ASR Publications, 1995.

Bashirul-Haq, "Naiki" [Good deeds]. *Nabat-e-Aisha*, September/October 2001, pp. 127–28.

Beiner, Ronald. *Theorizing Citizenship*. New York: State University of New York Press, 1995.

Beyer, Lisa. "The Women of Islam". *Time*, 25 November 2001, pp. 50–55.

Brohi, Nazish. *Summary Report on Harassment of Women at the Workplace*. Karachi: Working Women Support Center, December 2000.

Dawn. "WAF Withdraws from Body on Beijing Plan". 22 January 1998.

Democratic Commission for Human Development. *Auratun key Haqooq* [Women's Rights]. Lahore: Democratic Commission for Human Development, n.d.

Economist (The). "Putting Saudi Women to Work". *The Economist* 26 (September 1998): 48.

Fakar-ul-Islam. "Islam mein Khawateen key Siasi Haqooq" [Political Rights of Women in Islam]. Translation of an article by Barabara Stowesser. *Aaeen*, December 2001, pp. 20–23.

Fernea, Elizabeth. "The Challenges for Middle Eastern Women in the 21st Century". *Middle East Journal* 54, no. 2 (Spring 2000): 185–93.

Hashemi, Fatemeh. World Congress of Families II, Geneva, 14–17 November 1999. <http://www.worldcongress.org/gen99-speakers/gen99_hashemi.htm>.

Jahangir, Asma and Hina Jilani. *Lawyer to Lawyer Network.* <http://www.lchr.org/121/pakistan0599.htm>, May 1999.

Jamaat-i-Islami. <http://www.jamaat.org/Islam/WomaRights.html>.

———. <http://www.jamaat.org/qa/gender.html>.

Janoski, Thomas. *Citizenship and Civil Society: A Framework of Rights and Obligations in Liberal, Traditional and Social Democratic Regimes.* Cambridge: Cambridge University Press, 1998.

"Jordan's Clergy Say Family Planning Not Anti-Islamic". <http://www.unfpa.org/news/atwork/thaislam.htm>.

Kazemi, Farhad. "Gender, Islam and Politics". *Social Research* 67, no. 2 (Summer 2000): 453–74.

Moghadam, Valentine, ed. *Identity Politics and Women: Cultural Reassertions and Feminism in International Perspective*. Colorado: Westview Press, 1994.

———. *Women, Work, and Economic Reform in the Middle East and North Africa.* Boulder, CO: Lynne Rienner, 1998.

"Muslim Brotherhood Put Forth a New Image". <http://arabia.com/egypt/article>, 24 September 2000.

Naqvi, Talath. "Wanted Charity for Women's Police Stations". *The News*, 1 February 2000.

Nash, Kate. *Contemporary Political Sociology: Globalisation, Politics and Power.* London: Blackwell Publishers, 2000.

News (The). "WAF for Restoration of Women's Seats". 23 January 1994.

———. "WAF Demands Equal Rights for Women". 21 April 1998.

Oommen, T. K. *Citizenship, Nationality and Ethnicity: Reconciling Competing Identities.* London: Polity Press, 1997.

Patni, Ambika. "Behind the Veil". *Harvard International Review* 21, no. 1 (Winter 1998–99): 15–16.

Price, Susannah. "Boost for Pakistan's Women". *BBC News Online*, 2 September 2000.

Prior, David, John Stewart, and Kieron Walsh. *Citizenship-Rights, Community and Participation.* London: Pitman Publishing, 1995.

Rabbani, Saif Ullah. *Hijab ki Barakat: Noe Muslim Khawateen key Mushahedaat* [The Value of Hijab: Observations of Converted Muslim Women]. Lahore: Adara-e-Mutbuaat-e-Khawateen, 2000.

Revolutionary Association of the Women of Afghanistan. <http://rawa.fancymarketing.net/index.html>.
Siddiqui, Aziz. "A Vote for the 'Honour' Killers". *Dawn*, 8 August 1999.
Siddiqui, Mohammad Atta ullah. "Taraqqi pasand Islam ya Islam pasand taraqqi?" [Progressive Islam or Islamic Progress?]. *Khawateen*, January 2002, pp. 28–29.
South Asian Women's NETwork. <http://www.umiacs.umd.edu/users/sawwe/sawnet>.
Tetreault, Mary Ann. "Civil Society in Kuwait: Protected Spaces and Women's Rights". *Middle East Journal* 47, no. 2 (Spring 1993): 285–86.
United Nations Development Program. *Human Development Report 2000*. New York: United Nations, 2000.
———. *Human Development Report 2001*. New York: United Nations, 2001.
Women For Women's Human Rights. <http://www.undp.uz/GID/eng/TURKEY/NGO/wwhr_tr.html>.
Women of Pakistan: Struggling Against Violence Diary 2002.
Wright, Robin. "Iran's New Revolution". *Foreign Affairs* 79, no. 1 (January/February 2000): 133–45.

11

ISLAM, GENDER, AND POLITICS IN INDONESIA

Kathryn Robinson

Megawati Sukarnoputri was installed as Indonesia's fifth president on 23 July 2001 (see Mietzner 2000). Although her party, the PDI-P (Partai Demokrasi Indonesia–Perjuangan, or Indonesian Democratic Party of Struggle), won the largest number of seats in the 1999 general election (the first free election following the toppling of President Soeharto), her ascendancy to the presidency had been blocked by the political manipulations of Abdurrahman Wahid, who came to power as the fourth president on the strength of a coalition of Muslim-identified parties. There had been vigorous public debate in the period leading up to the general election in 1999 about whether a woman president was acceptable under Islamic doctrine and whether Indonesia, with a majority Muslim population, could accept a woman president. The negative arguments were based on textual interpretations of the Qur'an and Hadith.[1]

An analysis of this debate demands a broader context: to what extent has public debate in Indonesia about women's participation in public life rested on Islamic textual interpretation? To what extent has Islamic doctrine determined the limits and possibilities of women's political participation, in the way that it has done in many other countries which have a majority Muslim population?

INDONESIAN ISLAM AND DEBATES ABOUT WOMEN'S POLITICAL PARTICIPATION: THE HISTORICAL CONTEXT

To gain an impression about what has been written on this topic, I conducted a quick review of the Indonesian-published books dealing with "Indonesian women" which I had on my bookshelf — not a comprehensive or scientific survey, but a wide-ranging one, with a mixture of my own collection from the last twenty years — and those in the Australian National University Library, dating back to the 1950s. Many of them are government publications, others are commercially published. In these publications, where Islam is mentioned as a factor impacting on Indonesian women's social participation, it is in respect of family law although *adat* (custom, tradition) is also seen as relevant in this context. With regard to women's participation in public life, or political institutions, what is commonly invoked is historical precedent, in particular the historical cases of women who were rulers in pre-colonial polities such as Aceh (see, for example, Soewondo 1968; Department of Information 1987).

But Islam is generally absent not only from these Indonesian accounts of "the position of women". The standard English-language reviews of "the position of women" in Indonesia (written by scholars, mostly Westerners, from outside the country) rarely mention Islam as a factor influencing women's social position (see Robinson 2001). In the collections of studies on modern Indonesian women which have had considerable influence on understanding the status of women in Indonesia (for example, Atkinson and Errington 1990; Loche-Scholten and Niehof 1992; Sears 1996; Ong and Peletz 1995), Islam is not a major focus of interest or analysis.

A useful point of entry into the modern era is to examine the activities of women during the 1920s and 1930s when anti-colonial feeling was generating public political action. In women's organizations involved in the nationalist struggle, which included Islamic organizations — many connected to the major movements (such as Aisyiyah, the women's grouping within Muhammadiyah) — there was no difference of opinion about the importance of women being given equal citizenship with men. This was later reflected in the Indonesian Constitution which guarantees all citizens equal rights. Conflict among the organizations was related to the right of the state to impose uniform family law, in respect of issues like polygamy, age at marriage, and divorce. These issues split Islamic and non-Islamic (secular and Christian) women's organizations. Whereas discussion of marriage law reform had been an important issue at the first Indonesian Women's Congress in 1928, by the third congress, held in 1930, it had been dropped (Soewondo 1968).

By the 1950s, the major debates about women and Islam occurred in the Konstituante (Constituent Assembly, a committee to draft basic law) which deliberated between 1956 and 1959. Although its attempts to draft a truly representative constitution for the new republic ultimately failed, records of its deliberations give us some insights into the political thought of the time. Nasution reports that in its meetings, "Equality of rights between men and women was endorsed in principle by all parties in the Konstituante, with the exception of some individual members. However, as regards the position of women in family law, the Islamic political parties differed from the other parties" (1992, p. 218). The most extreme protagonist of the inferiority of women cited by Nasution is not, however, a representative of an Islamic party, but an independent member, Radja Kaprabonan. He held the view that "men ruled women because they were more noble and more intelligent. Men were the protectors of women" (1992, p. 219). Kaprabonan's statement received little expressed support, although Nasution comments that he "probably represented a widely-held view in Indonesian society" (1992, p. 219). He invoked religion in only the most general of terms, saying his view was "in accord with God's revelation as he had learned it" (ibid.). His views were directly challenged by a number of women delegates who do not appear, from Nasution's account, to have been very vocal in other debates. Indeed, one of his strongest opponents was Mrs Mangunpuspito from the Islamic party, Masjumi. She believed that:

> (t)he criteria to measure the high or low quality of a state was not based only on its political conditions, its being independent or not, its being wealthy or poor, but also on the high or low status which it accorded to women. Progress was impossible in a state where outdated regulations concerning women prevailed which curbed women's rights. It was not sufficient to acknowledge that God created all human beings equal, with the same fundamental rights to life and to the pursuit of happiness. It was necessary that these equal rights for men and women be implemented in the life of the nation. This was the aim of the movement for the emancipation of women, not only in the West, but also in the East (1992, p. 219).

Mrs Mangunpospito enjoined the Konstituante to improve on the rights of women guaranteed in the 1950 Constitution, by looking to the Qur'an (1992, p. 222). For her, it was other social and cultural elements of the varied cultures of the archipelago which led to the lower position of women: Islam would guarantee equality. Her emphasis on the position of women as an index of development mirrors the concern of many feminist nationalists (see Jayawardena 1986) (and the same point has been made by other Indonesian women, including the feminist civil rights lawyer, Nursyahbani Katjasungkana in 1998 in the debate which emerged over women and leadership in the lead-up to the 1999 Presidential election). Mrs Mangunpospito's comments about God creating men and women equal also prefigure much of the later debate at the time, where both male and female Islamic intellectuals countered the anti-woman position with the argument that Islam, in fact, guaranteed equality of the sexes, in that God created men and women equal.

Nasution identifies the Konstituante's uncertainties about the legal position of women as one of the concerns in the debate on human rights. However, any uncertainties referred to women's rights in regard to family law (including polygamy) and inheritance, due to inequities in both *adat* and *shari'a*. Tetilarsih Harahap Sudjanadiwirja, from the Christian party Parkindo, drew attention to inequities in family and inheritance law but commented that there was one field where she "did not see any problem for Indonesian women, namely the field of politics where she had the right to be elected" (1992, p. 220). Setiati Surasto, a PKI (Indonesian Communist Party) delegate reminded the Congress that the colonial Inlandsche Gemeente Ordonantie had barred women from election to the position of village head. This had prevented a woman twice elected from being authorized in her position, a contradiction with the Constitution of the independent nation, which guaranteed women the right "to elect and be elected" (1992, p. 220). (This colonial ordinance had also been the subject of criticism at the 1928 Women's Congress.)

The debate in the Konstituante mirrors the pattern which has characterized discussions about women in Indonesian politics and in the women's movement: Islam was seen primarily as influencing women's position in the family, not as influencing their right to participate in public life. This appeared to change in the discussions during the late 1990s about the candidature of Megawati Sukarnoputri for president.

The textual basis of most of the debate about a woman president needs to be seen against the background of the Islamization of Indonesia, in particular of the middle class, from the early 1990s when Soeharto's government encouraged the formation of ICMI, the Association of Indonesian Muslim Intellectuals. Western-educated Muslim leaders and Muslim scholars engendered debate about Islamic principles and social life, and the growth in Islamic educational institutions (especially the IAIN or State Islamic Institutes) contributed to the growing intellectual character of debate about Islamic doctrine. As well as a healthy local debate, Indonesian translations of books on women and Islam (from English, Urdu, and Arabic) have brought new dimensions to these deliberations, including in relation to debates about gender and power in Indonesia.

CAN A WOMAN BECOME A VICE-PRESIDENT?

This question gave rise to three hours of heated debate among the 100 *kiyai* (religious scholars) attending the regional conference of the East Java branch of the mass movement of Indonesian Muslims, NU (Nahdlatul Ulama), in November 1997. The debate seemed to be prompted by the possibility that Siti Hardijanti Rukmana (Mbak Tutut), Soeharto's daughter, would be a vice-presidential candidate. The debate determined that there was no obstacle to a woman holding this high office, and made a connection to the observed fact that Fatimah Achmad (of the official United Development Party, or PPP) held the office of Deputy Chair (Wakil Ketua) of the MPR (People's Consultative Assembly).[2]

In the debate one of the organizers of the meeting, K. H. Aziz Mashuri cited a Hadith from Abu Bakrah: "*Tidak akan sukses bagi suatu bangsa yang menyerahkan urusannnya kepada kaum wanita*" (Success will not come to a nation ruled by women). Aziz Mashuri commented that the implied lack of success could not be interpreted as meaning a woman leader was not lawful (*sah*). One of the *kiyai* from the Syafi'i school of jurisprudence (*mazhab*) allowed that high political office (*imamatul 'udzama)* or the position of judge (*qadli)* in the religious court (Mahkamah Syariah*)* could be held by a woman. On this basis, he argued, a woman could become vice-president. In regard to the Hadith cited above, it was argued that it had to be interpreted in the context of the manner of its transmission, that is *asbabul wurud.* Looking at the context in which the utterance was made, and the specificity of the circumstances, the conclusion was drawn that the Hadith applied specifically to the people of Persia at that time, and was not universal in its application.

Reporting on this story, the magazine *Gatra* sought the views of K.H. Ali Yafie, a member of the Majelis Ulama Indonesia (Council of Indonesian Ulama, a government-appointed body) who endorsed this view. In his opinion, the Hadith was in the nature of news (*berita*) and did not constitute either a legal judgement (*rumusan hukum*) or an instruction (*perintah*). He went on to say that such news must be looked at in context, to determine whether or not it constituted an instruction. He believed there were no reasons why women could not take high political office, provided they had the right personal characteristics for leadership, including clear thinking (*akal sehat*), broad knowledge, a sense of justice, and the support of the people. The magazine also sought the views of Professor Asjumi Abdurrahman, the co-ordinator of the Majlis Tarjih (Council of Consideration) of the central organization of Muhammadiyah, the group of religious scholars which issues *fatwa* on moral, ethical, and religious issues (Federspiel 1995, p. 150), who agreed that there was no problem if women were given the opportunity for high office. The scholar Dr Ratna Megawangi, described as a researcher on feminism, commented that the important factor in leadership was character.[3] The magazine report concluded by invoking a familiar discourse, invoking the precedent of women who have taken leadership roles in the history of Islam: from the Prophet's wife, Aisyiyah as a military leader, to Benazir Bhutto who was Prime Minister of a country with a constitution based on Islamic law.[4]

The interpretation, made in the political context in which Soeharto was still in power, was never put to the test. Tutut appeared on the hustings in East Java alongside NU leader Abdurrahman Wahid, but she was not selected by the ruling party, GOLKAR, as her father's presidential running mate. This honour went to B. J. Habibie, who assumed office after post-election political conflict forced Soeharto to resign, and Habibie was in power during the period of preparation for fresh general elections. These promised to be the first free election held in Indonesia since 1957. The restrictions on party formation were lifted, and 148 new parties were formed, expressing a diversity of political views. In the newly unshackled freedom of political debate, the issue of the suitability of women for high office came up again, as the PDI-P led by Megawati Sukarnoputri emerged as one of the front-running parties, and Megawati, who proved extremely popular with the mass of voters during the election campaign, looked like a serious prospect for the office of Indonesia's fourth president. It was in this political context that the debate about women and high office has to be understood.

The eventual outcome of the 1999 election disappointed many women activists in Indonesia. The proportion of women legislators actually fell, from 12 per cent in the Soeharto regime to 8 per cent in the so-called reform era. This was partly understood as a reflection of the fact that many of the women parliamentarians in the Soeharto era had been appointed, not so much on their own merits, but in accord with the workings of "the family principle": they were the wives, sisters, and daughters of Soeharto cronies — members of the political élite (Blackburn 1999). Despite the drop in percentage terms, Indonesian women are significantly better represented in the legislature than women in most other majority Muslim countries.

NOVEMBER 1998: THE KONGRES UMAT ISLAM INDONESIA

In the context of the increased political activity leading up to the 1999 election, a number of Islamic groups came together to hold the third Kongres Umat Islam Indonesia (KUII, or The Congress of the Indonesian Community of Believers). The first KUII was held in 1945, in the context of the struggle for national independence, and it converted the Japanese-period Masjoemi organization into a new united political party of Muslims (Masjumi) to fight for political independence (Federspiel 1995, p. 135). This was the third time the KUII had been planned. A meeting scheduled for 1966 fell through. The function of the KUII is not to make pronouncements on religious matters, but rather to consider contemporary social and political issues (*Forum Keadilan*, 30 November 1998, p. 26). Because of the large number of parties represented, there was no expectation that they would all hold the same views — in fact there was an expectation of diversity.

There had already been public debate about the issue of whether Indonesia as a majority Muslim country could have a woman president. Several Muslim figures had already endorsed the idea, for example, Matori Abdul Djalil, the head of the NU-associated party, the PKB (Partai Kebangkitan Bangsa, or National Awakening Party), had stated that it is the right of all citizens to become the leader of the nation, and the choice cannot be made on the basis of place of origin, religion, or gender (*Suara Pembangunan*, 9 November 1998). The Social and Political Commission of KUII called on the plenary to make a resolution that the president and vice-president should both be Muslim, and male, a resolution which was reportedly met with noisy acclamation by the assembly (*Gatra*, 14 November 1998, p. 45). (*Gatra* reported that the matter was discussed by two *Komisi* — the religious commission which came back recommending the request for a *fatwa*, and the social political commission which was divided in its view on the matter.) The supporters of the need for a resolution cited the Qur'anic chapter, *Surah An Nisā'*, verse 34.[5] They argued that this chapter states that men are the leaders/managers (*pemimpin*) of women. The statement is generalized to include politics, even though the verse actually refers to the organization of the household, comments the magazine *Forum Keadilan* (30 November 1998, p. 26). One of the members of this commission, K. H. Kholil Ridwan, strengthened his argument on this point by citing another Hadith which stated that a population (*Kaum*) would not be prosperous/happy (*bahagia*) if ruled by a woman. He concluded that the ban on women as leaders has existed since the time of Prophet Muhammad. The commission determined to send the matter to the Fatwa Committee of the Majelis Ulama Indonesia (*Forum Keadilan*, 30 November 1998, p. 26).[6]

According to the report published in *Gatra*, it was in fact the delegates from Aisyiyah, the women's organization associated with Muhammadiyah, and from another organization, Persis (Persatuan Islam, or Islamic Association) who raised the issue and later requested the *fatwa*. The Aisyiyah representative commented that the question of the Islamic position on a woman president was a pressing and sensitive issue, which was already the subject of a lot of discussion, and had strong supporters and opponents (14 November 1998).

The political intention of the decision was transparent in many people's eyes. They believed it was an intended attack on Megawati, following closely on an earlier attack on her Islamic credentials by the Minister for Agriculture in the Habibie Cabinet (A. M. Saefuddin) who argued she had worshipped in a Hindu temple. Another presidential aspirant, Amien Rais, as leader of the Islamic-based party PAN (Partai Amanat Nasional, or National Mandate Party), commented that even though there was clearly a consideration of politics, it was an important matter of religion for there to be a determination. He said, in principle, Islam did not recommend that women be heads of state, but in Islam there is always the *istisna'* (exception). This explained how Islamic countries like Pakistan and Bangladesh could have women leaders. He went on: "If in a particular country there is not one man who is capable of becoming the head of state, a woman who is more competent is allowed to fill in." (He did not clarify how this fits with a democratic electoral system.)

Khofifah Indar Parawansa, who became State Minister for the Empowerment of Women in the Abdurrahman Cabinet, in her capacity as deputy leader of the PKB, acknowledged that the recommendation of the congress was aimed at Megawati. She commented that even though Mega's name was not mentioned, the implication was clear. On the matter of interpretation, she said: "I am of the view that many of our *ulama* have not kept up with the development of jurisprudence in relation to women (*fiqh perempuan*). They interpret the Hadith without taking contemporary conditions into consideration." She said that in the light of the emergence of the gender movement, the *ulama* must bring their jurisprudence in regard to women up to date. She compared unfavourably the decision of the MUI (Indonesian Council of Ulama) with the earlier decision of Musyawarah Nasional (Munas) Alim Ulama (National Committee of Ulama) of the NU held at Situbondo which had determined that a women could be vice-president — the current decision was a step backwards (*Gatra*, 14 November 1998, p. 45). The head of the MUI, Quraish Shihab, said that the MUI was obliged to respond to the request, and they had to make their decision on purely religious grounds, with no political consideration of who might benefit or lose from the outcome (*Gatra*, 14 November 1998, p. 45).

The decision of the Kongres Umat Islam sparked an enormous outcry, with many people publicly taking up positions. First, there were many Muslim intellectuals who distanced themselves from the decision. Nurcholish Madjid expressed a view similar to that of the NU congress of the previous year — the matter was one of *fiqh* (Islamic jurisprudence) which invited many interpretations. "Not just in the matter of the President, but in relation to the correct ablutions for prayer (*wudhu*) there are many disagreements" (*Forum Keadilan*, 30 November 1998, p. 26). The news magazine *Tempo* reported that women held a demonstration at the roundabout outside the Hotel Indonesia in support of women assuming political leadership, and the Muslim social reform organization P3M (Perhimpunan Pengembangan Pesantren dan Mayarakat, or Centre for the Development of Islamic Boarding Schools and Society) held a seminar which rejected the consideration of gender as a basis for leadership (*Tempo*, 7 December 1998).

In 1999, as the election drew closer, there was even more public debate on the issue, in particular comments by groups who asserted the right of a woman (that is, Megawati) to head the nation. In April, Fatayat NU (the young women's association of NU) held a meeting to discuss women's leadership. They saw leadership as a matter of personal capacities. They reiterated the view that they had expressed at the KUII, that the relevant *ayat* (Qur'anic verses) had to be interpreted in a "contextual" rather than a "textual" manner ("Fatayat NU: Perempuan Bisa Jadi Presiden" [NU Young Women's Movement says a woman can become president], *Kompas Cybermedia*, 20 April 1999). Activist and scientist, Karlina Leksono spoke at a seminar entitled "Kebangkitan Pemimpin Wanita abad ke21" [Developing awareness of female leadership for the twenty-first century] on 20 April. She criticized the assumption women could not be political leaders as "patriarchal" and commented that Megawati's party had "made history" by overturning the New Order view of the primarily domestic role of women but the tragedy was that this achievement was being negated by the view that Islam proscribed women presidents ("Pandangan Patriarkhi, Menggangap Perempuan belum Bisa Memimpin" [Patriarchy believe women not yet able to lead], *Kompas Cybermedia*, 21 April 1999).

In addition, a number of male intellectuals not only rejected the interpretation that Islamic doctrine forbids women's political participation, but they have presented an alternative, text-based interpretation, seeing Islam as endorsing fundamental gender equity. A number of scholars were cited as arguing that the Qur'anic prescriptions used to argue against women becoming political leaders were misinterpretations of injunctions which related to domestic affairs, or to specifically religious activities (Parianom and Ariesdianto 1999).

As the counting of votes slowly proceeded after the elections and it became clear that the PDI-P under Megawati was the front-runner, the principal Islamic party under the New Order, the PPP (Partai Persatuan Pembangunan, or United Development Party) released a statement refusing to back a woman president (*Kompas Cybermedia*, 7 June 1999; "PPP refuses to back a woman as President", ABC Online, 16 June 1999).[7] The PDI-P won 30 per cent of the votes (the biggest share won by any single party), an outcome which Megawati's supporters interpreted as giving her the right to be supported by the electoral college (MPR) to become Indonesia's fourth president. The appointment of the president is determined by members of the MPR, and as the time for the presidential election grew closer, even more opportunities were created for public debate on the leadership, in particular by groups wanting to assert the rights of women (Megawati) to head the nation.

For example, in June 1999, the Central Organizing Committee of the Indonesian Islamic Students Association (Pengurus Besar Pergerakan Mahasiswa Islam Indonesia) held a press conference in the context of the presidential election campaign. They expressed the view that the issue of "gender and religion" was being manipulated by "status quo political groups" (shorthand for the Soeharto-Habibie forces). In their view, the issue of women leaders was, for Islam, a matter of *ikhtilaf* (differing interpretations) and should not confuse issues of a sacred nature with the worldly, the profane. Confusing these issues was in conflict with the desire for democracy and a strong civil society. They argued that religion was the basis for the moral behaviour of all mankind, not the basis of politics (*Kompas Cybermedia*, 19 June 1999). In a similar vein, Nurcholish Madjid commented that the decision of KUII was only one opinion — that there were many Islamic parties who did not see a problem with a woman president (*Kompas Cybermedia*, 24 June 1999).

Aisyiyah, the women's organization associated with the Muhammadiyah movement, discussed the matter at a congress in early July, and issued a statement that Islam did not serve as a barrier to a woman holding office, provided she was capable and credible ("Islam Tidak Pernah Hambat Perempuan" [Islam never hinders women], *Kompas CyberMedia*, 13 July 1999). The NU was also involved in a series of seminars in July. The first was "Fiqhunnisa: Tafsir Wacana Gender Dalam Kontekstualisasi Pemikiran Islam Klasik" [The interpretation of views on gender in classical Islamic thought], held by the general congress of the NU (*Muktamar*) in July 1999. The seminar was attended by, among others, Abdurrahman Wahid, leader of the NU (and subsequent victor in the presidential elections); Sinta Nuriyah Wahid (his wife, a noted women's activist in her own right); Khofifah Indar Parawansa (deputy chair of PKB, the party associated with the NU); and Chusnul Mariyah (a feminist political scientist, political activist, and self-proclaimed Muslim feminist). They discussed the topic "Gender in a theological perspective, gender in a cultural perspective, and gender from a political perspective". The head of the NU General Congress, Dr Said Aqiel Siradi (who had succeeded Abdurrahman Wahid), said in a subsequent press conference that the polemic concerning the attitude of Islam to women leaders showed that there was poor understanding of the overall attitude of Islam towards women. He denied the seminar was designed to assist Megawati's chances of election ("Pandangan Islam tentang Perempuan Belum Dipahami Secara Utuh" [Islam's view of women imperfectly understood], *Kompas CyberMedia*, 16 July 1999; "Ulama NU Dukung Presiden Wanita", [NU leader supports woman president], *Kompas CyberMedia*, 16 July 1999). Three days later, Said Aqiel Siradi was reported as stating that 70 per cent of NU *ulama* would accept a woman as president. This was announced at another seminar, held in Semarang by the Lembaga Studi Agama dan Pembangunan (Institute for the Study of Islam and Development) on "Women's leadership from the perspective of religion and political culture". Said Aqiel Siradi added, there had been four women rulers in Aceh, where they adhere to the Syafi'i school of law, and nicely brought together the customary arguments validating women's rights to assume leadership positions in terms of historical precedents, and Islamic textualism ("70 dari 100 Ulama NU Terima Perempuan Jadi Pemimpin" [70 of 100 NU religious teachers accept a woman as leader], *Kompas CyberMedia*, 20 July 1999).

The attempt to bring religious interpretation into the political scene as a strategy to neutralize Megawati as a political opponent may have influenced the political terrain on which gender equity is fought, but it is not clear that this is to the detriment of women. The last minister for women's affairs in the Soeharto period, Mien Sugandi, went on record as being opposed to a woman president, in spite of the fact that she herself was one of four female party leaders, her party (MKGR, or Musyawarah Kerja Gotong Royong) being a breakaway GOLKAR faction. She appeared to embody the criteria for success for women under the New Order, her political prominence resting on the influence and connections of her late husband. In her presentation of self, she embodied what Julia Suryakusuma labelled "The perfumed nightmare", with her heavy, elaborate make-up, her relentless self-promotion in ministry publications, and her lack of understanding or sympathy for ordinary Indonesian women (for example, her failure to respond to the reports of deaths of Indonesian women working as servants in the Middle East — see Robinson 2000). There was certainly nothing Islamic in her public persona. Her successor, in the Soeharto/Habibie Cabinet was Tutti Alawiyah, a woman preacher with impeccable Islamic credentials. She was a public persona in her own right, as an Islamic preacher, but perhaps better known for her religious rather than her social activities. While she was minister, the name of her ministry was changed from Menteri Urusan Peranan Wanita (Ministry for Managing the Role of Women) to Menteri Peranan Wanita (Ministry for the Role of Women).

The issue of gender was but one of the many used to undermine Megawati's claim on the presidency, and a coalition of Muslim parties was mobilized to support Abdurrahman Wahid (Gus Dur) in the deliberations of the electoral college in October 1999.[8] When the results were announced on 20 October and Gus Dur's success became known, there were displays of populist outrage on the streets (particularly in Bali) and perhaps this had a part in the outcome of the vice-presidential elections on the subsequent day, when the post went to Megawati.

In the Abdurrahman Wahid cabinet, Khofifah insisted on a change in title of the Women's Ministry to Menteri Pemberdayaan Perempuan, or Ministry for Women's Empowerment, reflecting both the language of the Beijing Conference on women and the language of the *Reformasi* (political reform) movement in Indonesia. But Khofifah has credentials which are unambiguously feminist. She built her political reputation as an activist in the Islamic student movement and became a parliamentarian at the age of twenty-seven. She was a vocal critic of the decision of MUII (at which she was a delegate).

Abdurrahman Wahid lost support of the major Islamic parties that had originally supported his presidency and he was forced to resign in June 2001 after losing the support of the MPR. Some of the politicians that had earlier found Megawati an unacceptable candidate on religious grounds now supported her, including Hamzah Haz, the leader of PPP who agreed to serve as her vice-president. However, some Islamic groups, including Partai Masyumi and the extremist Front Pembela Islam maintained an oppositional stance to the legitimacy of a woman president.[9]

An apparent attempt to place textual interpretation at the centre of public discussion about women's public roles did not appear to have the desired effect. It helped galvanize support for Megawati from people who disagreed with the anti-democratic sentiment implied by the invocation of Islam. It led to many Muslim intellectuals making public statements about Islam providing a moral basis for equality between men and women. So to the extent that Islamization has been associated with an appeal to sacred texts as a basis for understanding the nature of gender relations in Indonesia, the effect has not been the promotion of a view which limits women's participation in public life.

Notes

1. For an analysis of these arguments, see Bernhard Platzdasch, "Islamic Reaction to a Female President", in *Indonesia in Transition*, edited by Chris Manning and Peter van Dierman (Singapore: Institute of Southeast Asian Studies, 2000), pp. 336–50.
2. As described in "Perempuan Jadi Wapres" [Woman becomes Vice-President], *Gatra*, 14 November 1998, p. 104; *Tempo*, 22 November 1997.
3. Her comments are interesting as she has published a well-known book which was hostile to the idea of measures to bring about "gender equality" (Megawangi 1999).
4. *Gatra*, 22 November 1997, p. 104.
5. *Surah An Nisas*', or "The Women", is the fourth chapter of the Qur'an, and deals with "roles, responsibilities, and expected behaviour of Muslim women" (Federspiel 1995, p. 188).
6. These two texts were the subject of repeated focus in the discussion over the following months, with arguments back and forth in public forums and reported in the Indonesian media. See Parianom and Ariesdianto (1999) for a further sampling of the contributions to this debate.
7. The head of the PPP, Hamzah Haz, who made the statement, later reconsidered his position and agreed to become Megawati's vice-president in the political machinations that preceded the dumping of Abdurrahman Wahid by the MPR.
8. For further details, see Marcus Mietzner, "The 1999 General Session: Wahid, Megawati and the Fight for the Presidency", in *Indonesia in Transition,* edited by Manning and van Dierman, pp. 39–57.
9. "Masyumi dan FPI Tolak Presiden Perempuan" [Masyumi and FPI reject woman as president], *Republika Online*, 26 July 2001.

References

Atkinson, Jane M. and Shelly Errington, eds. *Power and Difference: Gender in Island Southeast Asia.* Stanford: Stanford University Press, 1990.

Blackburn, Susan. "The 1999 elections in Indonesia: Where were the women?". In *Pemilu: The 1999 Indonesian Elections*, edited by Susan Blackburn. Annual

Indonesia Lecture Series No. 22. Clayton, Vic: Centre of Southeast Asian Studies, 1999.

Department of Information, Republic of Indonesia. *The Women of Indonesia*. 3rd printing. Jakarta: Department of Information in Co-operation with the Minister of State for the Role of Women, 1987.

Federspiel, H. M. *A Dictionary of Indonesian Islam*. Southeast Asia Series No. 94 Athens, Ohio: Center for International Studies, 1995.

Jayawardena, Kumari. *Feminism and Nationalism in the Third World*. London and New Jersey: Zed Books, 1986.

Loche-Scholten, Elsbeth and Anke Niehof, eds. 2nd printing. *Indonesian Women in Focus: Past and Present Notions,*. Leiden: KITLV Press, 1992.

Megawangi, Ratna. *Membiarkan Berbeda?* Bandung: Mirzan, 1999.

Mietzner, Marcus. "The 1999 General Session: Wahid, Megawati and the Fight for the Presidency". In *Indonesia in Transition: Social Aspects of Reformasi and Crisis,* edited by Chris Manning and Peter van Dierman. Singapore: Institute of Southeast Asian Studies, 2000.

Nasution, Harun. *The Aspiration for Constitutional Government in Indonesia: A Socio-Legal Study of the Indonesian Konstituante 1956–1959*. Jakarta Pusat: Sinar Harapan, 1992.

Ong, Aihwa and Michael G. Peletz, eds. *Bewitching Women, Pious Men: Gender and Body Politics in Southeast Asia*. Berkeley, Los Angeles and London: University of California Press, 1995.

Parianom, Bambang and Dondy Ariesdianto, eds. *Megawati and Islam. Polemik Gender dalam Persaingan Politik*. Surabaya: PT Antar Surya Jaya Bersama LSK, 1999.

Platzdasch, Bernhard. "Islamic Reaction to a Female President". In *Indonesia in Transition: Social Aspects of Reformasi and Crisis*, edited by Chris Manning and Peter van Dierman. Singapore: Institute of Southeast Asian Studies, 2000.

Robinson, Kathryn. "Gender, Islam and Nationality". In *Home and Hegemony: Domestic Service and Identity in South and Southeast Asia*, edited by Kathleen Adams and Sara Dickey. Ann Arbor: Michigan University Press, 2000.

———. "Gender, Islam and Culture in Indonesia". In *Love, Sex and Power: Women in Southeast Asia*, edited by Susan Blackburn. Melbourne: Monash Asia Institute/ Monash University Press, 2001.

Sears, Laurie J., ed. *Fantasizing the Feminine in Indonesia*. Durham and London: Duke University Press, 1996.

Soewondo. *Kedudukan Wanita Indonesia dalam Hukum dan Masjarakat*. Djakarta: Timun Mas, 1968.

Law and Knowledge

12

PERSPECTIVES ON *SHARI'A* AND THE STATE

The Indonesian Debates

M. B. Hooker*

The last century saw the reformulation of *shari'a* into European forms (codes, statutes, and cases) throughout the Muslim world. As part of this, the sphere of the *shari'a* has also been restricted to family law and trusts.[1] The result is a triumph for secularization in that we now have laws for "Muslims" rather than "Islamic" law as such. That this is the case in the new millennium should not surprise us; it is an inevitable result of direct colonial rule added to — since the 1950s — by a voluntary acceptance of Western canons of jurisprudence especially in the Middle East. In a very real sense as well, it is the logical result of the works of Muhammad 'Abduh and his followers whose reduction of the classical *fiqh* to a "natural law" has been amply documented.[2] In short, the nation-state now determines the definition of *shari'a* in all the lands of Islam; the *ummah* is no longer the primary point of reference, instead it is the constitution(s) of the state(s) which defines Islam.[3]

This chapter attempts to answer two questions for Indonesia: firstly, how did the state come to dominate?; and secondly, is the apparent dominance of the state necessarily permanent?

STATE DOMINANCE IN THE TWENTIETH CENTURY

Before coming to the debates which form the subject of this chapter it is necessary to list in short form the institutional structures through which the state dominates and determines Islam. These have been discussed elsewhere but I give the appropriate references for those who are unfamiliar with the subject.

- *The Dutch colonial period.* In 1882 a "Priest Court" was established for Java and Madura. It had limited jurisdiction in marriage, divorce, and *wakaf.* It could not enforce its own decisions which had to be approved by the Landraad (civil) courts. The 1882 regulation was amended in 1937 with a wider jurisdiction and powers of enforcement in respect of dowry and maintenance. The system was extended to South and East Borneo in 1938. Overriding jurisdiction was always in the secular courts.[4]
- *The Republic of Indonesia 1946–91.* A Ministry of Religion was established in 1946 with supervision of the religious courts. The latter, based on the Dutch model, was extended to Sumatra and the Outer Islands until 1989 when a new Law on Basic Religious Justice was introduced. Its effect was to incorporate the religious courts within the general legal system. In 1991, the Kompilasi Hukum Islam (Compilation of Islamic Law) was introduced by presidential instruction. It is in three parts: marriage, divorce, custody, and guardianship; inheritance; and trusts. The content is a simplified *fiqh* written with reference to secular legislation, in particular the Marriage Law of 1974. It is a codified *shari'a* for Indonesian Muslims.[5]

What is Islam now? The agenda for an answer is determined from outside the classical texts. The various reform groups whether "modernist" or "traditionalist" all claim an "Islam". The problem here is that "Islam" becomes an object to be used for a purpose and inevitably this leads to secularism. This is the legacy of 'Abduh and Rashid Rida. The so-called fundamentalists in Indonesia, for example, authors of articles in *Media Dakwah*, clearly see this danger. Their view is that any reform agenda must be set from within the discourse of Islam itself. There are various versions of what this discourse might be.

First, the NU (Nahdlatul Ulama), the so-called traditionalists, rely on the classic texts (*fiqh*) of the Sunni *madhhab*. This is how one knows Islam. The argument is based on text commentary on Q. 4:157 and 72; to quote K.H. Mahfudz Siddiq, a former chairman of NU:[6]

> The opinion as expressed in the writings of these *ulama* are the products of their *idtjihad* as based on the Book of Allah; they do not make laws

> from their own reasoning so that it cannot be said that their opinions are not the laws of the Book of Allah in the sense that they make laws of their own. For if this is the case, and the people consider it so, the *ulama* have become *murtad.*

This is a response from within but its effectiveness is minimal because it does not directly engage with the reality of the state. Whilst it avoids reducing Islam to an object it has nothing practical to offer the Indonesian *ummah* who are colonial subjects or, subsequently, citizens of the new Republic.

Muhammadiyah, the oldest of the Indonesian reform movements founded in 1912, presents an agenda directly derived from Muhammad 'Abduh. It asserts that faith is prior to reason but holds that there is no *necessary* disjunction between the two. The essence of reason is the capacity to *select*; to select from past scholarship; to select from the Qur'an and Sunna but always to select for a purpose in the contexts of contemporary life. In other words, the acceptance or authority of an argument (selection) is to be judged on rational grounds, not on the status of the person proposing it. On the face of it, this is an appealing position but it carries the danger of an overly close compromise with secularism. The danger is in accepting the primacy of reason based on conditions of time and place. While one may propose that there is no necessary dysfunction between faith and reason, the quality of "necessary" remains undefined. This is a serious flaw in the argument as the following passage demonstrates:[7]

> We also call on all *ulama* to be willing to discuss the decisions of the Madjlis Tardjih, to point out its errors or the weakness of its arguments ... the matter will again be reviewed [by the Madjlis Tardjih] ... For a decision is only based on our knowledge and ability at the time it was made.
>
> The Madjlis Tardjih will not prohibit the study and discussion by the *madrasah* of the Muhammadiyah of the problems on which no decision has been given by the Madjlis, or to examine the arguments of the Madjlis in arriving at a decision.

When we take this with revelation versus reason, and the denial of disjunction then we are coming very close to an accommodation with secular dominance. The statement dates from 1932, the era of high colonialism, and shows the defensiveness which characterized Islamic thought in Indonesia at that time.

However, with Persatuan Islam (Persis), the third major intellectual group, we can see that a positive political philosophy from within Islam was also an alternative to secularism. It was vigorously pursued by Persis intellectuals from the 1930s to the 1960s. Their point of departure was "right analysis" by which they meant a careful examination of the Hadith to show its true meaning. Analysis was by way of language and the chains of transmission so that validity is wholly in the Islamic discourse. The latter is the reality and it follows, therefore, that any state other than the Islamic state is unacceptable. The will to act *(ikhtyār)* inevitably is the will to create a Muslim state given the internal imperative. One can easily verify this through the works of Hj. Moehamad Chalil (1908–61).[8] Perhaps a more accessible source is the celebrated debate between Moehamad Natsir and Sukarno of 1939–40 in which each defined his own version of what the independent Indonesian state should be. Dr Deliar Noer gives extensive citation[9] and a few examples of the arguments which illustrate the secular and Muslim positions at the time:

> Sukarno:
> … how do you realise your ideals [about this unity] in a country in which you will uphold democracy and in which part of its population are non-Muslims, as in Turkey, India and Indonesia in which millions of people are Christians or embrace another religion, and in which the intellectuals in general do not entertain Islamic thoughts? …
>
> If you become the government of the country in which many of its people are non-Muslim, do you want to decide by yourselves that the state be an Islamic state, the constitution be an Islamic *sjari'ah*? If the Christians and those professing other religions do not want to accept [your decision], what will you do? If the intellectual groups do not want to accept [your decisions], what will you do? Do you want to force them … to agree with your decisions? … do you want to play dictator, to force [them] with arms and cannons? If they will still not obey, what will you do? You do not want to eliminate them all do you? — for the present is a modern period and not a period of extinction of each other as was the practice of our former days.
>
> Natsir:
> Islam does not tolerate [nationalism] founded on fanaticism … which breaks up the bond of brotherhood of all Muslims of various nationalities; [it also disapproves of] the pride of a nation if this constitutes the criterion for deciding what is right and what is wrong in order not to diminish the glorification of the nation; if the wrong is considered right even if this is in the interest and for the success of one's own nation. If all that comes from one's own group is defended and protected, although it is wrong: [Islam does not agree with the slogan] "my country right or wrong".
>
> It is not wrong for a Muslim to make use of it [that is, the feeling of belonging to one group of nation] as a means for the concentration

> and strengthening of power ... if care is thereby taken to respect the interests and rights of other groups, if fanaticism which buries rightness, justice and humanity is put aside, and if ... the unity of the Muslim brotherhood is not lessened ...

There is no agreed definition of power, law, and how authority is to be legitimated. The secular position succeeded. The only concession to Islam was minimal, in the Piagam Jakarta of 1945, but as events unfolded this was also reduced to a position paper. Islam was not to be the foundation of the independent Republic and *shari'a* was not the law for the Republic. The 1945 Constitution is a purely secular document. However in the accompanying Pancasila (Statement of Five Principles) which is, in fact, incorporated into the preamble of the Constitution we read:

> [In] order to set up a government of the State of Indonesia which shall protect the whole of the Indonesian people and the entire native land of Indonesia, and in order to advance the general welfare, to develop intellectual life of the nation and to contribute in implementing an order in the world which is based upon independence, abiding peace and social justice, the structure of Indonesia's National Independence shall be formulated in a Constitution of the Indonesian State which shall have the structural form of a republic of Indonesia with sovereignty of the people, and which *shall be based upon: Belief in the One, Supreme God,* just and civilised humanity, the unity of Indonesia, and democracy which is guided by the inner wisdom in the unanimity arising out of deliberation amongst our representatives, meanwhile creating a condition of social justice for the whole of the People of Indonesia. [Emphasis added.]

The state is dominant and, from this point of view, the fate of *shari'a* in Indonesia is no different from that in other Muslim countries. Of course the process by which this position was reached is not the same as that in neighbouring Malaysia and the Philippines, nor is it the same as the so-called reforms in the Middle East. Nevertheless, the result is comparable; the reduction, indeed, trivialization of 1,400 years of *fiqh* to a simple code administered in a court with a carefully circumscribed jurisdiction.

The assumption is that something called "*shari'a*" can be narrowly defined as a certainty, and that state dominance is permanent. But is this true? I think it is at best problematic because it is constantly challenged from within Islam. *Shari'a* is not, in fact, reducible to codes. The basic terms (*ibadat, mu'amalat,* not to mention the technical phraseology) are always open to argument and debate. The intellectual initiatives of writers such as al-Rasi, Turabi, 'Ashmawi, and Fazlur Rahman are striking evidence[10] that the state dominance is challengeable. The "crisis of modernity" at the end of the twentieth century has in fact reinvigorated *ijtihad* to an unexpected degree.

The Indonesian response is quite remarkable.

THE CHALLENGE TO STATE DOMINANCE: *SHARI'A* AND THE STATE

Indonesian Islam has its own characteristics which include indigenous adaptations, Dutch colonial reformulations, and the political turmoil surrounding Independence. The huge variety of response from and within Islam has been described elsewhere,[11] but confining this discussion to law, four names, and hence four views, begin to suggest an original and Indonesian intellectualism.

The first is the legal philosopher Hazairin (1905–75) whose work has been much underestimated, even passed over or relegated to footnotes.[12] Up to a point this is understandable. He wrote and taught in the 1950s and 1960s in a period of great turmoil in Indonesian politics and during which time Islam was very much on the defensive. This is especially true for law. Further, his education was in the Dutch system and though he was a professor in the University of Indonesia his training and approach to law was not in sympathy with the times. His "rationalism" was seen to be tainted with what we now call "orientalism".

His initial proposition was that the future of Indonesian law, at the very least in family law, lay in the creation of a *madhhab nasional* (national school). By "*madhhab*" he truly meant *madhhab* and by "*nasional*" he truly meant Indonesian. His proposition actually rests on two assumptions: firstly, that there is a distinction between *'ibādāt* and *mu'āmālāt* which is sustainable; and secondly, that the fact of human existence (facts of life, social structures, and so on) while outlined in Revelation are not wholly explained by Revelation. Given these, all that Man can do is to begin from that which is directly known to him, that is, in this case, Indonesian social structures. Islam, in other words, was something to be moulded, used as a source for "practical" Islam. This was the subtext of his work in the 1960s — a completely new *madhhab*. How was this to be achieved?

Hazairin's answer is in three parts. First, the Shāfi'ī *madhhab* is but a source for *mu'āmālāt*. The particular provisions of Shāfi'ī, as such, have no binding force for Indonesian Muslims. As a matter of principle, this is, of course, unacceptable to the *ulama*. However, leaving that aside, what does this position imply from a strictly rational viewpoint? Can it be shown to be acceptable in such terms? For the answer to be "yes", the proposal must demonstrate a logical consistency from *within* the source, that is, from within Islam. An outside validation is not sufficient. To this, Hazairin never gave a convincing answer. His attempt was composed of an inconsistent, even eccentric, interpretation of the Qu'ran and Hadith which are historically and philosophically unsound. Obviously a dialogue with the *ulama* was not possible, a mutually acceptable framework for discussion of the idea of choice just did not exist. On the other hand, Hazairin's proposition did open up the possibility of recourse to other schools of *fiqh*, to the idea of *talf'īq* (opinions from different *madhhab*). The danger with *talf'īq*, as the *ulama* well recognized, is that it allows or even encourages recourse to the lowest common denominator of that which is socially or politically acceptable. It remains a subject of much debate in the Muslim world, especially in the Middle East. That debate is concerned, rightly, with establishing canons of and for choice. "Free" choice leads to trivialization of *shari'a*, of 1,400 years of jurisprudence and this is, in fact, what happened with the Kompilasi Hukum Islam although Hazairin had no part in the drafting of this document and there is no evidence that his views were considered. The Kompilasi is evidence of the current Indonesian recourse to the easy solution. Even Malaysia, where the Islamic debates are usually much less sophisticated, has not fallen into this trap. On the other hand, it is possible that he has not been totally without influence in this matter. Professor Fadhil Lubis has recently drawn attention to the work of Dr Ash-Shiddieqy which expresses similar ideas on Arabic and Egyptian sources. An assessment of their influence remains to be undertaken but Hazairin must have credit at least for first raising the issue in post-war Indonesia.

Second, Hazairin proposed that *shari'a* be subject to Indonesia-specific facts of legal life. A large part of Hazairin's early legal training was in *adat* law and the concept of *adat* as the basis for a national legal system. His own special topic was inheritance, including unilineal inheritance systems known especially in Minangkabau (matrilineal) and Batak (patrilineal) societies. It was in the area of inheritance, therefore, that he took a positive line for *shari'a* in national legal development. An extra factor was that bilateral (sometimes called "parental") succession is far more common than the unilineal systems in Indonesia. It also has obvious positive implications for women's status and the position of the child. It was here that *shari'a* was a positive source. But again, we come to the position of *shari'a* as source. A reformed adoption of *farā'id* (laws of inheritance) was not possible in Hazairin's view, because of Revelation. Bilateralism, by which he really meant female inheritance rights, was found in *shari'a* but the inequalities in male as opposed to female shares had to be corrected. Again, his attempts to extract principles from the Qur'an and Hadith were not acceptable to the *ulama*. How could they be? The *farā'id* rules are, in fact, set in Revelation. In essence, his argument from Indonesian facts to *shari'a* foundered because he saw *shari'a* as a source to be mined for a secular purpose and not as an absolute given.

This brings us to his third answer — that Indonesia required new *mujtahid* who must have a national (that is, Indonesian) perspective and must act collectively in a systematic way. In other words, *ijtihād* must be organized on a nation-wide basis. This was already partly the case at the time he wrote, with Muhammadiyah, the NU, and Persis. All claimed to act in this way and all continue the claim in their respective Fatwa Committees (see below). Since 1975 we also have Majlis Ulama Indonesia at national and state levels. In all these organizations there is now a collectivity of decision making for problems which impinge on *shari'a*. They all demonstrate a very local Indonesian perspective founded in consensus. Hazairin's achievement was to show the perils of approaching *shari'a* from the outside but also to emphasize the propriety of consensus long term.

In passing, I should indicate similar ideas put forward by Dr Munawir Sjadzali (Minister of Religion 1983–93) whose "Reaktualisasi" of *shari'a* is rather similar in that the given position is the facts of Indonesian social life. He bases himself, however, in the doctrine of *naskh* (abrogation) for the purposes of change. As one would expect, his views were and are controversial but from the point of view of *shari'a* are much more soundly based in *fiqh* than those of Hazairin.

I turn next to the philosopher Harun Nasution (1919–98) who was active from the 1960s to the 1990s. His education was primarily secular (in Cairo and at McGill University) though he did spend some time at Al-Azhar and at a private Islamic college in Cairo.[13] He was a follower of 'Abduh and he disseminated 'Abduh's views in a number of important works. These gained considerable influence in the IAIN (State Islamic Institutes). He was lecturer and later rector of the IAIN Jakarta, where his main accomplishment was a reform of the curriculum along "modernist" lines. His contribution to Islamic education was, and remains, notable. These two facts, his Western education and his sometimes aggressive reforms in Islamic education very much coloured how his work was received in modern Indonesia and they must be kept in mind when reading criticisms of his thought. As is to be expected, much of the latter has been politically inspired.

Nasution's fundamental position is that all religions, by which he meant revealed religions, have a commonality in that each recognizes the idea of the sacred and all have the same function which is to know and experience

God in so far as is possible for humankind. No religion, therefore, can be said to be prior to any other, or conversely, the completion of any other. This position is not at all acceptable to those learned in *fiqh* who take the standard position that Islam is the completion of God's message to humankind. This view has been put most forcibly by H. M. Rasjidi who attributes Nasution's position to "orientalist corruption" and maintains that as such it will lead to secularism and the evils thereof.

From the internal Muslim point of view the important conclusion for Nasution is that, historically, Islam is expressed in plural forms, and that this is a natural occurrence. In particular it is natural that social institutions vary from place to place and from time to time. None, therefore, can be more "true" than another. Approaches to "truth" are conditioned by time and place and rest on reason, not on a simple acceptance of predestination. In other words, he is theologically optimistic. The key to his optimism lies in the fact of the rich heritage of Mu'tazilite thought which is within Islam. Orientalism, as such, is completely irrelevant. His reading of Islamic history allows for spiritualism, even asceticism, which can be another form of rationalism. He maintains that it is not necessary to face a choice between reason and, for example, Sufism, as opposing ways of life.

It is notable that Nasution is not really all that concerned with the drafting of political or state institutional laws for Islam. His approach is actually via education, the function of which is to create an "Islamic state of mind". Although he is never all too clear on the point, he seems to be looking to inculcate an Islamic ethic into those best fitted to rule. From this will flow a just and rational Muslim society. The (Islamic) rule by the best suited is for the good of society. This was not the "religious utilitarianism" of his day and nor is it all that acceptable today.

The validity of Nasution's position rests on his definition of reason. Here the context is important; it is Indonesia from the 1970s to the 1990s with a state ideology — Pancasila — and an authoritarian regime coupled with quite startling economic growth directed by an all-powerful bureaucratic/military machine. If Islam can be reduced to an "ethic" or a "value" rather than being an alternative authority then it can obviously be subsumed into the state ideology.

Unfortunately Nasution's views do lend themselves to this use and he was a strong supporter of the New Order regime. He strongly disapproved of the previous (pre-1965) regime. This is the context within which Nasution developed his explanation of reason in Islam and, while not "politically directed" as such, it was certainly accommodating to the late twentieth-century Indonesian state ideology.

For Nasution, reason was human action and, while God gave the capacity, man determined it in its many shapes and forms. "Reason" and "capacity" are not synonyms but they can be merged or founded in a common ground by an act of will. It is the *will to action* which determines or shapes that which is possible and right. Nasution pays lip-service to *jabariya* and *qadiriya* but he does come up against the apparent internal contradiction — that the will to action must be within the parameters of Islam. On the other hand, the Mu'tazilite accepts that one can know by reason, and for Nasution this is demonstrated through the correct analysis of the Qur'an and Hadith; *aql* is the capacity to distinguish between oneself and "the other". Capacity has both intellectual and spiritual characteristics which determine that which is possible and that which is right. In his view, neither of these is necessarily determined by Revelation.

Nasution justifies the freedom of will to act by Qur'anic reference but the will is not absolute. It is limited in two respects. First, that which is naturally impossible (for example, to live forever) cannot be willed. Second, will is limited by the nature of things. For example, fire burns and one cannot will it otherwise. Though his language is not all that clear, Nasution appears to be referring to physical laws, including science, which govern the universe. So far as these are concerned, the will to action of both believer and unbeliever is equally conditioned by these laws. These limits on individual will ultimately derive from God's creation. But subject to these limitations, one may freely exercise one's will to choose alternatives in one's social relationships (in the widest sense to include politics).

A little earlier I indicated that the whole thrust of Nasution's thought made it relatively compatible with contemporary political ideology and he was not only aware of this, but became quite an active proponent of the then Pancasila ideology. He saw it as the intellectual justification for the modernization and development which was so successful in the Indonesia of the 1970s to the 1990s. This success was in itself a demonstration of the superiority of reason over the level of development in the Old Order society dominated by a sterile socialism. A "rational" Islam, therefore, was a natural element in a rational economy and ideology. Political representation as such for Islam was not necessary; it was sufficient that the élite had internalized the Islamic ethic. Pancasila is, in fact, a "manifestation of Islam in the context of the Indonesian State". This is a view according perfectly with government policy, which has always been opposed to institutionalized Islam. In other words, rationalism has a demonstrable social and political value which created a successful modernism for Indonesia. Islam's place, here, in Nasution's view, is that it is part of the wider national culture.

We turn now to the work of Nurcholish Madjid (1939–) for a separate but related view. Like Harun Nasution, this leading Muslim thinker has a background in Western Islamic study but, unlike Nasution, he also has a strong *santri* background by birth and educational upbringing.[14] It is also worth remembering that, unlike the previous generation of writers, he grew up in an *independent* Indonesia and this, combined with the remarkable breadth of his education, gives a quite distinct cast to his thought. He is avowably apolitical, being more concerned with education, but at the same time he is a political realist as his discussion of Islam and political pluralities in Indonesia indicates. The thrust of his thought is that Islam in Indonesia has developed Indonesian characteristics. These may be as simple and as obvious as linguistic adaptations and calendar systems or as complex as various social adaptations and manifestations which are "not Arabic". For Muslims to accept pluralism requires "a dialogue with temporal and spatial realities". The nature of man is one of these and it is required of Muslims, as of others, to accept and treat positively differences, "... supported by reasonable self confidence". In other words, there must be an acceptance of changed circumstances, and "classical Islam" itself exhibits these characteristics. Adaptation is not necessarily an attack on the authenticity of Revelation.

Madjid first came to the serious attention of Indonesian Islam when in January 1970, as chairman of the executive of HMI (Himpunan Mahasiswa Islam, or Islamic Students' Association), he presented a paper on the renewal of Islamic thought and the "integration of the Ummat". He proposes a liberalization of Islamic thought which consists of distinguishing between that which is eternal and that which is temporal. The *ummah* must be freed from the tendency to spiritualize the temporal because to do this is, in its own way, a deviation from the absolute transcendence (*tawhid*) of God. This view rests on showing that one can, in fact, distinguish between the eternal and the temporal. It implies further an acceptance of pluralism in the temporal affairs of Muslim societies, that is, that temporal values are culturally defined and subject to change. Unfortunately, as it turned out, he introduced the word *sekularisasi* into his discussion. In any discussion of Islam, the term generally has negative connotations and Indonesian Islam is no exception.

Madjid's paper aroused considerable controversy, and between 1970 and 1972 he published three more papers in which he clarified and elaborated his initial propositions. In the first of these, "More on Secularisation", he begins by way of an analogy between animism and Islam. For the former, inanimate objects have a religious meaning. On the other hand, for Islam the confession of faith imposes the view that only God is transcendent and only God must be worshipped. For the rest, the things of this world, they can be understood "... in accordance with what they are, whether in relation to their true nature or the laws governing them". This understanding is a function of Man's (God-given) intelligence.

Intelligence is primary to the nature of Man, and Man's duty is to exercise it rightly. However, it is limited because it cannot fully comprehend God. The most that can be hoped for is rightly guided action or, more fundamentally, the will to rightly guided action. Intelligence is, thus, a trust from God to be exercised in worldly matters. Madjid cites and interprets several verses from the Qur'an to this effect as well as providing an interpretation of the Confession of Faith — the use of *Ar-Rahman* and *Ar-Rahim* (see his Chapter 5 in this book). The point is that faith and knowledge are not the same and must be approached by different means. This is the crux of his whole argument and I return to it in due course.

The second paper in the series is his "Renewal of Thought in Islam" which focuses on the relation between the demands of social change and religiously derived value for the individual. What should be the nexus and how is it to work? His answer is that Islam must free itself from such unfortunate tendencies as sectarianism but, most importantly, from any attempt at institutionalization of belief. Religion is essentially an individual matter and must be understood by individuals in their own contexts and capabilities. Again, we have echoes of Nasution.

The third paper continues this theme — "Reinvigorating Religious Understanding" — with a call to get away from apologetics for religion. While these were useful in their time, now a psychological confidence, positive in nature, is required. The West can be approached in terms of equality. *Īmān* (faith) is more than static belief combined with *taqwā* (obedience), and the individual possesses a spiritual stability which is the basis of his will to action. That action is naturally (that is, by nature) to attain that which is good in God's eyes. The actions (*amal*) which then occur will be in spiritual harmony with man's whole environment. The translation of man's spirituality into concrete social action is the function of reason, not the domain of faith.

Madjid has developed these views in a consistent way over the past twenty-five years. However, the main sticking point for his critics remains the clear differentiation between "spiritual" and "temporal" Islam. His attempts to both differentiate and yet retain some sort of nexus is hotly disputed by such noted commentators as Muhammad Natsir, H.M. Rasjidi, and Endang Saifuddin Anshari who all, in their own ways, deny differentiation. Their arguments are both theological and historical and in essence come to the issue of authority — who, and on what criteria, can rightly judge the world of temporal affairs? The question is as old as

Judaism, Christianity, and Islam, and it is for each generation to answer it in turn.

Religion in the nation-state or, for Islam, the "Islamic State" is the modern manifestation of the authority issue. For Madjid the concept has to be rejected on two grounds. First, its proponents are merely apologetic and imitative in the face of Western ideological dominance — democracy or socialism — in contemporary national life. Islam does not, in fact, lend itself to ideologization because it is a true religion for which a state, as such, is not necessary. This is the distinction between religion and ideology, the latter is the justification for a state *and* is supported by it. Islam is neither, and strained interpretation of, for example, the "Constitution" of Medina is neither relevant nor helpful for contemporary Indonesia. I have perhaps put more here into Madjid's comments than he has, but what I have said is the logical outcome of his position. The second reason for rejecting the Islamic state idea is that for Islam to be at all able to inform the institutions of state, an undue degree of legalism would be required. "Undue" here means undue for the circumstances of Indonesia.

On the other hand, as with Nasution, the arguments of Madjid do lend themselves quite happily to whatever ideology contemporary Indonesia happens to possess. The "Islamic State" is really a state of mind. Pancasila, for example, can be accommodated in the same Islam and, in turn, it can accommodate Islam. Indeed, some of his colleagues, for example, Djohan Effendi have been quite positive in promoting a Pancasila-Islam nexus. But which Pancasila and which Islam? In the present flux of Indonesian politics there is no firm answer.

Where does this leave us with Madjid? Has he, as Professor Hallaq asks, (see above) given us a methodology? The answer, if there is one, will have to wait until we look briefly at the last of the modern *ulama* in Indonesia. These are Abdurrahman Wahid and Achmad Siddiq. Conventionally these two authorities are usually described as "traditionalist" or "conservative" Muslim thinkers. In so far as these adjectives have any meaning they may be taken to refer to the fact that both are leading figures in the NU, a movement which is largely Javanese and based in *pesantren*. The terminology "traditionalist" is unfortunate and misleading. As Abdurrahman Wahid himself says:

> traditionalists are widely supposed to be backward in orientation and ossified in their understanding of Islamic society and thought. It is held that their persistence in holding orthodox Islamic law (i.e., the Sunni *madhhab* or legal schools) leads them to reject modernity and a rational approach to life. Similarly, in matters of theology, their determined adherence to the scholasticism of al-Asy'ari and al-Maturidi is said to

> have resulted in a fatalistic understanding of submission to God's will and a disregard for the exercise of free will and independent thinking. Traditionalists are furthermore accused of being too other-worldly in their practice of ritual Islamic mysticism (*tasawuf*). Their activities within the *sufi* orders (*tarekat*) give the appearance of forsaking the present world in the hope of gaining eternal happiness in heaven. Thus, the commonly held view of traditionalists is that they are a wholly passive community unable to cope with the dynamic challenges of modernisation, the sort of community that scholars regard as belonging to a dying tradition.[15]

There is much that is justified in this complaint. While it is true that in the decades preceding Independence and even for a considerable period after 1949, the NU could be described as defensive of Islam, this is no longer the case. In recent NU *fatāwā*, especially from the 1970s to the 1990s, the charge of a lack of dynamism is clearly unjustified. There is instead a considerable creativity. Other commentators, for example, Dr Greg Barton have also noted the presence of *ijtihād* although the term is not normally used. The NU incursion into active politics (1952–84) as part of a larger grouping was brief and unsatisfactory.[16] For the past decade or so, therefore, the efforts of NU members has gone into redefining itself and "its" Islam. The process has been and remains uneven, being comprised of real differences of opinion, personal self-seeking, government intervention, and plain uncertainty. All of these factors have been discussed by competent authorities.

For now, the NU seems to have decided the main issue for itself. When asked what was the most important task facing the future Indonesia — what should be done? — Abdurrahman Wahid has said: "Indonesians have to understand the meaning of the Rule of Law." In a general sense he meant efficient judicial administration and an open and transparent administration of justice. It is a European fallacy to suppose that the "rule of law" in this sense is a European invention. All the great legal cultures, Islam included, know the meaning of the term though they may express it differently. Given his background (*pesantren*, Al-Azhar, and Baghdad University), Wahid's frame of reference is in Islam although this does not mean that he is unfamiliar with Western scholarship — on the contrary, he has read widely.

To understand Wahid's position it might be useful to begin by noting that he is essentially a moral philosopher, rather than a strict practitioner of the philosophy of (Islamic) law. His interest is in the moral good of society within the parameters of Islam. Whilst he shares a commitment to rationalism with Madjid and his colleagues, he tends to take the practice of rational thought as a natural given. It is the *use* to which this is put which is his main concern. This is an important distinction; to conflate the two is to impose confusion. There is no necessary causal link between the naturally given and the use to which it is put. There may be a commonality in "rational" but it can beg the question of what is meant by "rational". This is by way of a caution.

A further point to bear in mind is Wahid's "protective yet critical impulse" (Dr Greg Barton's phrase) towards the *pesantren* culture from which he comes. One may call it protective though this is to underestimate its fundamental importance in forming a whole view through which the world is refracted. Like Nasution before him he sees the curriculum, the basic source of knowledge, as crucial for Islam in this time of transition. And so it is — all social, political, or law reform starts with a curriculum, not with impractical legislation. Wahid's position is that: firstly, the *pesantren* system is valuable and needs preservation; and secondly, through its leadership, it must *demonstrate and deliver* a value to the social good. By the latter he means an ascertainable and qualitative contribution to the nation. To a Western reader this appears a vague prescription but in the Indonesian context it places quite considerable demands on its proponent. The reason is obvious; as is well known, the Indonesian legal system is chaotic, and not even an operative system at all. Its institutional structures are weak and it is plagued by endemic corruption. The place and function of *shari'a* within such a system has been and remains debatable and the concessions to Islam, in the form of *fiqh*, are minimal to the point of trivial.

Wahid's remedy, first suggested in a seminal paper "Making Islamic Law Conducive to Development", which is now almost twenty-five years old, is to align *shari'a* with the development of a national law. The theory of the past ages cannot be expected to provide solutions to the contemporary context of Indonesia. He comes very close to suggesting that the past *uṣūl al fiqh*, as formulated by the great jurist as-Shāfi'ī (767–820 CE) is, as such, irrelevant — too closely tied to the literalism of a bygone age. Instead, the profound truths of religion must be accommodated within the social and personal necessities of the day. While the *fiqh* is known in text form, its idiom is historically of other times and places. This does not mean to say that one disregards "rules" but that "rules" are not always unambiguous. Ambiguity is, of course, an important characteristic of *fiqh* in the contemporary nation-states, including Indonesia. The nature of ambiguity is to give options in social and political life which may vary and even contradict one another over time or by changed circumstance. Wahid recognizes this, whilst at the same time holding fast to the primacy of *shari'a* at the most fundamental level. Similarly one knows *shari'a*, at its most formal, in the great texts of the past. What one does with this knowing is quite another matter. In Wahid's case the political imperative appears to have led him towards an accommodation with the approved Pancasila ideology which is founded in a quite different legitimating source, the (secular) state. This is an ambiguous position; the circumstances just described are abnormal for Islam in the sense that Revelation has become a subordinate condition. Ambiguity has given to Islam the character of extreme relativity. A withdrawal from active politics is a partial option and this has been taken by the NU, the organization of which Wahid is head. This has the advantage of forcing attention to the more fundamental issues, and the debate at the moment is concerned with establishing or perhaps re-establishing the fundamentals of NU thought. Unfortunately this is less helpful for the philosophy of law — the main interest is in social philosophy. It is a legitimate programme, but not sufficient in legal theory.

Such a comment requires justification and now, by returning to Professor Hallaq's question — "where is the method?" — we may be able to give an answer. It is not to be found in speaking in terms of "traditional Islam", "responses to modernity", "humanistic pluralism", or the like. Instead, can we identify general principles which embody the rationale behind a *fiqh* rule, and then use this creatively? The nature of Revelation means that argument must be by deduction to determine the validity of a prescription which is particular to a time and place. Only Nurcholish Madjid attempts to provide a method to do this and his reasoning, as I understand it, is as follows.

Givens:

(a) The Qur'an is absolute and inviolate. The Sunna of the Prophet is an exemplification of the absoluteness of Revelation.
(b) Qur'anic hermeneutics show that Revelation consists of ideals and principles for man not regulating every last detail of life; hence the scholarly jurisprudence of the four Sunni schools.
(c) The idiom of Revelation is in seventh-century Arabic language and culture.

Method:

(d) Isolate those principles in the Qur'an which relate directly to social justice prescriptions.
(e) Specify the seventh-century cultural context of these prescriptions.
(f) Specify our own cultural context(s) in which these prescriptions are to (purportedly) apply.

The result will be a rational hermeneutic which will also be an internally consistent prescription. It is not secularism. Nor does it demand that we ignore the traditional scholarship. That which is appropriate (such as Ibn Taymiyah) should be retained, at least as an example.

Before looking at this in a little more detail, there is one further point. This discussion is about creating the methodology of a legal system for Indonesian Islam in the early twenty-first century. I am restricting the discussion because the *fatāwā* lay down rules, and it is essential to know how they are defined and arrived at. This is not an exemplar of Western cultural distinction or an orientalist reading of Islamic prescription. All legal systems rest upon this basic endeavour (in this case, *uṣūl al-fiqh*) without which there is no system. *Shari'a* in Indonesia raises this issue in a very frank and brutal way. Does Indonesia actually have a legal system in the formal sense? The usual test is efficacy in time and place, though degrees can never be exactly specified. This is not a new question, but it has become one of great importance in the twenty-first century. Indonesia certainly fails the efficacy test: laws are generally not known; they are in a state of internal confusion; and they do not determine behaviour. In short, neither public nor private law commands a general obedience. These comments may or may not apply fully to the religious courts; it is notable, however, that *fatāwā* from the NU and Muhammadiyah clearly reject the authority of the courts. At best *fatāwā* ignore the existence of the religious courts. In short, the efficacy test for the national legal system is not accepted by the Mufti or Fatwā Committee: efficacy is "in" Islam. We now come back to Madjid in more detail.

Givens:

(a) The Qur'an is not problematic; the Sunna is open to issue. The point is that Madjid is prepared to admit that the Sunna has a normative value independent of Revelation. He does not define this in detail nor is it necessary to consider it further here. The point is that in building his system, Madjid is allowing rational hermeneutics into the discussion at a very early stage. His view is that the Sunna, as such, is not a necessarily binding source of law in all its (the Sunna's) aspects. "Binding" here means binding for Indonesian circumstances. This certainly addresses the argument on efficacy of rulings (*ahkām*) but whether the basis for this is to be found in *istiḥsān* or *istislāḥ* is not clear — probably the latter. In any case, the position is sustainable within limits.

(b) A further issue is the status of 1,400 years of jurisprudence — *taqlīd*, *ijmā'*, and *istiḥsān*. The issue in Indonesia is the same as in all parts of the Muslim world. Perhaps the most striking example is in *takhayyur* (blending from different schools/doctrines), a sort of quasi-*ijtihād*. The Compilation of Islamic Law is an example, and not a happy one.

(c) The Qur'anic idiom is, in Madjid's view, self-evident. The importance of this given, however, really lies in the fact that it is stated at all. It is a reminder that for him, true reform must start with the basic text.

Method:

(d) Prescription and ethics can be separately identified. This is a defensible position but one not without problems for laws based in Revelation. The various views on Natural Law, which one finds in the standard textbooks, illustrate the dilemmas. Briefly, while Divine Wisdom directs man, Revelation by definition is not fully intelligible. However, as a rational being, man has the ability to distinguish between good and evil and the rules on these we call Natural Law. Human prescription derives from this but it *must be read with* those parts of Revelation which themselves contain prescriptions. Obvious examples in *shari'a* include those passages which deal with family and inheritance. The man-made positive law must not contradict these prescriptions. Madjid himself refers to "social justice", a pure Natural Law concept. It is the "limits of human authority" which are the issue here.

(e) Assuming the identification of prescription, however defined, we can only properly understand them in the context of seventh-century Arabia which is their idiom. We have to understand that idiom 1,400 years later. There is a huge assumption here; that history is truly objective and that a meaning in a particular context can be properly identified. It assumes, indeed, that the historian is a purely rational being without bias. But in the present instance, for Madjid, this is rather less than probable because his enquiry has a purpose which is not objectivity as such, but meaning for "social justice". The purpose, therefore, directs if not sets the criteria for "objectivity". One has to make a choice in such circumstances. Either one gives up because of the logical difficulties or one persists on the grounds that some conclusion, even if flawed in a Cartesian sense, is better than none at all. History, after all, is not science and we are bound to do the best we can with whatever evidence of the earlier time remains to us. Underlying everything is the fact that we are not dealing with a fixed corpus of material. New evidence gives rise to new explanations, in this case the formulation of prescriptions in a religious law. The 1,400 years of *fiqh may* be significantly modified but al-Shāfi'ī early recognized the danger of this in his objections to *istiḥsān.*

(f) Allowing that we can find some universally agreed position, the specification of the contemporary Indonesian cultural context bristles with difficulties. Essentially, what is "context"? Is it properly in philosophy, sociology of Islam, its political manifestation, or efficacy in a national legal system? Are these mutually exclusive or linked, and in any case is one or all to be linked to the seventh century; indeed, can such a link be considered appropriate?

These are the issues which, in various forms, are debated today in Indonesia. It is a rich and complex debate and one is reminded of the account which Professor Hallaq gives of the thought of Fazlur Rahman (d. 1988) with whom Madjid has much in common. One can agree that we now have the beginnings of a methodological system. However, the real Indonesian problem lies in whether or not Indonesia actually has a so-called proper legal system. It is doubtful and the methodology proposed by Madjid may, in fact, be stillborn.

I have attempted to describe "contexts" but one might actually make a case to show that the "contexts" described are, in fact, much more than that. They really amount to a variety of definitions of Islam. Each definition is "Islam" in its own way but, having said that, none is totally separate from any other or others. The key to understanding the variety of definitions — indigenous, colonial, post-Independence — lies in the scholasticism of the twentieth century. While the Egyptian reformers certainly set the agenda for this 100 years ago the Indonesian use of that agenda can only be understood through Indonesian scholastic effort.

The scholasticism of the past century, like the scholasticism of the preceding history of Islam, is concerned to explain or translate *shari'a* to the world while maintaining the integrity of Revelation. In this sense it is not new. However, in twentieth-century Indonesia we must distinguish between a responsive scholasticism and a creative scholasticism.

The first is characteristic of the colonial period and is characterized by a defensiveness in law and dogma. Such an attitude is perfectly understandable. For the first time in Indonesian history, the conditions within which Islam had to exist were not susceptible to answers from within. Indeed, even the texts were open to questions as to their validity in the nineteenth century. Answers from within Islam were not sufficient in the new conditions. The solution was to advocate changing the conditions — to look for an Islamic polity, to encourage or force the individual to become a good (better) Muslim. In other words, to change the contexts within which Islam found itself. The assumption was that Islam itself did not need and was not subject to the same demand. It was already perfected. This was the view associated with the NU and Persis, but even in Muhammadiyah one has to reach a point at which perfection is a given. The responsive scholasticism went into defending and demonstrating the perfectness of Islam in the face of the obvious fact of its subject status in colonial Netherlands East Indies.

We have to wait until well into the post-Independence period — say from the late 1960s — to find clear indications of a creative scholasticism. By this I mean one which is self-confident enough to propose serious change, alteration, or adaptation of classic scholasticism. Whatever the language used (Hazairin, Sjadzali, Nasution, Madjid, Wahid), the common intention is to explain the truths of Islam from within in a way which is positive and useful for the Indonesian *ummah*. The emphasis is on the creativity inherent in Islam, the true flowering of which can be achieved through rational thought which is itself God-given. Creativity is a duty but, as is recognized, it also has its dangers. Here are two:

Firstly, Islam as object: creativity means selection and choice. For Indonesian Islam, as for Islam elsewhere, it raises yet again the Mu'tazilite–Asharite positions. Whilst it is premature to say that there is a common Indonesian position, it is certainly true to say that all streams of Muslim thought accept creativity as a possibility. However, each has a separate emphasis on reification. The spectrum is wide from the little-known "progressive" fringe groups, on the one hand, through Muhammadiyah contextualization, to Persis scripturalism, to NU *taqlīd*. But these are misleading classes, each varies in time and place and in particular subjects. However, none denies creativity and all run the risk of turning religion into an object — a "thing outside".

Secondly, Islamic studies: by what criteria does one approach the "thing outside"? For the responsive *ulama* the answer was found internal to Islam but it was not sufficient. For the creative thinkers, one has *ijtihād* — but what sort of *ijtihād* is it? We can find an answer when we look at the books cited in the post-Independence studies. Western philosophy and social sciences are well represented. It is hard to escape the conclusion that an internalized orientalism is present in Indonesian Islam. The degree of this presence must always be open to debate. Whether it is right or wrong in terms of some criteria is another matter. The answer is always going to be personal and ideological.

It is difficult not to conclude that the contemporary state dominance of *shari'a* may be more apparent than real.

Notes

*Parts of this chapter were written in 1999–2000 and have appeared in M. B. Hooker, *Indonesian Islam: Social Change through Contemporary Fatāwā* (Sydney: Allen & Unwin; Honolulu: University of Hawaii Press, 2003), pp. 30, 33–46.

1. There are partial exceptions (for example, in Saudi Arabia, Pakistan, and others) allowing greater scope for *shari'a* but these are crisis-driven and highly unstable. Sudan is an excellent example of the latter.
2. See Malcolm Kerr, *Islamic Reform* (Berkeley, California: University of California Press, 1966).
3. For the Middle East, see, for example, the essays in D. H. Dwyer (ed.), *Law and Islam in the Middle East* (New York: Bergin and Garvey, 1990). For India, see Asaf A. A. Fyze, *Outlines of Muhammadan Law* (London: Oxford University Press, 1964). For Southeast Asia, see M. B. Hooker, *Islamic Law in South-East Asia* (Kuala Lumpur: Oxford University Press, 1984).
4. See M. B. Hooker, *Islamic Law in South-East Asia*, pp. 249–55 for outline and references.
5. For outline, see M. B. Hooker, "The State and Syariah", in *Indonesian Law and Society*, edited by T. C. Lindsey (Sydney: Federation Press, 1999).
6. Cited in Deliar Noer, *The Modernist Muslim Movement in Indonesia 1900–1942*. (Kuala Lumpur: Oxford University Press, 1973), p. 234.
7. Cited ibid., p. 83.
8. Especially in his *Definisi dan Sendi Agama* (Jakarta: Bulan Bintang, 1970).
9. Noer, *Modernist Muslim Movement*, Note 7 on pp. 275–90.
10. See Wael Hallaq, *A History of Islamic Legal Theories* (Cambridge: Cambridge University Press, 1997), especially Chapter 6 "Rises of Modernity: Toward a New Theory of Law?".
11. See the essays in Robert W. Hefner and Patricia Horvatich, eds., *Islam in an Era of Nation States* (Honolulu: University of Hawaii Press, 1997).
12. An exception is the recent article by R. Michael Feener, "Indonesian Movements for the creation of a 'National Madhhab'", *Islamic Law and Society* 9, No. 1 (2002): 83–116.
13. For biographical details, see Saiful Muzani, "Mutazilah Theology and the Modernization of the Indonesian Muslim Community: Intellectual Portrait of Harun Nasution", *Studia Islamika* 1, no. 1 (1994): 91–132.
14. For further details, see Greg Barton, "Indonesia's Nurcholish Madjid and Abdurrahman Wahid as Intellectual 'Ulama': The Meeting of Islamic Traditionalism and Modernism in Neo-Modernist Thought", *Studia Islamika* 4, no. 1 (1997): 29–82.
15. Abdurrahman Wahid, "Foreword", in *Nahdlatul Ulama, Traditional Islam and Modernity in Indonesia,* edited by Greg Barton and Greg Fealy (Melbourne: Monash Asia Intitute, 1996), p. xiii.
16. Barton, "Indonesia's Nurcholish Madjid", p. 17.

References

Barton, Greg. "Indonesia's Nurcholish Madjid and Abdurrahman Wahid as Intellectual '*Ulama*': The Meeting of Islamic Traditionalism and Modernism in Neo-Modernist Thought". *Studia Islamika* 4, no. 1 (1997): 29–82.

Chalil, Moehamad Haji. *Definisi dan Sendi Agama.* Jakarta: Bulan Bintang, 1970.
Dwyer, D. H., ed. *Law and Islam in the Middle East.* New York: Bergin and Garvey, 1990.
Feener, Michael R. "Indonesian Movements for the Creation of a 'National Madhhab'". *Islamic Law and Society* 9, no. 1 (2002): 83–116.
Fyze, Asaf A. A. *Outlines of Muhammadan Law.* London: Oxford University Press, 1964.
Hallaq, Wael. *A History of Islamic Legal Therories.* Cambridge: Cambridge University Press, 1997.
Hefner, Robert W. and Patricia Horvatich, eds. *Islam in an Era of Nation States: Politics and Religious Renewal in Muslim Southeast Asia.* Honolulu: University of Hawaii Press, 1997.
Hooker, M. B. *Islamic Law in Southeast Asia.* Kuala Lumpur: Oxford University Press, 1984.
————. "The State and Syariah". In *Indonesian Law and Society,* edited by T. C. Lindsey. Sydney: Federation Press 1999.
————. *Indonesian Islam: Social Change through Contemporary Fatāwā.* Sydney: Allen & Unwin; Honolulu: University of Hawaii Press, 2003.
Kerr, Malcolm. *Islamic Reform.* Berkeley, California: University of California Press, 1966.
Muzani, Saiful. "Mutazilah Theology and the Modernization of the Indonesian Muslim Community: Intellectual Portrait of Harun Nasution". *Studia Islamika* 1, no. 1 (1994): 91–132.
Noer, Deliar. *The Modernist Muslim Movement in Indonesia 1900-1942.* Kuala Lumpur: Oxford University Press, 1973.
Wahid, Abdurrahman. "Foreword". In *Nahdlatul Ulama, Traditional Islam and Modernity in Indonesia,* edited by Greg Barton and Greg Fealy. Melbourne: Monash Asia Institute, 1996.

13

THE ROLE OF MUSLIMS IN THE NEW MILLENNIUM

Mohamed Aris Othman

We have just emerged from an American century, whatever that means. It could have been a German century had the Allied forces lost the Second World War, or a Japanese century had Hiroshima and Nagasaki been spared the atomic bomb. What happened, of course, happened by the will of Allah. The point is that military superiority was one of the deciding factors in the determination of world power on the cusp of the present millennium.

What about this new millennium? It could be an Asian millennium — and by Asia, of course, Australia is included. For Muslims, there is nothing very special about the new millennium. It will merely continue an arbitrarily defined periodization and pose even greater challenges for Muslims in particular and the world in general. However, Islam could be a unifying force for the entire world, in the sense that it could be used to foster a meaningful relationship between Muslims and non-Muslims. To wield such a force, Muslims must be advanced in all fields.

In this chapter I will discuss the challenges that Muslims face in the new millennium. There is a need to resolve the issue of the reconstruction of knowledge in line with the Islamic vision so that this knowledge can be fully utilized for the needs of the *ummah*. In Islamic universities this is being achieved by integrating courses on revealed knowledge (such as *Fiqh* and *Usuluddin*) with human and physical sciences courses. While being prepared for professional careers, students are also being exposed to the religious vision. Muslim intellectuals were preoccupied with this issue in the last quarter of the twentieth century. The effort to reconstruct knowledge is in line with the need to produce professionals in all fields who are morally upright. There is also a need to reduce friction among Muslims. In this context, the *ummah* should not be divided by trivial differences, and the *ummatic* vision should be fully exploited. Moreover, there is a need for non-Muslims to understand more about Islam, which will bring them into a closer and more meaningful relationship with Muslims.

Lack of knowledge was the fundamental problem that was faced by Muslims in the previous millennium, and this caused various socio-economic and political problems for the *ummah*. It is the task of all Muslim intellectuals to resolve this issue. The Muslim call for the reconstruction of knowledge happened as early as the Abbasid Khulafa (eighth century CE), when scholars were charged with the task of reconstructing Greek, Persian, and Indian knowledge in line with the Islamic vision.

At the Second International Conference on the Reconstruction of Knowledge in accordance with the Islamic Vision, which was held in Islamabad, Pakistan, in Rabiul Awal 1402/January 1982, the participants agreed to conduct a post-mortem of the dilemma that was faced by the *ummah*, and their poor intellectual, political, and economic conditions. Islamic minds must be awakened, and various territories must be explored to ascertain how the general principles of knowledge reconstruction can be applied to the Arts and Sciences. There is a need to reform and develop Islamic thought and methodology, and the basic content, principles, goals, and values of the Islamic vision.[1]

In this exercise, it will be important to re-examine and remould knowledge in line with the Islamic vision. Indeed, it will be important to integrate modern disciplines into the Islamic vision. There is a definite need to promote the contributions of Muslim social thinkers in the fields of Sociology, Anthropology, History, Political Science, Psychology, Communication, and English.

Knowledge of the Qur'an and Sunna must be applied to the contemporary situation. Islamic religious disciplines need to be humanized in the sense that they must be relevant to contemporary issues. Islamic religious knowledge can, for example, address the issue of environmentalism, and many political issues can be addressed from Islamic perspectives. Thus, Islamic religious knowledge can also be a science to solve human problems.[2]

By the time that the Third World Conference was held in Kuala Lumpur, Malaysia (1404/1984), it was clear that the need to reconstruct knowledge in line with the Islamic vision had gone beyond the frontiers of academia, and had become the concern of the general public, institutions, and government.

It is not my intention here to glorify our past, but it is worth remembering that Muslims did their fair share of contributing towards the development of science and technology in the West. With this contribution from the Muslim world, the scholars of the Renaissance were able to develop their knowledge in the various branches of science and technology, such as navigation, astronomy, mathematics, chemistry, medicine, and pharmacy, thereby gaining political and economic superiority.[3] Today, Muslims are learning from the West, and they will do so well into this new millennium. What they will contribute to the West is an integrated outlook and a wholeness of life that the West has relinquished in its thought and lifestyles. The Islamic approach to the use of science and technology will further reduce the danger of war and the use of weapons for human destruction. Scientific discoveries should also help Muslims (both *iman* and *taqwa*) to strengthen their faith in Allah.

As far as science and technology are concerned, there are two perspectives to be considered — their use and misuse. In many respects science and technology have been used for good purposes that are in line with social and moral values, but their misuse has had destructive effects. This became evident during the Industrial Revolution and has affected the peace and security of the world. Needless to say, more money has been spent on weapons than on food. The use of science and technology in line with Islamic values is necessary to fulfil the needs of the Muslim *ummah*. The last millennium was marked by the failure of the Muslim world to be on par with the advanced nations in terms of science and technology. Hence, there is much work in store for Muslims in the new millennium, and in science and technology they can benefit from the West. By reconstructing knowledge in line with the Islamic vision, Muslims do not have to reject everything that is Western. It is due to the need to produce morally upright men and women that a religious vision must be infused into modernity.

It is a gross misrepresentation to suggest that Islam rejects science and technology.[4] The period that immediately followed the Hijr (from the ninth century to the twelfth century CE) saw great advances in science and technology.[5] Indeed, science and technology have been regarded as crucial elements in Islam, behind which lies the recognition of Allah as the Almighty, the Absolute, and the Master of mankind. The decline in Islam's ability to shape world history began with the Scientific Revolution in western Europe, and the subsequent growth in military and economic power had adverse socio-economic effects on the Muslim world. Moreover, internal problems helped to accelerate Western colonization from the seventeenth century.

Thus, the reconstruction of scientific knowledge in line with the Islamic vision does not mean that we must change the basic laws of physics, chemistry, and so on. We must still study the structure of matter. The study of atoms and beyond is necessary. We can explain how water is formed but we cannot explain why it is formed. There must be a power beyond human comprehension, and that power is Allah.

Another major problem that is faced by the Muslim *ummah* is their failure to organize themselves as a united front. The need to reduce friction has long featured in the agendas of Islamic movements, which have had the common objective of producing a socio-economic and socio-political model of development in line with Islamic principles and *shari'a*.[6] These movements should not be looked upon as threats to the West. Pan-Islamic organizations such as the World Muslim Congress that was established in Mecca during 1926, and the Muslim League that was formed in Mecca during 1962, are examples of these movements.[7]

By the sheer weight of their numbers, Muslims have been perceived as a collective threat to the West. Islam is a majority religion in 42 nations, with 700 million believers in Muslim majority areas and 400 million Muslims in the rest of the world. One would expect that there is a conflict between Islam and the West in terms of moral values and principles, but there are also areas in which there is no conflict, and in which they can co-operate. In response to Western hegemony, the Muslim world has to develop its own strategic, political, and economic interests. Thus, the effort to rebuild and reconstruct Muslim society should not be looked upon as a threat to the West.

The need to restructure Muslim society is necessary because certain factors have caused it to become disorganized. Firstly, the disorder that was created by colonialism resulted in the exploitation and suppression of indigenous populations. Secondly, the process of alignment to the West because of the vested interests of some leaders has caused disunity in the Muslim world. Thirdly, the failure of the secular leadership in the Muslim world to work for the *ummah*. This leadership is characterized by secularism, corruption, and autocracy, and must be replaced. The need for reorganization should not be looked upon as a threat to the world. The role of Muslims in the new millenium must be understood in the context of realizing the *ummatic* vision.

Islamic movements, especially in the last quarter of the twentieth century, have always been looked upon as "fundamentalist threats".[8] NATO (North

Atlantic Treaty Organization) generals have claimed that the most likely military confrontation of the future would come from Islam in the form of a north-south conflict and not an east-west conflict. The West must come to terms with Muslims. It must realize that Muslims need to have a share of such things as raw materials, international trade, and Western markets for their commodities.

In contradistinction, Muslims must re-examine themselves. They must learn to resolve their socio-political and socio-economic problems through negotiation, and remember the Qur'anic maxim that Allah will not change their destiny unless they make the effort to change. According to the saying of one of the Prophet's companion (Ibn Mas'ud), they must fulfil their obligations to Allah as if they are going to die tomorrow, and struggle for worldly gain and economic prosperity as if they are going to live for another 1,000 years.

The relationships between nations have taken on new meanings amid the phenomenon of globalization. Muslims in the new millennium will have to come to terms with this phenomenon, and Islam can provide spiritual values both to believers and non-believers. The idea of a borderless world should benefit both Muslims and the West. Globalization should not be used to exploit developing nations that happen to be Islamic by appropriating their sophisticated technology and capital.

There have been signs of positive change in the attitudes of Western Orientalists towards Islam. According to Murad Hofmann, there has been a conscious effort on the part of European academics to embrace Islam, and a number of them are on the brink of pronouncing the *shahadah*. On the part of Muslims, there are wealthy leaders who can contribute materially to the *dakwah* movement.

Today there are about 2 million Muslims each in the United States and Germany. In Great Britain there are about 1 million, whilst in France there are about 2.5 million. There are mosques from Los Angeles and Moscow to Rome and Zagreb. In 1994, Spanish Muslims established the International Islamic University, the "Averoes" of al Andalus. Five centuries after the fall of Muslim Spain, the *azan* or calling for prayer can be heard again not far from the old mosque of Cordoba.[9] This may seem like a provocation in the West. However, Islamic movements in the new millennium should not be looked upon as threats, but as healthy competition that will reciprocally contribute to world peace.

We must not forget the role of Muslim social scientists in the new millennium, and their role in working for the welfare of the *ummah* in particular, and the world in general. It is necessary for these social scientists to be properly equipped with the religious vision that will enable them to solve the problems of the *ummah.* Muslim social scientists must study Islamic values and ideals that are consistent with progress. For example, the economic goal of becoming prosperous is tied to the basic tenet of the pilgrimage to Mecca. The search for wealth and material gain is certainly not incompatible with Islam.[10]

Research must also be conducted into the positive effect of the communal life of Muslims in modern industrialized and commercialized societies. Muslim social organization at all levels is based on the spirit of co-operation: we live in *jama'ah* (communities). We know that many social problems result from family break-ups and suicide that mar the individualistic modern societies of the West. Muslim social scientists should also embark on research projects in areas such as health and education. The literacy rate is still low in Muslim nations, and resistance to modern health care is thought to be associated with illiteracy. In this context, social scientists can be agents of change and deal with the human dimensions of development.

In conclusion, it must be emphasized that non-Muslims need to understand more about Islam, and this calls for a more concerted effort to spread the Islamic message to the world. It is also necessary for Muslims to put their own house in order and face the challenges of the new millennium.

Notes

1. The need for a paradigm shift in the human sciences was felt in the early 1970s when this issue was raised by Muslim social scientists in the United States. The First World Conference on Muslim Education in Mecca in 1977 then reasserted the need to bring the human sciences in line with Revelation (*wahyu*), the need to realize the symbiotic relationship between Revealed Knowledge and acquired knowledge. See *Toward Islamization of Disciplines,* Islamization of Knowledge Series No. 6 (2nd ed.) (Herndon, Virginia: The International Institute of Islamic Thought, 1995).
2. Mohd Aris Othman, "Paradigm Shift in Human Science", Keynote Address to the International Conference on Islamisation of the Human Sciences, International Islamic University of Malaysia, 4–6 August 2000.
3. Seyyed Hossein Nasr, *Science and Civilization in Islam* (New York: The New American Library, 1970).
4. Sohail Inayatullah, "The Future of Science in the Islamic World (Reflections)", *The American Journal of Islamic Social Sciences* 14, no. 3 (1977): 77–81. See also Mehdi Golshani, "Philosophy of Science from the Qur'ānic Perspective", in *Toward Islamization of Disciplines.*

5. Seyyed Hossein Nasr, *Science and Civilization.*
6. Zeenath Kausar, ed., *Political Development: An Islamic Perspective* (Petaling Jaya, Malaysia: The Other Press, 2000).
7. On the future relations of Muslim countries, see M. Kamal Hassan, *Intellectual Discourse at the End of the 2nd Millennium: Concerns of a Muslim-Malay CEO* (Kuala Lumpur: International Islamic University of Malaysia Press, 2001), pp. 79–100.
8. On Islamic Fundamentalism, see Ahmad H. Sohr, "Islamic Fundamentalism", in *Muslims and Islamization in North America: Problems and Prospects*, edited by Amber Haque (Maryland: A. S. Noordeen and Aman Publications, 1999).
9. Murad Hofman, *Islam 2000* (Maryland: Aman Publications, 1996), p. 8.
10. Mohd Aris Othman, "Non-Economic Factors which Affect Economic Development of Rural Malays", *Akademika* 13 (1978): 1–9.

References

Golshani, Mehdi. "Philosophy of Science from the Qur'anic Perspective". In *Toward Islamization of Disciplines.* Islamization of Knowledge Series No. 6. Herndon, Virginia: International Islamic Publishing House, 1995.

Hassan, M. Kamal. *Intellectual Discourse at the End of the 2nd Millennium: Concerns of a Muslim-Malay CEO.* Kuala Lumpur: International Islamic University Press, 2001.

Hofman, Murad. *Islam 2000.* Maryland: Aman Publications, 1996.

Inayatullah, Sohail. "The Future of Science in the Islamic World (Reflections)". *American Journal of Islamic Social Sciences* 14, no. 3 (1977): 77–81.

Kausar, Zeenath, ed. *Political Development: An Islamic Perspective.* Petaling Jaya, Malaysia: The Other Press, 2000.

Nasr, Seyyed Hossein. *Science and Civilization in Islam.* New York: The New American Library, 1970.

Othman, Mohd Aris. "Non-Economic Factors which Affect Economic Development of Rural Malays". *Akademika* 13 (1978): 1–9.

———. "Paradigm Shift in Human Science". Keynote Address to the International Conference on Islamization of the Human Sciences, International Islamic University of Malaysia, 4–6 August 2000.

Sohr, Ahmad H. "Islamic Fundamentalism". In *Muslims and Islamization in North America: Problems and Prospects,* edited by Amber Haque. Maryland: A. S. Noordeen and Aman Publications, 1999.

Toward Islamization of Disciplines. Islamization of Knowledge Series No. 6. 2nd ed. Herndon, Virginia: The International Institute of Islamic Thought, 1995.

Conclusion

14

DEVELOPING ISLAMIC ARGUMENTS FOR CHANGE THROUGH "LIBERAL ISLAM"

Virginia Hooker

> Preserve the fire of Islam not its ashes! Discover the fire of Islam! (President Sukarno, 1958).[1]

The last decade of the twentieth century saw the publication of many writings by Muslims who argued that extremists were causing violence not only to people but also to the basic precepts of Islam. In 1997 for example, Bassam Tibi, well-known analyst of contemporary Islam, concluded the Preface to his book *The Challenge of Fundamentalism*, with the sentences: "As the 'open society' has its enemies, to use the phrase of Sir Karl Popper, so too does an 'open Islam' have its enemies: the fundamentalists. They are a challenge not only to world order but also to us liberal Muslims".[2] Tibi's response to "the burgeoning global phenomenon of religious fundamentalism" is "a compact based on secular democracy and human rights". If this were to become the basis for "an international cross-cultural morality", he argues, different civilizations and cultures might be brought together into more peaceful forms of coexistence.[3]

The last chapter of Tibi's study canvasses the possibility that human rights might become the means of establishing "a cross-cultural international morality" which could be shared by individuals in Muslim and Western civilizations. In reaching this position, Tibi acknowledges the "inspiring" discussions he enjoyed in Jakarta with Indonesian Muslim intellectuals. That experience led him to believe that "Southeast Asian Muslims offer us some hope for easing the desperate situation of Islamic civilization and the disintegrating order of the world at the turn of the new century".[4] Tibi uses the term "liberal Muslims" and he singles out Southeast Asia, in particular Indonesia, as the region which might produce ideas for cross-cultural understanding, which could underpin a new sense of morality for all mankind. His optimism is the starting point for this final chapter which will encompass many of the themes of the previous chapters but present them through the eyes of a recently formed group of "liberal Muslims" in Indonesia.

In his book, Tibi was referring to the late twentieth and early twenty-first century and he may not have realized that, a century earlier, Indonesian Muslims were already engaged in debates about how to combine the principles of Islam with the demands of a modern world.[5] Their argumentation and writings were greatly influenced by the intellectual movements in Cairo which, responding to Western ideas of progress, were advocating that Muslims pay greater attention to the achievements of the West or risk being left behind in a rapidly changing world.

Many Muslims in Indonesia are still inspired by the modernizing Muslims of the late nineteenth century and by their successors, the neo-modernist Indonesian thinkers (especially Nurcholish Madjid and Abdurrahman Wahid) who developed their philosophies during the 1970s. The group of Indonesian liberal Muslims has been chosen as representative of other similar groups who are actively engaging with the challenge of how to be true to Islam and at the same time use concepts developed by the non-Muslim West (secularism, equal rights for women, scientific rationalism, capitalism).

One of the reasons why Tibi and others have remarked on the vibrant nature of discussions in the Muslim intellectual milieu of Indonesia is that there has always been a tradition of serious debate in Muslim communities of the archipelago. This has strong roots in the many societies which make up Indonesia and demonstrates a genuine tolerance of diversity of thought and respect for informed opinion. Religious debate is considered a normal part of religious life and the Indonesian tradition has long drawn on intellectual trends beyond its own region, encountered by its scholars and savants in their contact with foreign visitors or on their own extensive travels. The group to be discussed in this chapter exhibits the same flair for eclectic argumentation, a flair they share with many other groups in the Muslim world of the early twenty-first century.

However, in Indonesia, unlike some Muslim countries, there is also the legacy of Dutch colonialism and the Japanese occupation, which insisted on separation of religion and politics in all matters of governance. This separation which, although not unchallenged, was maintained by the secular nationalists who governed Indonesia after independence and during the 1950s. Under the second president, General Soeharto, religion was restricted in its political expression to one, government-dominated party, and Islamic political activity was virtually banned. President Soeharto's policies of economic development and social engineering (mass literacy campaigns, improved communications for domestic security, population control, and political ideology of unity in diversity) supported by the armed forces which duplicated all civil positions of governance, resulted in quite spectacular economic growth.[6] Servicing this growth, through an expanding bureaucracy, an uncontrolled finance system, and burgeoning military activity, was an active and ambitious middle-class who had access to higher education (at home and abroad), international travel and expensive consumer goods. However, among the Muslims in this economically advanced group were a number who realized they did not understand their own religion sufficiently, were uneasy with the pace of change, and were thus motivated to attend discussion groups and seminars about their religion. One of the most active of the organizations providing these instructional courses was the Paramadina Foundation (1986) whose star was Nurcholish Madjid.[7] On state university campuses, students formed discussion groups to learn more about Islam and to discuss its role in the nation-state. Although this kind of debate was discouraged by New Order ideologies it was nevertheless sustained within the narrow confines of campus mosques and in private discussion circles. In some Islamic tertiary institutions, academics (led by Harun Nasution as described in M. B. Hooker's Chapter 12 in this volume), introduced their students to the writings of modernists in the Middle East and in the West.[8] In short, economic prosperity and individual uncertainty had resulted in many of the élite, the holders of power, searching for deeper meaning for the life of the nation.

Unable to engage in politics, many Muslims, young and old, devoted some of their time and money to helping the less fortunate in their communities not only in material terms but also through religious outreach activities, termed *dakwah*. President Soeharto was not unaffected by the uncertainty and increased interest in Islam, and in the early 1980s employed a Muslim teacher to work with his family, set up a foundation to subsidize the building of mosques throughout Indonesia, and made the pilgrimage to Mecca in 1991.[9] In 1990, the President supported a move to establish a national association for Muslim intellectuals, ICMI (Ikatan Cendekiawan Muslim Se-Indonesia, or Association of Indonesian Muslim Intellectuals). With presidential approval and led by Dr B. J. Habibie, the energetic (also erratic) Minister for Research and Technology, ICMI attracted a diverse membership which encompassed ministers, military figures, academics, journalists, and students. In their first national conference in December 1990, the theme was "To Build a Twenty-First Century Indonesian Society" in which many contributors urged Muslims to master the new technologies that would be needed to operate in the new millennium.[10]

The high public profile which the New Order regime allowed ICMI to develop led to considerable speculation in the early 1990s about its purpose and "true" significance. The diversity of ICMI's membership and the range of public statements made by some of its leading members about ICMI's aims — education, democratization, Muslim unity and so on — only ensured that speculation would persist.[11] Of longer term significance was the fact that many ICMI members had political clout and their interest in Islam ensured that Islam was not only a legitimate topic for public debate but that its potential as a political tool was again highlighted. The socio-economic context of the mid-1990s, however, became increasingly tense. The benefits of rapid economic growth evident from the late 1980s were not evenly spread throughout Indonesian society. The businesses reaping enormous profits were largely those which had collusive relationships with the government bureaucracy, politicians, and especially with relatives of President Soeharto, and to protect their interests there was a "proliferation of policy-generated barriers to domestic competition".[12] Under the New Order, power was based on wealth and violence was the means by which wealth was both obtained and maintained. Any public criticism of what was later referred to as KKN (*korupsi, kolusi, nepotisme*, or corruption, collusion, and nepotism) often resulted in state-condoned action to silence the critics.[13] Violence was used to demand and extort money on small and large scales in criminal networks which dominated urban life in Indonesia.[14] At the national level, the centralized policies of the Soeharto government, particularly the exploitation of natural resources in Kalimantan, Irian, Riau and Aceh, enabled income from those resources to be channelled to the élite in Jakarta, thus fuelling anger and disaffection among the affected populations.[15] At the root of this entrenched system of cronyism, monopolies, corruption, and violence was the ineffectual state of the law and institutions incapable of sustaining good governance.[16]

The Asian economic crisis of 1997 exacerbated the sense of inequality and injustice felt by increasing numbers of Indonesians. By May 1998, public criticism of the president and his closest advisers was reinforced by massive student protests, civil disorder and even more violence, which was ended only by the resignation of Soeharto as president on 21 May 1998.[17] The demands for *reformasi* or reform prompted the new president, B. J. Habibie, to respond with legislation for greater regional autonomy and to hold a new general election in 1999. Although Megawati Sukarnoputri's party was the popular winner she did not gain the presidency. Instead, an unexpected alliance of Muslim parties brought Abdurrahman Wahid to the top position. Many Muslims believed he would favour a greater role for Islam and for his Muslim supporters in the government and were disappointed when this did not happen. For these and other reasons, dissatisfaction with his style of government grew and, in June 2001, he resigned and was replaced by Megawati.

The close association between ICMI and key figures in the New Order meant that the advantages of being a member of ICMI and close to leading power-brokers in the regime no longer had the same benefits when the president stepped down. The ending of the New Order and the opening up of the formerly tightly controlled political sphere signalled the beginning of renewed struggles for power as well as calls for social and economic justice. A strong feature of the *reformasi* movement which had worked for the ending of the New Order was the emphasis on improving public understanding of the importance of good governance and democratization. A host of new non-governmental organizations (NGOs) were formed to respond to the impacts of the economic crisis and implement civic education programmes. Among them was a plethora of new Muslim organizations which provided practical assistance to victims of the economic collapse or tried to educate Muslims about their responsibilities as good citizens. A few, such as Jemaah Islamiyah, had been underground organizations during the New Order and after its fall, operated more openly.

The freedom to actively debate the role of Islam in a more democratic Indonesia was reflected in an outpouring of articles, books, television discussions and public lectures organized by a wide range of groups. One of these, held in February 2001, was attended by about 100 people who met at one of Jakarta's best known arts centres to listen to the first of a monthly series of talks about "liberal Islam". The term quickly became synonymous with a movement and group of the same name. The discussions about "liberal Islam", its meaning, its contribution to the contemporary expression of Islam, its relevance for Indonesia, its place in the life of individual Muslims, had the support of key media professional, Goenawan Mohammad, who facilitated their access to public fora. The "liberal Islam" debates and discussions were carried into the wider community through articles in the newspapers *Jawa Pos*, *Tempo*, and their networks, a Jakarta radio station, and an Internet website and mailing list. The mailing list, started in March 2001 with about 70 members but quickly grew to more than 400, representing Indonesians at home and abroad, Muslims and non-Muslims, and some foreign academics. The Indonesian members came from a variety of Islamic groups, think-tanks, institutes, and universities, and included journalists, activists, and researchers. A few were studying for postgraduate degrees in the Netherlands, Canada, the United States, and Australia.

A year after the launch of the on-line website, Luthfi Assyaukanie, one of the founders of the group, assembled and edited a representative collection of "liberal Islam" writings and interviews with leading Muslim intellectuals.[18] It was entitled *Wajah Liberal Islam di Indonesia* (The Face of Liberal Islam in Indonesia) and has a startling cover illustration of an old-fashioned set of timber wall-lockers, some open to show a variety of ticking clocks and one which holds a small time bomb. The clocks are traditional, modern and neo-modern (Mickey Mouse and "Endangered Species" feature on two of the clock faces) and suggest urgency and danger. The old-fashioned nature of the lockers is at variance with the zany, post-modern faces of some of the clocks and the viewer may wonder what lies behind the doors of the unopened lockers — are there more surprises?

The cover illustration is an effective introduction to the contents of the book, which are diverse, up-to-date in their concerns, and ready to challenge many traditionally held assumptions about the interpretation of Islam. The time bomb, readers will probably assume, represents religious fundamentalism but contributors to the book make it clear that the principles which underpin fundamentalism are diametrically opposed to the creativity of thought which they espouse. The contributors and Luthfi Assyaukanie, the editor, provide a range of definitions for their understanding of "liberal Islam".[19] In the summary which follows below, the views of the Liberal Islam group will be treated collectively, and individual viewpoints will not be identified specifically, although it should be understood that quite heated debate between members of the mailing list is a feature of the movement.

The term "liberal Islam" is understood by many Muslims to refer to the practice of *ijtihad* — the creative interpretation of Islam which enables it to remain relevant to the changing needs of conditions and times, place and history. However, the Indonesian group goes to some lengths to present their own understanding of the term. It is important to understand how they think of the concept "liberal" and how they position themselves in relation to other groups. It becomes clear that their understanding of terms such as "liberal", "left", and "conservative" is relative, and differs from the understanding of many non-Indonesians as well as their critics in Indonesia. When describing "liberal Islam" they stress that "liberal" must be differentiated from "liberalism". In Western thinking, they explain, liberalism is often identified with the right, whereas in the discourse of Islamic thinking liberal Islam is associated with movements of the left. (It should be noted that the contributors' use of these terms is not defined clearly.) They argue that the terms left and right are useful in the context of liberal Islam to distinguish more readily between thinking which is progressive and inclusive in contrast to that which is conservative and closer to traditional interpretations of Islam. Liberal Islam is Islam which is critical, progressive, and dynamic. The qualities associated with it, according to its proponents, are openness, pluralism, tolerance, and inclusion. The roots of this approach are found within Islam itself because Islam is liberating. And exploring the sense of *liber* (Latin: free), they argue that liberal Islam encourages its followers to be free to interpret and be critical of the classical scholars of Islam and be free to take the best of the old and jettison what is not appropriate for the present. Although there is considerable debate about the range of thinking covered by the term, several members of the group believe it is not productive to keep returning to questions of definition because if a term becomes too limited by its definition it is no longer liberal.[20]

There is also discussion concerning the intellectual genealogy of the movement. One member argues that the liberal views of the Mu'tazilis (eighth century CE) give the movement a very old pedigree.[21] Several agree that the main impetus for the movement can be traced to the Western-influenced Muslim intellectuals who had experienced life in Cairo and in France. Rif'at Tahtawi, Muhammad Abduh, Rashid Rida, Hasan al-Banna, and Sayyid Qutb are mentioned. Assyaukanie judges that the last three emphasized the "rightist" or traditional aspects of Muhammad Abduh's thinking, whereas Qassim Amin (1865–1908, often described as the first Muslim champion of women's rights) and Ali Abdul Raziq could be called "leftist" and thinkers in the tradition of modernist liberal thought. Here, Assyaukanie is clearly using "left" and "right" in a non-political sense.

In more contemporary times, the group identifies the following intellectuals as being associated with liberal Islam in the Arab world: Hasan Hanafi, Mohammed Arkoun, and Muhammad Abid Jabiri. Popularization of the term "liberal Islam" is ascribed to the book by Charles Kurzman, entitled *Liberal Islam: A Source Book*, while the concepts contributing to the development of liberal thought in the Middle East are said to be outlined in Leonard Binder's *Islamic Liberalism* and Albert Hourani's *Arabic Thought in the Liberal Age*.[22] However, the work which is given most credit for inspiring the thinking of many members of the Indonesian movement is A. A. Asaf Fyzee's *Modern Approach to Islam*.[23] His sentiment of understanding Islam in its present context rather than in its past or future manifestations is noted as having particular appeal to the Indonesian movement. Fazlur Rahman, they claim, built on and extended Fyzee's programme for a liberal approach to understanding Islam.[24]

The writings collected in *Wajah Liberal Islam di Indonesia* cover many issues: the relationship between Islam and democracy; human rights and Islam; inter-religious harmony; the status of women; the rights of religious minorities; Islam and secularism. Many individual points of view emerge in the samples of on-line debates which are included in the book. The debates surrounding two particular issues, however, provide a strong sense of the guiding principles and motivations of the movement. The first concerns the Qur'an and its interpretation and the second is the implementation of *shari'a* law in Indonesia.

In his Introduction to the collection, Luthfi Assyaukanie explains that the Qur'an was revealed gradually, over twenty-three years, and was "created" in space, in time and out of the interaction between the Prophet and Arab society. The Qur'an, he suggests, is not an encyclopaedia or a reference text, but a source of moral guidance and it is this which gives it the quality of universality. For Assyaukanie, the theories of intellectuals such as Mahmud Mohammad Taha, Nashr Hamid Abu Zayd, Mohammed Arkoun, and Fazlur Rahman, who have personally experienced the tensions between tradition and modernity and have tried to resolve them, carry more weight than the words of isolated religious teachers whose experience is confined to life in remote villages.[25] Following on from this, Ahmad Sahal contributes a chapter on the method of interpreting the Qur'an practised by the second Caliph, Umar, whose interpretations of the Qur'an were based on the principle of *maslahah* (for the general good, for the welfare of the people) and involved the exercise of his power of reason (*ra'y*, rational thought). Caliph Umar's method of rational thought (as opposed to literal interpretation) can be traced through Ibn Rushd to Muhammad Abduh and is characterized by three positions which are critical starting points for liberal Islam. First, the body of the Qur'an cannot determine all aspects of life and the most important things are not able to be covered by technical stipulations. It is the Qur'an's abiding moral principles which can be used as the basis for guidance. Second, the use of human reason to interpret the Qur'an automatically gives value to the plurality of humankind and allows for interpretation based on differing contexts. Third, the text (in this case the Qur'an) always remains the text and it is only interpretations which vary. Interpretations are relative and cannot claim to be absolute so that a literal interpretation is only one of many ways of interpreting the Qur'an. As interpretations are diverse, so too is Islam.[26] The points made in this explanation of a particular method of Qur'anic interpretation recognize the primacy of the Qur'an as the source of guidance for humankind but, following the model of the Caliph Umar and later scholars, insists on the importance of rational thought, contextual considerations and the validity of pluralism (variety within Islam is to be expected).

A further contribution of understanding the Qur'an comes from Taufik Adnan Amal who summarizes recent research on the history of the compilation of the Qur'an as a text or document. One of his sources for information about texts of the Qur'an is al-Khu'i's *The Prolegomena of the Qur'an.*[27] The issues are not only differences of opinion based on the orthography, linguistics, and grammatical principles of the text but more substantial questions concerning different versions of the Qur'an. At present two versions exist (the standard Egyptian version which is used by the majority of Indonesians and another which is used in the Yemen and some parts of northwest Africa). While attempts to produce a new critical edition of the Qur'an have failed in the past, renewed interest in using a rational approach to Qur'anic interpretation may support such an enterprise now.[28]

The issue of "reconstructing the history of the Qur'an" was the topic of a public forum organized in Jakarta by the Liberal Islam Network in July 2001. Some of the heated interchanges between speakers are included in Assyaukanie's book.[29] One of the issues considered most critical was as follows. While it was recognized as important to have a version of the Qur'an which was as close as humanly possible to the Revelations received by the Prophet, the investigations and research leading to a "new" Qur'an might disturb and upset many Muslims, whose faith rested on the understanding that the Qur'an was immutable. Added to this was the probability that restoring other versions of the Qur'anic text would lead to increased plurality of interpretation and this may not always be helpful to believers. These views echo those of al-Ghazzali who in the eleventh century CE "had denounced the corrupting of the simple faith of the multitude with intellectualist arguments".[30]

We can summarize the positions of followers of Liberal Islam by extending al-Ghazzali's focus on the specific audience which would be affected by change. In the twenty-first century CE, the Indonesian liberal thinkers focus on three groups: first, Muslim intellectuals who have the training to engage in textual reconstruction of the Qur'an and whose method must take account of the principles of *kalam* (Islamic scholastic theology, an extremely specialized branch of the Islamic sciences); second, non-scholastic Muslims or ordinary believers whose needs must be handled with great care; and third, non-Muslims, for whom the inclusiveness and pluralism of the Qur'an are qualities to which they can respond.[31] What is noteworthy in the broader context of Islamic thinking in the contemporary Muslim world is the breadth of approach in the one "package". The liberal thinkers try to encompass the technical aspects of Islamic philosophy and theology (*kalam*) recognizing that the research required for Qur'anic study must not exclude this fundamental basis of Islamic knowledge. They also acknowledge the distress and anger which ordinary Muslims might feel when confronted with alternative readings of the holy scripture. Finally, their concern includes non-Muslims and an awareness that the possibility for greater mutual understanding should be explored.

The issue of whether or not the body of Islamic law loosely called *shari'a* should be formally implemented is the second issue which demonstrates many of the attitudes of the Liberal Islam group. As outlined in M. B. Hooker's chapter in this volume, during the period of New Order government (1966–98), the *shari'a* was codified and restricted in its application to marriage, divorce, custody and guardianship; inheritance; and trusts. In the post-Soeharto period and specifically under the provisions of the Regional Autonomy Law (No. 22/99), there have been greater opportunities for regional concerns to be expressed. The people of many regions in Indonesia have seen this as the opportunity to openly practise local customs and ceremonies which had not been encouraged under the New Order's cultural policies. Some Muslim groups in regions of Java and Sulawesi, in particular, have campaigned at the local level for the implementation of *shari'a* law. The "Committee for the Enforcement of Islamic Law" (Komite Penegakan Syariat Islam) is one example of such a group. Established towards the end of 2000, it was formed in South Sulawesi to lobby for special autonomy in South Sulawesi and the authority to implement *shari'a* law. The group's intimidation tactics and failure to prepare a well-developed programme to explain to the local Muslim community what would be involved in a programme of *shari'a* implementation has meant that to date it has not received wide support.[32] Nevertheless, the Indonesian and foreign media give prominence to regional movements calling for implementation of the *shari'a* and it remains an emotive issue in domestic politics. The Liberal Islam group devotes a special interview section of their book to the topic "The implementation of Islamic Law in Indonesia" and has published the views of leading Muslim intellectuals.[33]

The definition of *shari'a* is itself a matter of debate, but some in the group suggest it be understood in the broadest terms — that *shari'a* is the order or framework for all social life, including economic and political and aims to create a just society so that any system which guarantees justice will include the *shari'a* of Allah.[34] In practical terms, notes Musdah Mulia, the only woman interviewed on this topic, the implementation of *shari'a* in its broadest sense is not feasible. If we talk about implementation, she suggests, then we are discussing *fiqh* (jurisprudence) which involves the application of independent judgement by jurists when they have to interpret points of law for specific purposes. *Fiqh*, therefore, is an assemblage of very specific points of view and it is extremely difficult to say which is the "best" interpretation of the juristic principles of the Qur'an.[35] Her comments highlight the complexity of attempting to implement principles which can have such a range of interpretation.

Most Muslims accept that *shari'a* is at the heart of Islam and without it there is no Islam. However, interpreting and implementing the *shari'a* is a major issue for modern-minded Muslims and the subject of intense concern and controversy. The diversity of opinions among jurists is reflected at a higher level by the diversity which exists between different "schools" of Islamic law (*madhhab*). It is in fact the different interpretations of Qur'anic principles which differentiates between *madhhab.* It is this degree of internal variance which is identified by the liberal Islam followers as capable of causing contestation and dissension between Muslims which would be harmful to the community and to Indonesian society.

The experts interviewed in the Liberal Islam book also consider the reasons behind the calls for greater use of *shari'a*. They suggest that there is a close link with Indonesia's current socio-economic condition of anxiety and uncertainty which has followed the ending of the Soeharto regime and a massive financial collapse. In Professor Azyumardi Azra's view, it is precisely during such times of instability and transition that the *shari'a* may be seen by some Muslims as the solution to problems which have not been resolved by secular processes and institutions.[36] In other words, when there is a perceived failure of law and order and a decline in moral behaviour, some Muslims believe the implementation of *shari'a* would improve the situation. Masdar Mas'udi adds a further perspective to the link between *shari'a* and socio-economic conditions. He believes that if the concept of *shari'a* implementation is to be taken seriously, it would be essential first to resolve basic socio-economic problems, particularly poverty, so that people were no longer forced to commit crime in order to survive. If *shari'a* were to be implemented in a society in which there was social injustice and inequalities of any kind, then it would be unjust to punish the victims of poverty and discrimination. He also suggests that the supporters of *shari'a* implementation should be working to ensure a just system for all Indonesians, not only the Muslim majority.[37]

Concerns for the "audience" or individuals who would be affected by increased application of *shari'a* is again a feature of the liberal Islam responses. The points are made that the majority of "ordinary" Muslims do not understand the complexities of *shari'a* and would, therefore, not understand the purpose or meaning of many of the stipulations. One of the results of this imperfect understanding would probably be a failure to follow all aspects of the *shari'a*, thus leading to non-compliance. Second, in practical terms, it is very difficult to apply *shari'a* in a plural society which includes non-Muslims. Discrimination on a number of levels could occur leading to social (as well as political) fragmentation.

These responses to calls for the implementation of some form of *shari'a* reveal also the concern of liberal Islam supporters with the concept of liberty. The calls to *enforce* the *shari'a*, they argue, can be interpreted as a failure by those Muslims to persuade Indonesian Muslims to follow *shari'a* of their own volition. Forcing Muslims to follow a particular form of the *shari'a* (were the supporters of its implementation to be successful in drafting a workable system of Islamic law) could be construed as infringing their personal freedoms and basic human rights. It is a short step from concerns for individual liberties to the basic principles of democracy and the Liberal Islam collection does devote considerable space to discussions about the relationship between Islam and democracy. Of interest to a discussion of Islamic arguments for change are the group's advocacy of democracy as the political system most likely to sustain the highest values of Islam.

The group's arguments for suggesting a symbiosis of Islam and democracy rest on the premise that one of the highest values in Islam is justice. If the goal of an Islamically based society is to achieve justice for all people by providing access to education and economic opportunities, then a democratic system offers real potential for realizing these goals.[38] And, the supporters of liberal Islam argue, the growth of a culture of democracy is rooted in a culture of liberalism and acceptance of pluralism as a normal (rather than abnormal) condition.[39] As Bassam Tibi, among others, points out a recognition of the relationship between democracy and the "political culture of pluralism, human rights, and liberal tolerance" arises from acceptance of "cultural modernity".[40] This concept of cultural modernity has been rejected by many fundamentalist Muslims and marks a critical difference of attitude between them and other Muslims who seek common ground between Islamic and democratic principles.

Many of the contributors to *Wajah Liberal Islam di Indonesia* seem to focus on finding counterparts in Islam for concepts or principles developed by Western thinkers. For example, an Islamic counterpart is sought for the "live and let live" principle ascribed to John Stuart Mill.[41] Identifying these commonalities may facilitate interaction between Muslim and Western intellectuals but it will probably fail to make a long-term contribution to the discourse of liberalism in either intellectual milieu. Equally importantly, the search-and-find enterprise of matching concepts across intellectual traditions does little to build on and extend very strong intellectual traditions within Islam. A re-reading of works by Muslim scholars, particularly the *mutakallim*, of the pre-modern era will provide a rich lode of stimulating material to inspire creative approaches to contemporary issues. To suggest just one possibility for further exploration: the early Mu'tazilites (ninth and early tenth centuries CE) are credited with extending the theories of atomism first posited by Democritus and Epicurus. The theories they propounded have been described as "Islam's most original contribution to philosophy".[42] Their understanding of the universe was based on manifestation through monads, the ultimate unit of being. They theorized that monads occupy a position which is surrounded by a void, the hypothesis applying to monads of time as well as space. "The Muslim monads are, and again are not; all change and action in the world are produced by their entering into existence and dropping out again, not by any change in themselves".[43] Al-Ghazzali did not incorporate these concepts into his thinking and the Mu'tazilite approach was viewed with suspicion resulting in its exclusion from mainstream Islamic thinking. In Indonesia, Harun Nasution and others have reopened the possibilities which Mu'tazilite perspectives can offer modern thinkers and their theories of monads and their relationship with change may well repay further examination.

Mainstream Islam has generally not been receptive to theories of modernization. In their efforts to stimulate change, the members of liberal Islam have also been criticized for their ideas. As one contributor to the book asks, is liberal Islam so liberal that it is like plastic? Can it just be bent this way and that according to the interests of each of its interpreters? The same contributor also warns of the dangers of using the concept of "presentism" to evaluate the past, when concepts vital to modern society might have had no meaning for earlier societies. And when followers of liberal Islam debate points with Muslims who are not followers of that approach, who is to say which interpretation of the Qur'an is better?[44] The network of liberal Islam supporters state that they do not have all the answers and that liberal Islam is not a kind of "utopia". However, it does claim to create a climate which encourages new interpretations of Islam and at the same time to extend an understanding of this approach to wider groups within society.[45]

It should be noted that the wide-ranging nature of the debates and "free-thinking" of key members of the group have provoked quite intense reactions from some more conservatively minded Muslims. Some of these responses have been expressed in the media and through contributors to the Islam Liberal website. However, others have taken more sinister forms and a death threat was even issued against Ulil Abshar-Abdalla for his liberal views.

To return to the issues raised in the present volume, *Islamic Perspectives on the New Millennium*, each of the chapters has described both extremist and more moderate positions that have been adopted by members of a range of Muslim groups in the Middle East, South Asia, and Indonesia. The metaphor of the spectrum has been used in several of the chapters to describe the spread of opinion on each of the issues raised for analysis. Diversity of interpretation of the Qur'an and Sunna is the feature which is striking in all discussions of responses to modernities. The views of extremists have often stimulated those who do not agree with them to define and articulate alternative interpretations, just one example of which is the Liberal Islam movement in Indonesia.

The Indonesian Liberal Islam group draws on both Middle Eastern and Western sources for its interpretations of Islam and its views on the role of Islam in contemporary life. Many members of the group have a strong working knowledge of both the classical sources of Islam and Western critical theory. On many issues, such as human rights, use of natural resources, corruption, and transparency in financial and judicial institutions, the position of women and good governance, their views have much in common with non-Muslim thinkers. In particular, there is shared ground on views concerning the benefits and advantages of the secular state and plural societies.

However, it would be a mistake to assume that because there is much that is shared, the views of these Muslim intellectuals and non-Muslim intellectuals are identical. Muslims, moderate or not, have as their basic points of reference, the Qur'an and the Sunna, which would not be accepted as such by non-Muslims. And even within the liberal Islam network the metaphor of the spectrum is still valid. Some of its members would not go as far as others in their degree of acceptance of radical interpretations of the Qur'an.

The liberal Islam network provides just one example of the debates among young Muslim intellectuals who are grappling with developing a new understanding of Islam. Central to this understanding is a desire to give more prominence to those principles in Islam which support the ideals of democracy. In their current debates, they explore options for the kind of political organization which offers freedom of religious expression without disturbing the freedom of others. In their view, thinking should not be restricted to current structures such as the secular state but should try to envisage a form which allows space for human creativity, the quality described in earlier chapters in this volume. The aim of the ideal socio-political programme would be the solution to the issue of how all humankind, despite their differences of experience and history, could live equitably on this planet with its limited space and resources. The group's aims will have been realized if one day the word "Islam" will be synonymous with the spirit which works for the well-being of all humankind without exception.[46]

The slogan of the liberal Islam network, run as a banner on its website, reads "*Menuju Islam yang membebaskan*" (Towards a liberating Islam). The network, while still growing, represents a tiny percentage of Indonesian Muslims. Although their discussions are circulated on the Internet, on radio, at public meetings, and in the print media, they have made little impact on grassroots organizations. But this may be happening. Hefner has argued that a distinctive feature of Islam in Indonesia is the efforts made by intellectuals and other exemplary figures to link into and form "coalition structures" with mass-based organizations in society.[47] The contributors to *Wajah Liberal Islam di Indonesia* indicate that they acknowledge the challenge of transferring their liberal approach beyond their own circle. If the principles of the movement fail to be translated into practice they would consider liberal Islam to have failed.[48] The socialization of its ideas is perhaps the greatest challenge the group faces.

The liberal Islam movement exemplifies an interesting tension. Claiming that Indonesia's Muslim population exceeds that of the total Muslim population of the Middle East, the supporters of liberal Islam believe if they can establish an Islamic social system based on liberal principles, then Indonesia will lead the way in showing that they have achieved something which Afghanistan, Saudia Arabia, Iran, and Sudan have failed to do.[49] However, although presenting Indonesia as part of the wider Muslim world, there is a strong sense that the focus for change should be Indonesia and priority should be given to addressing the problems which confront Indonesians.[50] The movement expresses a strong sense of nationalism and localization which marks it as a very Indonesian expression of Islam, and a re-expression of the concerns of earlier Indonesian Muslims that society and people were the primary foci for change. For the earlier generations as well as the followers of liberal Islam, the concept of an Islamic state is not integral to the religion of the Prophet and is not in keeping with the Indonesian idiom of religious pluralism and cultural diversity.[51]

Bassam Tibi, like other foreign scholars who visit Indonesia, was impressed with the quality of the debates among the younger generations of

Muslim intellectuals he met there. He suggested in his own analysis of political Islam that the concept of human rights might be used to find common ground for an international cross-cultural morality. The Liberal Islam network is perhaps more realistic in its efforts to make contact with other Muslim groups in Indonesia and to engage with non-Muslims. They recognize that Muslim "hardliners" (as they are often termed in Indonesia) are unlikely to change their views and that many "ordinary" Muslims will also not agree with their very flexible attitude to Qur'anic interpretations. While many in the group believe strongly that the liberal Islam agenda should be spread as widely as possible through the Muslim community in Indonesia, nearly all of them seem to believe that what is of crucial importance in their movement is its tolerance of diversity and difference.[52] Their debates suggest that their primary concerns are wider than those of Bassam Tibi. Their debates suggest that, rather than using a concept such as human rights as the basis for finding commonalities with people and groups who do not share their ideas, they would prefer to recognize that differences do exist on even very basic issues. It is the acceptance of that right to differ which lies at the very heart of their beliefs. Some of the members of the Liberal Islam network ascribe the basis for this belief in pluralism to the modern-minded Muslims of the late nineteenth century, whose message is encapsulated in the words of Indonesia's first president and champion of a secular state, Sukarno, when he urged Indonesians not to preserve the ashes but rather to discover "the fire of Islam". In this, they are his heirs.

Readers who feel sympathetic to the aspirations and approach of "liberal Islam" need to be aware of the opposition and hostility such an approach can attract within the Muslim world. The Indonesian group described in this chapter has provoked strong criticism, some of which appears on its own website.[53] Other groups in Indonesia, with aims which are very similar to those of Jaringan Islam Liberal, do not receive the same level of publicity and interest but nevertheless initiate local study groups and sponsor public meetings and discussions which address the same issues as those which circulate among members of Jaringan Islam Liberal.[54] Such groups are increasing and they are matched by groups who strongly disagree with their aims and method of argumentation.

Preceding chapters in this book have described the diversity of current understandings of Islam. This final chapter has described the strength of feeling among Indonesian Muslims concerning the interpretation and implementation of Islam and the challenges this poses for active engagement with all areas of life in the twenty-first century. It stands as an example of the eclecticism of argumentation which underpins contemporary debates and the massive challenge of defining and understanding the *shari'a* in the postmodern age.

Notes

1. The original Indonesian reads, "Warisilah api Islam dan jangan kita warisi abunya! Galilah api Islam!" and was first used by Sukarno in letters to Islamic leaders written during his period of Dutch detention on the island of Endeh (Flores) between 1934 and 1936. He repeated the sentiment on various public occasions after he became President, one of the most notable being in his speech entitled "Religion and Science" to mark the opening of the Faculty of Islamic Law, Nahdlatul Ulama Institute of Higher Education, Solo, 2 October 1958. I am grateful to Yudi Latif for tracking down the reference and for constructive comments on an earlier draft. I would also like to thank Luthfi Assyaukanie for correcting several factual errors.
2. Bassam Tibi, *The Challenge of Fundamentalism: Political Islam and the New World Disorder* (Berkeley, Los Angeles, London: University of California Press, 1998), p. xv.
3. Ibid., p. xii.
4. Ibid., pp. 210–11 and xiv. Similar recognition of the importance of debates by Indonesian Muslims appears several years after Tibi's book in Esposito and Voll's "Abdurrahman Wahid: Scholar-President", in *Makers of Contemporary Islam*, edited by John Esposito and John O. Voll (New York: Oxford University Press, 2001), pp. 199–216.
5. As described, for example, in Anthony Milner, *The Invention of Politics in Colonial Malaya: Contesting Nationalism and the Expansion of the Public Sphere* (Cambridge: Cambridge University Press, 1995), pp.167–92.
6. See further Hal Hill, ed., *Indonesia's New Order: The Dynamics of Socio-Economic Transformation* (St Leonards: Allen & Unwin, 1994); Adam Schwarz, *A Nation in Waiting: Indonesia in the 1990s.* (Sydney: Allen & Unwin, 1994, revised 1999); and Donald K. Emmerson, ed., *Indonesia Beyond Suharto: Polity, Economy, Society, Transition* (Armonk, New York, London, England: M.E. Sharpe, 1999).
7. For background to Nurcholish Madjid's position, see Robert W. Hefner, *Civil Islam: Muslims and Democratization in Indonesia* (Princeton and Oxford: Princeton University Press, 2000), pp. 113–19.
8. In addition to the description of Harun Nasution's thinking given by M. B. Hooker in his chapter in this book, see also Prof. Dr Harun Nasution (Saiful Muzani, editor), *Islam Rasional: Gagasan dan Pemikiran*, 5th ed. (Bandung: Penerbit Mizan, 1998).
9. Robert W. Hefner, "Islamization and Democratization in Indonesia", in *Islam in an Era of Nation-States*, edited by Robert W. Hefner and Patricia Horvatich (Honolulu: University of Hawai'i Press, 1997), footnote 38, p. 120 and p. 88. For further details of the mosque-building programme, see Hugh O'Neill,

"Islamic Architecture under the New Order", in *Culture and Society in New Order Indonesia*, edited by Virginia Matheson Hooker (Kuala Lumpur: Oxford University Press, 1993), pp. 151–65.

10. Hefner, "Islamization and Democratization", p. 101.
11. For analyses of the aims and influence of ICMI see Douglas E. Ramage, *Politics in Indonesia: Democracy, Islam and the Ideology of Tolerance* (London and New York: Routledge, 1995), Chapter 3 and Robert W. Hefner, *Civil Islam: Muslims and Democratization in Indonesia* (Princeton and Oxford: Princeton University Press, 2000), Chapters 6 and 7.
12. For a fuller picture of this period, see Thee Kian Wie, "The Soeharto Era and After: Stability, Development and Crisis, 1966–2000", in *The Emergence of a National Economy: An Economic History of Indonesia, 1800–2000,* edited by Howard Dick, Vincent J. H. Houben, Thomas Lindblad, and Thee Kian Wie (St Leonards: Allen & Unwin 2002), p. 213.
13. For a recent study of corruption in Southeast Asia, see *Corruption in Asia: Rethinking the Governance Paradigm*, edited by Tim Lindsey and Howard Dick (Leichhardt: The Federation Press, 2002) and in particular Gary Goodpaster, "Reflections on Corruption in Indonesia", pp. 87–108.
14. For a graphic description of networks of local violence, see Tim Lindsey, "The Criminal State: *Premanisme* and the New Order", in *Indonesia Today: Challenges of History*, edited by Grayson Lloyd and Shannon Smith (Singapore: Institute of Southeast Asian Studies, 2001), see especially p. 288.
15. For more details, see Howard Dick, "State, Nation-State and National Economy", in *The Emergence of a National Economy*, edited by Howard Dick et al., pp. 9–34.
16. Thee Kian Wie, "The Soeharto Era and After", pp. 241, 242.
17. For descriptions of the ending of the New Order regime, see Geoff Forrester and R. J. May, eds., *The Fall of Soeharto* (Bathurst: Crawford House Publishing, 1998).
18. Publication details: Luthfi Assyaukanie, ed., *Wajah Liberal Islam di Indonesia*, (Jakarta: Jaringan Islam Liberal/Teater Utan Kayu, 2002), 315 pp., written in Indonesian. All English translations used in this chapter are my own.
19. Luthfi Assyaukanie provides some biographical details about himself, as an introduction to the collection, so that readers may see how his background has influenced his thinking. Born into a family of religious scholars and Islamic educators in Jakarta, his tertiary education was at Jordan University where he studied both religious and secular subjects. His seven-year stay in the Middle East was coloured by the debates of the late 1980s when intellectual positions on Islam were characterized as being either traditional, modernist/secularist or "eclectic" (also "neo-modernist", the term preferred by Fazlur Rahman). While there, he says, he witnessed Islam being regarded as an all-encompassing solution for any issue, yet the Muslim Brothers, members of Jordan's Parliament, failed when they tried to apply Islamic solutions to real problems. It exemplified for

him, an example of idealism clashing with the complexities of reality, particularly when Muslims tried to use rulings from the classical period of Islam in contemporary contexts for which, in his view, they were inappropriate. For Assyaukanie, the rise of liberal Islam in contemporary Indonesia is an attempt to face the realities of life using the basic Islamic principles of justice and equality (see Luthfi Assyaukanie, "Islam Liberal: Pandangan Partisipan", in Luthfi Assyaukanie, ed., *Wajah Liberal Islam di Indonesia*, pp. xv–xxvii.
20. Assyaukanie, *Wajah Liberal Islam di Indonesia*, pp. 158, 164, 200, 202, 203, 219, 225.
21. Mu'tazilis are credited with establishing the theological movement which created speculative dogmatics and with the strictly grammatical interpretation of the Qur'an, see further H. A. R. Gibb and J. H. Kramers, *The Shorter Encyclopaedia of Islam* (Leiden, New York: E.J. Brill, 1991), pp. 421–27.
22. For full bibliographic details, see entries in the References at the end of this chapter.
23. A. A. Asaf Fyzee, *A Modern Approach to Islam* (London: Asia Publishing House, 1963).
24. Assyaukanie, *Wajah Liberal Islam di Indonesia*, pp. 157–59, 163, 219.
25. Ibid., pp. xix, xx, xii.
26. Ibid., pp. 4–8.
27. Al-Khu'i, *The Prolegomena of the Qur'an*, translated by Abdulaziz A. Sachedina (New York: Oxford University Press, 1998).
28. Assyaukanie, *Wajah Liberal Islam di Indonesia*, pp. 78–91.
29. Ibid., pp. 174–96.
30. Gibb and Kramers, *Shorter Encyclopaedia of Islam*, p. 214.
31. In particular, the work of the South African, Farid Esack is cited. He has reconstructed the pluralist theology of the Qur'an to promote inter-faith solidarity in South Africa, see *Wajah Liberal Islam di Indonesia*, p. 204.
32. Further details about this group are given by Jennifer Donohoe, "Islamic Law and Competition for Power in the *Reformasi* Era" (unpublished Honours Thesis, Faculty of Asian Studies, The Australian National University, 2002).
33. *Wajah Liberal Islam di Indonesia*, pp. 96–119.
34. The definition is that of Masdar Mas'udi, in *Wajah Liberal Islam di Indonesia*, p. 103.
35. Ibid., p. 132.
36. Ibid., p. 99
37. Ibid., p. 103–105.
38. Ibid., p. 117.
39. Ibid., p. 207.
40. Bassam Tibi, *The Challenge of Fundamentalism*, pp. 24–25.
41. *Wajah Liberal Islam di Indonesia*, pp. 223–24.
42. Gibbs and Kramer, *Shorter Encyclopaedia*, p. 212.
43. Ibid., pp. 38–39.

44. *Wajah Islam Liberal di Indonesia*, p. 213.
45. Ibid., p. 230.
46. Ibid., pp. 210, 296.
47. Robert Hefner, "Civil Islam, Democratisation, and Violence in Indonesia: A Comment", *Review of Indonesian and Malaysian Affairs* 36, no. 1 (2002): 71.
48. *Wajah Liberal Islam di Indonesia*, pp. 207, 230.
49. Ibid., p. 224.
50. Ibid., p. 16.
51. Ibid., p. 291. Robert Hefner refers to the success with which "Indonesian Islam managed to keep its centre of gravity in society, rather than in a more direct union with the state". He mentions how some Indonesian Muslim scholars during the late 1950s argued strongly "against the idea that Islam requires the establishment of an 'Islamic' state", "Civil Islam, Democratisation, and Violence in Indonesia", p. 69.
52. For statements about the movement's aims and purpose, see its website <Islamlib.com>.
53. See Haidar Bagir, "Andai Aku Seorang Muslim Liberal", <Islamlib.com>, 17 August 2002, accessed 7 May 2003.
54. To take just one example, the Humanist Islam (Islam Humanis) group which is exploring how the concept of humanism can be sacralized especially by more actively drawing on the power and energy of Allah.

References

Al-Khu'i. *The Prolegomena of the Qur'an*. Translated by Abdulaziz A. Sachedina. New York: Oxford University Press, 1998.

Assyaukanie, Luthfi, ed. *Wajah Liberal Islam di Indonesia*. Jakarta: Jaringan Islam Liberal/ Teater Utan Kayu, 2002.

Binder, Leonard. *Islamic Liberalism: A Critique of Development Ideologies*. Chicago: University of Chicago Press, 1988.

Jennifer Donohoe. "Islamic Law and Competition for Power in the *Reformasi* Era". Honours thesis, Faculty of Asian Studies, The Australian National University, 2002.

Emmerson, Donald K., ed. *Indonesia Beyond Suharto: Polity, Economy, Society, Transition*. Armonk, New York and London: M.E. Sharpe, 1999.

Esposito, John and John O. Voll. *Makers of Contemporary Islam*. New York: Oxford University Press, 2001.

Forrester, Geoff and R. J. May, eds. *The Fall of Soeharto*. Bathurst: Crawford House Publishing, 1998.

Fyzee, A. A. Asaf. *A Modern Approach to Islam*. London: Asia Publishing House, 1963.

Gibb, H. A. R. and J. H. Kramers. *The Shorter Encyclopaedia of Islam*. Leiden and New York: E. J. Brill, 1991.

Hefner, Robert W. "Islamization and Democratization in Indonesia". In *Islam in an Era of Nation-States: Politics and Religious Renewal in Muslim Southeast Asia*, edited by Robert W. Hefner and Patricia Horvatich. Honolulu: University of Hawai'i Press, 1997.

———. *Civil Islam: Muslims and Democratization in Indonesia*. Princeton and Oxford: Princeton University Press, 2000.

———. "Civil Islam, Democratisation, and Violence in Indonesia: A Comment". *Review of Indonesian and Malaysian Affairs* 36, no.1 (2002): 67–76.

Hill, Hal, ed. *Indonesia's New Order: The Dynamics of Socio-economic Transformation*. St Leonards: Allen & Unwin, 1994.

Holt, P. M., Ann K. S. Lambton, and Bernard Lewis. *The Cambridge History of Islam*. Vol. 2A. Cambridge: Cambridge University Press, 1977.

Hourani, Albert. *Arabic Thought in the Liberal Age, 1798–1939*. Cambridge, New York: Oxford University Press, 1962.

Kurzman, Charles, ed. *Liberal Islam: A Sourcebook*. New York: Oxford University Press, 1998.

Lindsey, Tim. "The Criminal State: *Premanisme* and the New Order". In *Indonesia Today: Challenges of History*, edited by Grayson Lloyd and Shannon Smith. Singapore: Institute of Southeast Asian Studies, 2001.

——— and Howard Dick, eds. *Corruption in Asia: Rethinking the Governance Paradigm*. Leichhardt: The Federation Press, 2002.

Milner, Anthony. *The Invention of Politics in Colonial Malaya: Contesting Nationalism and the Expansion of the Public Sphere*. Cambridge: Cambridge University Press, 1995.

Nasution, Harun. *Islam Rasional: Gagasan dan Pemikiran*. 5th ed. Bandung: Penerbit Mizan, 1998.

O'Neill, Hugh. "Islamic Architecture under the New Order". In *Culture and Society in New Order Indonesia*, edited by Virginia Matheson Hooker, pp. 151–65. Kuala Lumpur: Oxford University Press, 1993.

Ramage, Douglas E. *Politics in Indonesia: Democracy, Islam and the Ideology of Tolerance*. London and New York: Routledge, 1995.

Schwarz, Adam. *A Nation in Waiting: Indonesia in the 1990s*. Rev. ed. Sydney: Allen & Unwin, 1999.

Thee Kian Wie. "The Soeharto Era and After: Stability, Development and Crisis, 1966–2000". In *The Emergence of a National Economy: An Economic History of Indonesia, 1800–2000*, edited by Howard Dick, Vincent J. H. Houben, Thomas Lindblad, and Thee Kian Wie. St Leonards: Allen & Unwin, 2002.

Tibi, Bassam. *The Challenge of Fundamentalism: Political Islam and the New World Disorder*. Berkeley, Los Angeles, and London: University of California Press, 1998.

GLOSSARY

ahl al-sunnah wa al-jama'a	Sunni Muslims
al-Hijrah	the migration (or flight) of the Prophet Muhammad from Mecca to Medina in 622 CE, the year which Muslims recognize as the beginning of the Muslim era, signified by the letters AH (*anno hijrah*)
al-jama'a	the community
al-Qur'an	the divinely revealed scripture of Islam which provides a complete religious, moral and ethical system for Mankind
'amal	practice, action
'aql	intelligence, reason, rationality
Ar-Rahim	in relation to Mankind, God the Giver of Compassion
Ar-Rahman	God, the Compassionate One
Asharite	followers of al-Ash'ari, 9th century founder of Islamic scholasticism known as *kalam*, which he developed in opposition to the Mu'tazilites (see below) and in which he was supported by the Shafi'ites (see below) — "conservative" in method
bay'	contract of sale
CE	Common Era (of dating)
dakwah	Islamic outreach

DPR	Dewan Perwakilan Rakyat (People's Representative Assembly)
FIBE	Faisal Islamic Bank of Egypt
fiqhi, fiqh	of law; legal prescriptions
fatwa (plural: *fatawa*)	opinion given by an *ulama* (see below) in response to a question concerning a matter of law or doctrine
G-7	Group of Seven (Canada, France, Germany, Britain, Italy, Japan, the USA), the world's seven leading industrialized democracies
GOLKAR	Golongan Karya (Functional Groups), the ruling political party under President Soeharto
Hadith	saying or act of the Prophet as witnessed by a contemporary and passed on by transmitted accounts which are a source of Islamic law
halal	permissible
haram	forbidden
IAIN	Institut Agama Islam Negri (State Institute for Islamic Studies)
ibadat	prescribed religious duties which are not to be varied in any way
ICMI	Ikatan Cendekiawan Muslim Indonesia (Indonesian Muslim Intellectuals' Association)
ijara (Arabic: *ijra'*)	legal enforcement
ijma'	consensus of juristic reasoning/opinion
ijtihad	the "effort", or "struggle" of using scholarly reasoning to interpret the sources of Islam
ikhtilaf	differing interpretations of Islamic sources
iman	faith, religious belief
intifadah	uprising
istihsan	the method of legal reasoning which allows deviation from one ruling to a more relevant position (juristic preference)
istisna'	exception
jabariya	the doctrine that Man's acts are predestined

jama'ah	community, gathering
JIB	Jordan Islamic Bank
jihad	to exert every effort to live according to God's ways including opposing His enemies
kadi	judge
khilafat / khulafa	Caliphate: union of the Muslim world under one ruler who will fulfil God's Will
KISDI	Komite Indonesia untuk Solidaritas Dunia Islam (Indonesian Committee for Islamic World's Solidarity)
KKN	*korupsi, kolusi, nepotisme* (corruption, collusion, nepotism)
madhhab	"school" of Islamic law
mahram	intermediaries
MPR	Majelis Permusyawaratan Rakyat (People's Consultative Assembly)
mu'amalat	social relationships, conduct can vary unlike the practices of *ibadat* (see above)
mudharabah	contracts based on profit and loss sharing
mujtahid	experts qualified to make independent legal and religious judgements
murabaha	a contract of sale in which the bank buys on behalf of a client but retains an interest
musharakat	joint venture contract
MUI	Majelis Ulama Indonesia (the Indonesian Council of Ulama)
murtad	an apostate
mutakallim	theologians, scholastics
mutashabihat	a legal issue requiring further study
Mu'tazilite	group of 8th century Muslim thinkers who developed speculative dogmatics based on a strictly grammatical interpretation of the Qur'an (see also Asharite above)
NGOs	non-governmental organizations

NU	Nahdlatul Ulama ("Renaissance of the Ulama"), largest Islamic social movement in Indonesia, founded in 1926
PAN	Partai Amanat Nasional (National Mandate Party)
Pancasila	the Five Basic Principles of the Republic of Indonesia
pbuh	peace be upon him (epithet used after the name of the Prophet Muhammad)
PDI	Partai Demokrasi Indonesia (Indonesia Democratic Party)
PDI-P	Partai Demokrasi Indonesia-Perjuangan (Indonesian Democratic Party of Struggle), under the leadership of Megawati Soekarnoputri it surpassed its predecessor, the PDI
Persis	Persatuan Islam
Piagam Jakarta	Jakarta Charter; a document prepared in June 1945 stating that the Republic of Indonesia would be based upon belief in the One God with the obligation for Muslims to follow *shari'a*. In the Constitution adopted as official in August 1945 the reference to following *shari'a* was dropped.
PKB	Partai Kebangkitan Bangsa (National Awakening Party)
PLS	profit and loss sharing
PPP	Partai Persatuan Pembangunan (United Development Party)
Q.	common abbreviation for Qur'an
Qadariyah	theological school in early Islam asserting Man's free will
qadli	judge; see also *kadi*
riba	"increase", now usury, unjustified
Reformasi	"Reform" referring to the movement against the regime of former President Soeharto which

	led to his stepping down (21 May 1998) and continued to demand the end to corrupt practices in Indonesia
Shafi'ite	followers of the third school of Muslim law
shahadah	the confession of faith
shari'a	the Law in its broadest sense
Shi'a	those Muslims who recognize Ali (the Prophet's son-in-law) and his line as the legitimate successors of the Prophet Muhammad
Sunna (Arabic: *al-Sunnah*)	the deeds and behaviour of the Prophet Muhammad (pbuh)
Sunni	the four schools of Islamic Law (Hanafi, Maliki, Shafi'i and Hanbali)
takhayyur	blending views or opinions deriving from different Islamic schools or doctrines
taqlid	the opposite of *ijtihad*, i.e., strictly adhering to the accepted authorities of one of the four Sunni schools
taqwa	piety, complete submission to God
tawhid	the Oneness (unity) of God which encompasses all aspects of human life
ulama	scholars, learned
ummah	the totality of people who profess to follow Islam
ushul al-fiqh (usul al-fiqh)	principles of law/of ascertaining law
wakaf	gift for pious and charitable purposes
wali	guardian, often with legal powers
WTO	World Trade Organization
zakat	compulsory payment (2.5 per cent) of one's annual income, due at the end of the fasting month

INDEX OF NAMES

A
Abduh Muhammad, 44, 199–201, 206, 237–38
Abdurrahman, Asjumi, 188
Abshar-Abdalla, Ulil, 244
Achmad, Fatimah, 187
Adam, Yahya b., 114
Ahmad, Ziauddin, 118
Al-Afghani, Jamal al-Din, 22, 44, 135
Al-'Alim, Mahmud Amin, 48
Al-Banna, Hasan, 22, 237
Al-Din, Ahmad Baha', 58
Al-Duri, 'Abd al-'Aziz, 59
Al-Farouqi, Ismail, 51
Al-Ghazzali, 239, 243
Al-Jabiri, Muhammad 'Abid, 6, 51, 53, 57
Al-Kawakib, 'Abd al-Rahman, 135–36
Al-Khattab, Umar Ibn, 135
Al-Khitab, Omar Ibn, 21
Al-Khu'i, 239
Al-Marzuqi, Abu Ya'rub, 53
Al-Mawdudi, Abu al-A'la, 135–36
Al-Nabhani, Shaykh Taqi al-Din, 136
Al-Qaradawi Yusuf Shaykh, 51
Al-Rasi, 203
Alawiyah, Tutti, 194
Ali, Abdullah Yusuf, 116
Amal, Taufik Adnan, 239
Amin, Qassim, 237
Amin, Samir, 48-49
Anas, Malik b., 114
Anshari, Endang Saifuddin, 210
Arafat, Yasser (Palestine), 24
Arkoun, Mohammed, 237–38
Asad, Muhammad, 117
'Ashmawi, 203
Assyaukanie, Luthfi, 236, 238–39
Azra, Azyumardi, 9, 12, 241

B
Bakr, Abu, 135
Bakrah, Abu, 187
Balqziz, 'Abd al-Ilah, 57
Barton, Greg, 212
Basri, Faisal, 33
Battuta, Ibn, 45
Bhutto, Benazir, Prime Minister (Pakistan), 171, 188
Bin Laden, Osama, 26–31, 44
Binder, Leonard, 237
Bush, Geroge W., President (United States), 1, 28, 30

C
Chalil, Hj. Moehamad, 202
Chapra, Muhammad Umar, 117

D
Dahlan, K. H. Ahmad, 106
Djalil, Matori Abdul, 144, 189
Doualibi, 117

E
Effendi, Djohan, 211
El-Halafawi, Jihan, 173
El-Saadawi, Nawal, 171

F
Fatwa, A. M., 143
Faysal, Shukri, 50
Forrester, Geoff, 108
Fyzee, A. A. Asaf, 237–38

G
Ghannoushi, Rashid, 6, 51–53
Ghazali, 51

H
Habermas Jürgen, 48
Habibie, President (Indonesia), 34, 96, 138–40, 142, 146, 188, 190, 194, 233, 235
Hallaq, 211, 214, 217
Hanafi, Hasan, 51, 237
Hashmi, Farhat, 174
Hatta, Mohammad, Vice-President (Indonesia), 104
Haz, Hamzah, Vice-President (Indonesia), 145, 194
Hazairin, 204–206
Hefner, Robert W., 134, 245
Hill, Hal, 94
Hofmann, Murad, 225
Hooker, M. B., 13–14, 240
Hooker, Virginia, 1, 231
Hourani, Albert, 237
Huntington, Samuel P., 2, 33
Hurgronjie, C. Snouck, 101, 138
Hussein, Saddam, President (Iraq), 1, 25, 29–30
Huxley, Julian, 78

I
Iskandar, Muhaimin, 143
Ismail, Nur Mahmudi, 34, 143–44

J
Jabiri, Muhammad Abid, 237
Jadaane, Fehmi, 52
Janoski, Thomas, 163

K
Kaprabonan, Radja, 185
Karzai, Hamid, President (Afghanistan), 29
Katjasungkana, Nursyahbani, 186
Khaldun, Ibn, 114
Khatami, President (Iran), 10, 28, 153
Khofifah, 194
Khomeini, Ayatullah (Iran), 23
Khoshroo, Gholamali, 9–10
Kurzman, Charles, 237

L
Leghari, Farooq, President (Pakistan), 174
Leksono, Karlina, 191
Liddle, William 133
Lubis, Nur Ahmad Fadhil, 7–8, 205

M
Ma'arif, Syafi'i, 95, 143
Madjid, Nurcholish, 5–7, 9–10, 13, 93, 191–92, 209–12, 214–17, 232–33
Mahendra, Yusril Ihza, 143–44
Makhmalbaf, Samira, 175
Mangunpuspito, 185–86
Mannan, M. A., 109
Mardjono, Hartono, 144
Mariyah, Chusnul, 193
Marshall, T. H., 163
Mashuri, K. H. Aziz, 187
Massoud, Ahmed Shah, 26
Mas'udi, Masdar, 241
Mawdudi, Maulana, 50, 174
McLuhan, Marshall, 46
Megawangi, Ratna, 188
Mernissi, Fatima, 58
Mill, John Stuart, 243
Mohammad, Goenawan, 235
Mujani, Saiful 133
Mulia, Musdah, 241
Musharaf, Parvez, General (Pakistan), 29, 170
Muzadi, K.H. Hasyim, 143

N
Nasution, Harun, 185–86, 206–11, 213, 243
Natsir, Moehamad, 202, 210

Noer, Deliar, 143, 202

O

Othman, Aris, 13–14

P

Pamungkas, Sri Bintang, 96
Panggabean, Samsu Rizal, 5
Parawansa, Khofifah Indar, 190, 193
Popper, Karl, 231

Q

Qutb, Sayyid, 50, 135, 237

R

Rahardjo, M. Dawam, 96
Rahman, Fazlur, 116, 203, 217, 237–38
Rais, Amien, 32–33, 93, 96, 143–44, 190
Rasjidi, H. M., 207, 210
Raziq, Ali Abdul, 237
Rida, Rashid, 44, 135–36, 200, 237
Ridwan, K. H. Kholil, 189
Robinson, Kathryn, 12
Rukmana, Siti Hardijanti (Mbak Tutut), 187–88
Rushd, Ibn, 114, 238

S

Saeed, Abdullah, 8–9
Saefuddin, A. M., 190
Sahal, Ahmad, 238
Said, Edward, 59
Saikal, Amin, 4–5
Sarakhsi, 114
Sarwar, Samai, 171
Sasono, Adi, 96
Shah, Mohammed Reza (Iran), 22
Sharabi, Hisham, 53, 58
Sharif, Nawaz, 171
Sharon, Ariel, Prime Minister (Israel), 30
Shboul, Ahmad, 2, 5–7
Shiddieqy, Ash, 205
Shihab, Alwi, Minister of Foreign Affairs (Indonesia), 33, 144
Shihab, Quraish, 190
Siddiq, Achmad, 211
Siddiq, K. H. Mahfudz, 200
Siddiqi, Muhammad Nejatullah, 118
Sidjabar, Walter Bonar, 87
Siradi, Said Aqiel, 193
Sjadzali, Munawir, 206
Soeharto, President (Indonesia), 8–9, 32, 34, 93, 96, 101–102, 108, 133, 136–39, 142, 144, 146, 183, 186–88, 193–94, 233–34, 240–41
Sudjanadiwirja, Tetilarsih Harahap, 186
Sugandi, Mien, 193
Sukarno, President (Indonesia), 101, 103, 138, 142, 146, 202, 246
Sukarnoputri, Megawati, President (Indonesia), 9, 12, 136, 139, 142–43, 146–47, 183, 186, 188, 190–94, 235
Sumargono, Ahmad, 143
Surasto, Setiati, 186
Suryakusuma, Julia, 193

T

Taha, Mahmud Mohammad, 238
Tahtawi, Rif'at, 237
Tibi, Bassam, 231–32, 242, 245–46
Toffler, Alvin, 83
Turabi, 51, 203

U

Uzair, Mohammad, 117

W

Waheed, Saima, 176
Wahid, Abdurrahman, President (Indonesia), 9, 12, 32, 93, 139, 142–44, 183, 188, 190, 193–94, 211–14, 232, 235
Wahid, Salahuddin, 143
Wahid, Siti Nuriyah, 193

Y

Yafie, K. H. Ali, 187
Yasmeen, Samina, 10–12
Yusuf, Abu, 114

Z

Zainuddin, M. Z., 145
Zayd, Nashr Hamid Abu, 238
Zurayk, Constantine, 63

INDEX OF SUBJECTS

A
Aceh, 36
Afghanistan, 1, 25–27, 29, 35
  jihad call, 26
  Revolutionary Association of the Women of Afghanistan (RAWA), 170
  Taliban, 26–30, 35
Al-Jazeera, 3
Al-Qaeda, 1, 4, 28–30, 44
Angkatan Mujahidin Indonesia, 134
Arab world and globalization, 43–63
Arab-Israeli conflict, 23–24
Arabic publications, 54
Australia
  intervention in Indonesian politics, 34–35

B
Bali attack, 28
Bank Mal wat Tamwil (BMT), 36, 106
Bank Muamalat Indonesia (BMI), 36, 107–108, 138
Bank Perkreditan Rakyat Syariah (BPRS), 36, 106–107, 138

C
caliphate, 134–37
Casablanca attack, 28
Christianity, 20
  crusades, 4, 21–22
citizenship, 163–68
colonialism, 4, 21–22

D
Dow Jones Islamic Market Index, 124

E
East Timor, 34–35
Egypt
  Faisal Islamic Bank, 119, 121
  feminist movements, 173
European Union (EU), 55

F
Faisal Islamic Bank, 119, 121
feminist movements, 168–76
  Egypt, 173
  Iran, 173
  Kuwait, 171
  non-governmental groups (NGOs)
    Arab Women's Solidarity Association, 171
    Kuwait Democratic Forum (KDF), 171
    National Commission for Pakistani Women, 170
    Revolutionary Association of the Women of Afghanistan (RAWA), 170
    Women for Women's Human Rights (WWHR), 170
    Women's Action Forum, 170–71

Pakistan, 170–71, 173–76
Saudi Arabia, 175
financial activism, 91–110, 113–25
Front Pembela Islam (FPI), 134, 194

G
Gama'ah Tafkir wa al-Hijrah, 135
globalism, 5, *see also* globalization
globalization, 5–7, 10, 43–63, 225
approaches, 45–46
Arab discourse, 46–47
effect on nation-state, 54–56
Islamic factor, 43–45, 49–54
threat to cultural identity, 56–59
vehicle of consumerism, 59–63
westernization, 47–49
GOLKAR, 140, 142, 144, 188, 193
Gulf War, 6, 32

H
Hizb al-Tahrir, 134, 136
humanitarianism and religion, 78–79

I
Ikhwan al-Muslimun, 135
Indonesia
Asian economic crisis, 234
caliphate or modern nation-state, 134–37
Christian party
Parkindo, 186
colonialism, 13, 200
development of Islam, 7–9, 81–88, 92–94, 133–47, 232–47
domestic instability, 33–34
economic activism, 105–108
economic challenges, 36, 94–97
Indonesian Association of Muslim Intellectuals (ICMI), 96, 138–39, 186, 233–35
Indonesian Committee for the Islamic World's Solidarity (KISDI), 32
Indonesian Council of Ulama (MUI), 100, 103, 190, 206
Islamic banking, 7–9, 36, 102–104
Islamic banks
Bank Mal wat Tamwil (BMT), 36, 106
Bank Muamalat Indonesia (BMI), 36, 107–108, 138
Bank Perkreditan Rakyat Syariah (BPRS), 36, 106–107, 138
Islamic economics, 97–100, 105–10
Islamic law, 8, 12–13, 100–105, 133–47, 145–47, 199–218, 240–42
Islamic state, 92–94, 211
Islamic Students' Association (HMI), 209
Jakarta Charter, 140, 145–146, 203
Javanese Islam, 37
jihad call, 36
KKN practices, 95, 234
Kongres Umat Islam Indonesia (KUII), 189, 191–92
Liberal Muslim network, 240, 244, 246
Muslim groups
Angkatan Mujahidin Indonesia, 134
Front Pembela Islam (FPI), 134, 194
Gama'ah Tafkir wa al-Hijrah, 135
Hizb al-Tahrir, 134, 136
Ikhwan al-Muslimun, 135
Jamaah Tarbiyah, 136
Jemaah Islamiyah, 235
Lasykar Jihad, 134, 147
Muslim responses to the New World Order, 32–38
nation-state, 134–37
New Order government, 38, 91–92, 95–96, 108, 136, 138, 192–93, 207, 233–35, 240
Pancasila, 134, 137–41, 143–44, 203, 207–208, 211, 214
Paramadina Foundation, 233
People's Consultative Assembly (MPR), 32, 93–94, 103, 139, 142–144, 146–47, 187, 192, 194
Persatuan Islam (Persis), 35, 201, 206, 217–18
political Islam, 133–47
political parties, 140–45
GOLKAR, 140, 142, 144, 188, 193
KAMI, 141
Muhammadiyah, 32, 94–95, 103–104, 106–107, 137, 141, 143–44, 188, 192, 201, 206, 215, 217–18

Musyawarah Kerja Gotong Royong (MKGR), 193
Nahdlatul Ulama (NU), 32–33, 93–94, 103–104, 107–108, 137, 141, 143, 187–88, 190–93, 200, 206, 211–12, 214–15, 217–18
Partai Abul Yatama, 141
Partai Amanat Nasional (PAN), 94, 141–42, 190
Partai Bulan Bintang (PBB), 140, 142, 144
Partai Cinta Damai (PCD), 141
Partai Demokrasi Indonesia (PDI), 140
Partai Demokrasi Indonesia — Perjuangan (PDI-P), 142, 144, 183, 188, 192
Partai Indonesia Baru (PIB), 141
Partai Islam Demokrasi (PID), 141
Partai Islam Indonesai (PII), 144
Partai Keadilan (PK), 94, 144
Partai Kebangkitan Bangsa (PKB), 94, 141–42, 144, 189–90, 193
Partai Kebangkitan Ummat (PKU), 141
Partai Masjumi, 185, 189, 194
Partai Masyumi Baru, 141, 194
Partai Nahdlatul Ummat (PNU), 141
Partai Persatuan (PP), 140
Partai Persatuan Pembangunan (PPP), 94, 140, 142, 144–46, 187, 192, 194
Partai Persatuan Pembangunan-Reformasi (PPP-Reformasi), 145
Partai Politik Islam Indonesia Masyumi (PPIIM), 140
Partai Solidaritas Uni Indonesia (Partai SUNI), 141
Partai Syarekat Islam Indonesia (PSII), 140
Partai Syarekat Islam Indonesia 1905 (PSII 1905), 141
Partai Umat Islam (PUI), 141
Partai Umat Muslimin Indonesia (PUMI), 141
proposed trade relations with Israel, 33, 136
reformasi, 9, 32–33, 37, 194, 235
secessionist movements, 34, 36
Aceh, 36
East Timor, 34–35
Irian Jaya (West Papua), 34
State Islamic Institutes (IAIN), 105, 186, 206
State Islamic University Syarif Hidayatullah (UIN), 9
Syarikat Dagang Islam (SDI), 106
women's political participation, 183–95
International Monetary Fund (IMF), 36, 95
Iran, 10
Constitution, 10, 154–56
feminist movements, 173
Foreign Investment Bill, 10, 156
Islamic state, 152–157
jihad call, 23
revolution, 10, 22–23, 153
Iraq
UN sanctions, 25
US-led invasion, 1, 22, 28–30
Irian Jaya (West Papua), 34
Islam
and globalization, 5–7, 43–63
and nation-state, 10, 151–52
definition, 92
fatawa, 13, 45, 100, 212, 215
fundamentalist, *see* Islamic fundamentalism
hajj, 45
history, 4, 21–22, 92
in Indonesia, 7–9, 81–88, 92–94, 133–47, 232–47
in Iran, 152–57
jihad, 21, 23, 45, 50, 52
liberal, *see* liberal Islam
political, *see* political Islam
Qur'an, 2, 4–7, 20, 50, 63, 74–77, 79–86, 93, 97–101, 104, 110, 113–14, 119, 124, 141, 155, 174, 183, 185, 189, 191–92, 200–201, 205–206, 208, 210, 214–16, 222, 225, 238–41, 243–44, 246
role in world politics, 150–51
Sunna, 75, 113–14, 124, 141, 155, 174, 201, 214–15, 222, 244
ulama, 33, 100, 103, 107, 135, 142, 190, 204, 211

ummah, 3, 6, 10, 21, 45, 107, 151–52, 155, 199, 201, 209, 221–26
Islamic banking, 7–9, 102–104, 113–25
development, 115–16
investment in companies, 123–25
principles, 114–15
profit, 120–22
profit and loss sharing (PLS), 8, 115, 118, 120, 122
riba, 8, 104, 107, 114–21, 123–24
sale-based banking, 122–23
Islamic Development Bank (IDB), 102, 123
Islamic economics, 97–100, 105–10
Islamic finance, *see* Islamic banking
Islamic Fiqh Academy, 123
Islamic fundamentalism, 23, 44, 49–54, 231
Islamic law (*shari'a*), 8, 12–13, 45, 100–105, 145–47, 199–218, 240–42
Islamic principles, 20–21, 97–100
Islamic state, *see* Indonesia and Iran
Islamic teachings, 74–77, 79–81
"Islamicphobia", 23
Israeli-Palestinian conflict, 23–24, 29–30, 32–33

J
Jamaah Tarbiyah, 136
Jemaah Islamiyah, 235
Judaism, 20

K
Kuwait
feminist movements, 171
Kuwait Democratic Forum (KDF), 171

L
Lasykar Jihad, 134, 147
liberal Islam, 231–47

M
modernity, 6
modernization, 47–49
Muhammadiyah, 32, 94–95, 103–104, 106–107, 137, 141, 143–44, 188, 192, 201, 206, 215, 217–18
Muslim brotherhood, 74–77, 173
Muslim Brothers, 22, 24, 50–52, 173
Muslim humanitarianism, 74–77
Muslim women, 10–12, 161–77
citizenship, 163–68
Economic Activity Rate (EAR), 164, 166
feminist movements, 168–76
literacy 164–65
political participation, 164, 183–95
Muslim world
anti-West sentiments, 19–29
relationship with the West, 19–31
Afghanistan, 25–27
Cold War rivalry, 4, 22, 24
colonialism, 21–22
invasion of Iraq, 22, 28–30
Iranian revolution, 22–23
Israeli issue, 23–25
mending of ties, 29–30
religious differences, 20–21
Second World War, 4, 22
UN sanctions against Iraq, 25
Muslims
challenges, 221–26
contributions, 223
role, 221–26

N
Nahdlatul Ulama (NU), 32–33, 93–94, 103–104, 107–108, 137, 141, 143, 187–88, 190–93, 200, 206, 211–12, 214–15, 217–18
nation-state, 10, 54–56, 134–37, 151–52
New Age, 5
New World Order (NWO), 4–5
Indonesian Muslim responses, 32–38
non-governmental organizations (NGOs), 162, 171, 235
Arab Women's Solidarity Association, 171
Kuwait Democratic Forum (KDF), 171
National Commission for Pakistani Women, 170
Revolutionary Association of the Women of Afghanistan (RAWA), 170
Women for Women's Human Rights (WWHR), 170

Women's Action Forum, 170–71
North Atlantic Treaty Organization (NATO), 38, 224–25

O
Omar Agreement, 21

P
Palestine
conflict with Israel, 23–24, 29–30, 32
Hamas, 24, 27, 44
Islamic Jihad, 24, 27, 44
Oslo peace process, 24, 30
Palestine Liberation Organization (PLO), 24
Pakistan, 25–27, 29
Al-Huda movement, 174
Council of Islamic Ideology, 117–18, 121
feminist movements, 170–71, 173–76
honour killings, 171
Islamic banking, 118
Jamaat-I-Islami, 44, 173–74
military police (ISI), 26, 29
National Commission for Pakistani Women, 170
Women's Action Forum, 170–71
Pancasila, 134, 137–41, 143–44, 203, 207–208, 211, 214
Paramadina Foundation, 233
Partai Kebangkitan Bangsa (PKB), 94, 141–42, 144, 189–90, 193
Partai Persatuan Pembangunan (PPP), 94, 140, 142, 144–46, 187, 192, 194
Persatuan Islam (Persis), 35, 201, 206, 217–18
political Islam, 47–48, 133–47

Q
Qur'an, 2, 4–7, 20, 50, 63, 74–77, 79–86, 93, 97–101, 104, 110, 113–14, 119, 124, 141, 155, 174, 183, 185, 189, 191–92, 200–201, 205–206, 208, 210, 214–16, 222, 225, 238–41, 243–44, 246

R
Revolutionary Association of the Women of Afghanistan (RAWA), 170
Riyadh attack, 28
religion and humanitarianism, 78–79

S
Saudi Arabia
feminist movements, 175
September 11 attack, 1, 19, 28–31, 136, 147
social movements, 161–62

T
Taliban, 26–30, 35

U
United Nations (UN), 24, 162
intervention in Indonesian politics, 34–35
sanctions against Iraq, 25
Security Council, 1, 29
UNAMET, 34
UNHCR, 34
United States
bombing of Afghanistan, 1
Bush administration, 28–29
Central Intelligence Agency (CIA), 22, 26, 35
Clinton administration, 27–28
CNN network, 3
dominant world power, 4, 22, 38
intervention in Indonesian politics, 34–35
invasion of Iraq, 1, 22, 28–30
September 11 attack, 1, 19, 28–31, 136, 147
strategy in Afghanistan, 25–27
support of Israel, 23–25
universal civilization, 2
universalism, 45–46

W
Westernization, 47–48
women's political participation, 183–95
women's rights, *see* feminist movements
World Bank, 36, 95
World Trade Organization (WTO), 10, 156

www.ingramcontent.com/pod-product-compliance
Lightning Source LLC
Chambersburg PA
CBHW020811100426
42814CB00001B/19